TALKING AMERICAN:

Cultural Discourses
on DONAHUE

COMMUNICATION AND INFORMATION SCIENCE

Edited by
BRENDA DERVIN
The Ohio State University

Recent Titles

TALKING AMERICAN:

Cultural Discourses
on DONAHUE

Donal Carbaugh

ABLEX PUBLISHING CORPORATION
NORWOOD, NEW JERSEY

The materials contained herein are produced with the consent of Multimedia and Phil Donahue.

Library of Congress Cataloging-in-Publication Data

Carbaugh, Donal A.
    Talking American : cultural discourses on Donahue / by Donal Carbaugh.
        p. cm.—(Communication and information science)
    Based on the author's doctoral dissertation, University of Washington.
    Bibliography: p.
    Includes index.
    ISBN 0-89391-492-4 (ppk); 0-89391-477-0 (cloth)
    1. Oral communication—United States. 2. Conversation.
3. Donahue (Television program) 4. United States—Popular culture.
I. Title. II. Series.
P95.C38   1988
001.54′2′0973—dc19   88-10455
                                                            CIP

Ablex Publishing Corporation
355 Chestnut Street
Norwood, New Jersey 07648

TABLE OF CONTENTS

*To the Communal Voice
and Every Person Who Creates
With It*

The whole enterprise in cultural analysis starts with our own society as a point of departure, not only because we know it (or can know it) in both accuracy and depth, but because it is precisely our own society which is problematic in our lives (Schneider, 1976, p. 212).

PREFACE

To the reader:

The two major parts of the book introduce first, American notions of personhood, then, American notions about speaking. I organize my comments this way primarily because notions of the person received slightly more attention than did those about speaking. But both are intimately related, as will become clearer throughout. The first chapter provides a general introduction. The heart of the book is oriented to a detailed discussion of some "talk" that is "shown" on "Donahue" and has a broad cultural currency (chaps. 2, 3, 4, 5, 7, 8, and 9). Other parts of the book are oriented more to a discussion of various theoretical issues (the introductions to units 1 and 2, chaps. 6, 10, and 11). Those readers interested more in descriptions of American life may wish to skim or skip the more theoretically oriented material. However, I hope most readers will welcome the full force of the book and will read the chapters consecutively, as they are written, keeping in mind that chap. 11 sketches and illustrates five properties of cultural discourses.

What I present should be considered more a productive portrait than a mere mirror. Consider, for example, the woman who was married and living with two men at the same time. She explained her "choice" of mates, as did her partners. They described how each partner freely chose to live this way, were honest about their style of life (called a "free-form marriage"), expected others to allow each their own choice, and expressed self-satisfaction in the arrangement. How is it that "marriage" is portrayed this way? Does this portrayal vary that much from others? Persons seem to be saying that they each are "their own person," but many are saying this same kind of thing! Persons, at least those observed in this contemporary American scene, tend to say what they think as individuals, to think what they say as individuals. Rarely do they hear what they say as the expression of a cultural voice. This study explores prominent tribal idioms of America today, idioms that sound individualistic, but are accomplished communally. This cultural performance of individuality contains of course an irony, which runs through my cultural account, and an irony that if wholly grasped, takes one beyond the mere mirroring of common sense (as an individual act), to its productive portrayal (as a cultural performance). What I hold up to my compatriots then is not merely a mirror, but a portrait that has been carefully crafted to embrace communal aspects of living that may otherwise remain hidden.

The strived-for effect was best exemplified by one of my informants who said, after hearing part of what follows: "That's right, but I hadn't thought of it that way." Others have responded similarly (and others not) with all reactions serving to instruct me further. But always it was this type of reaction toward which I aimed.[1]

Human lives, and communication about them, are fraught with complexities, logical loops, multiple layers of meanings, and contradictions. I hope to have captured some of these dynamics in the contemporary American scene. As Schneider suggests in the opening quote, our lives are, at least on some occasions, "problematic." But I do not attempt to offer a way out, nor of course to offer a final interpretation of this delightful process. What I offer is a way of hearing cultural voices where others have heard only individuals. But because of the great resourcefulness in these common resources, I cannot offer a complete picture, only a kind of snapshot. It appears cultural analysts must work within this limit (Geertz, 1973, p. 29). I do hope however to present a productive interpretation to you; one that orders routine daily moments in a new way, throwing sensibilities into another light, making what people commonly say an object of critical reflection, and entering that reflective voice into the communal conversation.

---

[1] Gergen (1978) has described this general process of contributing to the social phenomena of investigation as "generative theory."

ACKNOWLEDGMENTS

I am grateful to many who have contributed to this project, as friends, critics, informants, family, sometimes all at once.

At the University of Washington in the Department of Speech Communication, I am especially indebted to Gerry Philipsen, who directed the doctoral dissertation which initiated this study and who provided reactions from pointed criticism to friendly encouragement. The example of his scholarship will be with me for a long time to come. To John Stewart, who was frequently encouraging and helpful, I also extend my thanks. In the Department of Anthropology, I wish to thank Carol Eastman and Charles Keyes, who read and reacted to early parts of the study. The graduate school of the university and the Department of Speech Communication provided various forms of financial support early on, for which I am very grateful.

A special thanks goes to Dell Hymes who encouraged my work and with whom I had a few inspirational discussions during this project. His pioneering scholarship has grounded much of my own. My intellectual debt goes similarly to the works of Don Cushman, Clifford Geertz, David Schneider, and Victor Turner.

I have benefited from discussions with several persons who read (or heard) earlier parts of the study and provided useful comments. To all I extend my thanks: Robert Bell, Charles Braithwaite, John Campbell, Dwight Conquergood, Vern Cronen, Stan Deetz, Brenda Dervin, Bill Donaghy, John Fiske, Rom Harré, Glen Hiemstra, Robert Hopper, Tamar Katriel, Scott Jacobs, Deborah Kelm, Wendy Leeds–Hurwitz, Tom Nilsen, William Rawlins, George Ray, Robert Sanders, Stuart Sigman. A special thanks to Frank Millar of the University of Wyoming who gave an extremely careful reading of the manuscript, which resulted in a more refined argument and a final product that is much more readable.

At the University of Massachusetts, my academic home, I want to thank my chair, W. Barnett Pearce, my colleagues, and my students, who have provided an excellent environment in which to test and develop ideas. The Department of Communication has also provided a small research grant which helped in the final stages of preparing the manuscript.

At the University of Pittsburgh, I wish to thank two of my colleagues, Sally Murphy and Lester Olson, for their interest and lively discussions. A faculty research grant from the university provided an opportunity to refine some of my thoughts about native genres of speaking.

Several departments of communication created opportunities for me to discuss some of my ideas, an opportunity for oralizing that I found stimulating and for which I extend my thanks: Montana State University, State University of New York at Buffalo, University of Arkansas at Little Rock, University of North Carolina at Wilmington, and University of Montana.

Several persons, early on in my education, posed questions to me that have proven productive and complex. I must acknowledge a special debt to my undergraduate mentor, Paul Keller of Manchester College, Indiana, who is a very gifted teacher. Others have helped similarly, as colleagues and special friends. To Joyce Hocker, Wes Shellen, and Bill Wilmot, thanks.

The process of publication was facilitated through the friendly and skillful efforts of Barbara Bernstein and Carol Davidson to whom I extend a sincere thanks.

Finally, I am forever grateful to my family, which has encouraged and supported me throughout. To my wife, LuAnne, the memory of my mother, my father, David, Pushpa, Mary, Betsy, Ted, and my grandma (who at 88 gives a tremendous sense of continuity and perspective to it all), my heartfelt thanks.

Donal Carbaugh
Seattle, Pittsburgh, Amherst
1982–1987

1

DONAHUE: A CULTURAL APPROACH TO THE "TALK" OF A "SHOW"

Every epoch has certain places that are marked especially for communication. In Athenian society, the place was the Assembly. The Greeks gathered there to hear great deliberative discourses such as those between Demosthenes and Aeschines. Orators spoke through patterns of rational speech and oral persuasion, giving a particular flair to the public drama. At another time, in Colonial America, people came to the town hall. Here citizens could exercise their right to speak publicly, discuss the social, political, and economic policies of their infant nation, and negotiate various points of view. In each place and time, one can hear particular forms of communication used, such as rational persuasion for the Greeks and individual assertions for the Colonial American. One can hear further in each place particular models for speakers, be it the model of the orator for the ancient Greek or the participative citizen for the colonial American. By studying human scenes through their patterns of communication, we can understand both the forms of communication people use when speaking and the models for being that they embody when speaking. Both concerns—which following others I will call genres of speaking and symbols of personhood—inform us about the social lives of individuals and societies as they are communicated in time and place.

This book explores these concerns (i.e., genres of speaking and symbols of personhood) as they give shape to the communication patterns in a contemporary American scene. Throughout the inquiry, I am asking: What are the cultural resources that are used in the routine "talk" of a prominent American scene? What I present is an ethnographic case study of the communication resources that some Americans use when talking in public. It is an effort to step back and look at some of the ways we—I include myself—talk to each other, both at what we are saying and how we are saying it. It is not a study of psychological differences between persons; cultural differences between

1

social groups; ideological differences between political institutions; nor is it a study of the marketplace of television and the role of economics in its creation. It is a study of the ways some Americans talk to each other (Hymes, 1974), and as a result of talking this way, differentiate themselves one from another, group from group, belief from belief, and if their talking is displayed on television, it sells a product (in this case, a "talk show"). I want the focus to be clear, early on. Thus I repeat, the study explores the communication patterns commonly used in a prominent American scene, especially the symbols used for constructing a sense of personhood and the native genres used for speaking. My focus is upon these patterns of talk. Thus, I am exploring the *talking* that is American, more than an *American* that is talking. I am asking, what if any are some of the common resources that persons use when talking in public? What does the use of these communicative resources accomplish in this scene?

This book deals with American (generally mainstream North American) patterns of communication. It is important in studies of this kind to differentiate individual Americans from the cultural patterns which they must live in, or by. I will be describing symbols for personhood such as "being an individual" and "having a self." I will describe generic forms of communication such as "being honest." But what I am describing are cultural patterns that are commonly intelligible and widely accessible across American scenes, not aspects within personalities of individual Americans. As Varenne (1986, p. 6) has put it: "America," here, is the pattern in terms of which human beings must construct their lives when they interact in the United States." What is of general interest here is the historically rooted and widespread patterns themselves, more specifically, the things we as Americans say to ourselves, about ourselves, that distinguishes us from others.

One cannot find places in history where millions have gathered daily, to talk. But in contemporary America, we have such a place, where persons gather to talk, and to witness each other talk. We call it the talk show—a popular genre of television programming. If for no other reason than the sheer numbers of persons involved, it warrants serious study.

There are perhaps at least two types of talk shows. On the one hand there are the personality-centered shows, such as those of "Johnny Carson," "Dick Cavett," and "Merv Griffin," which interview a popular figure in order to tell us something about his or her life.

A second type of talk show is more issue-centered and proceeds more through audience (lay folk) discussion and commentary than through the interview of a popular personality. Examples include the shows of "Donahue," "Dr. Ruth" (Crow, 1986), "Sally Jessy Raphael," and "Oprah Winfrey." This type focuses generally on social issues (although each occasionally conducts a personality-type show) through discussions, including telephoned comments. Multiple voices can be heard (often using audience members' reactions and callers, or persons who telephone from their homes). As Donahue put it in his best-selling autobiography:

> While we are very pleased that Bob Hope and Johnny Carson and a host of other biggies have done our show, the fact remains that our program survives on issues. We discuss more issues, more often, more thoroughly than any other show in the business. We also involve the audience in our act more than any other show on the air, period. Without the audience, there's no "Donahue" show! (Donahue & Co., 1979, p. 236)

Where the personality-type programs "talk" takes place primarily within dyads about topics that are more personal and noncontroversial, the issue type displays a kind of group discussion about topics that are more social and often controversial.

Chief among the issue type on American television is, of course, the "Donahue" show, named after its host, Phil Donahue. The show is extremely popular. It airs in more than 200 markets, including Alaska, Hawaii, and Puerto Rico. It has won several awards, including Emmys for "best show," "best host," and "outstanding achievement for a creative technical craft." It consistently ranks No. 1 among syndicated talk shows and it is watched by about 5 million households, or 7 to 7.5 million viewers per day ("Donahue" staff, 1983; Robinson, 1982). The show is credited by some for ushering in a second generation of talk shows, from the more personality interview type, to the more issue discussion type (Harrison, 1983). The show regularly receives national news attention, for example, when it moved from Chicago to New York; when it found a heart for "Baby Jesse," an infant whose life was in jeopardy; and when it showed a son and father, whose ex-wife happened to watch the show, and consequently alleged that the son had been "kidnapped," with "Donahue" being an accessory to the crime. More recently, and for the first time, Donahue and his staff have gone to a foreign country, the Soviet Union, to tape several shows with Soviet guests and audiences.

The host, Phil Donahue, is as prominent a figure as is the show. For some, he is the embodiment of the "trying to be liberated male," open and honest about his opinions and personal life (Donahue & Co., 1979). For others, he is a kind of caricature of "knee-jerk liberalism," that embodies a backboneless philosophy of pluralism (Chenoweth,

1982). But, however one expresses an opinion about Donahue, one cannot escape his presence and influence on American media today. In fact, a recent Gallup poll reported that he was ranked second, only behind Walter Cronkite, as the most identifiable media name (Craig, 1986). He has been interviewed on the popular television newsmagazine, "60 Minutes," and apparently because of his ability to coordinate "talk," was asked during the last presidential campaign to host (along with "Nightline" host Ted Koppel) a debate among Democratic candidates. To add to his list of media accomplishments, during the summer of 1986, he saw all 5 shows of his series titled, "The Human Animal," make the top 20 ratings, the first time NBC had swept the 10 o'clock prime-time slot in six years (Phil . . ., 1986). Even Reed Irvine, chairman of the conservative Accuracy in Media, has praised Phil Donahue and the "Donahue" show for the open and fair treatment of controversial issues (Irvine, 1984).

In addition to these personal accomplishments, "Donahue" has become a symbol that is used by and intelligible to Americans. For example, the title character in a 1983 movie, *Mr. Mom,* defined himself during the movie as "a regular Phil Donahue." In a Funky Winkerbean comic strip, after Betty found out that Ann might be living with a boy she explained, "Hey! It's okay, Ann! I watch Phil Donahue a lot and I've learned not to be judgmental."

Because of the prominence, popularity and coherence of "Donahue" (the show) and Donahue (the man) in American society today, and because the show is designed for talk, it is a rich context for the study of communication. As a television genre and as a scene that engages millions of Americans every weekday, "Donahue" warrants an especially serious and sustained study. Just as we have learned about Roman society by studying orations in the Assembly, and Colonial society by studying negotiations in the town hall, so we should learn much about contemporary American society by studying the kind of talk that is heard on "Donahue."

Talk as a Cultural Resource

I want to say a few words about the general approach used in this study, which in general combines some features of interpretive anthropology with the ethnography of communication in order to study "cultural communication" (Philipsen, in press) in this contemporary American scene. As I listened to people talking, what I looked for was the "native" view of persons and of the talk that was getting done (Hymes, 1972, 1974). I listened for the ways that speakers discussed cultural actors. I asked: How are persons symbolized in this talk? What model of persons is used here to evaluate issues and actors? As for talk, I resisted translating utterances into etic, or "experience distant," frameworks, for example, as "pre-indexes," "repairs," "side-sequences," and the like, and asked instead the emic, or "experience near," questions (Geertz, 1976). Is there a native view of the type of talk that is getting done? When persons talked about their talk, as when they said, "that's a very honest statement," I asked what kind of routine talk does this native saying, "very honest statement," refer to? Thus, what I attended to systematically was the terms that speakers used naturally, and asked of them, what views of persons and communicative actions do these folk terms organize, what do they accomplish for American speakers, and what do they mean?

Let me give a more detailed example of symbolizing about talk. One discussion on "Donahue" centered on the rights of individuals to walk through suburban neighborhoods without being asked by police officers to "identify themselves." The specific case under discussion involved a long-haired Black man who had been arrested more than 10 times for, using his word, "walking." The studio and viewing audience was asked if they would call the police if a man like this was walking in their neighborhood. One woman said she would call the police, not because of this man's appearance, but because "normally there is nobody in our neighborhood." This raised the ire of a guest, the Black lawyer of the "stroller," who said in disbelieving astonishment: "You would call the cops because nobody walks in your neighborhood? Please spare me!" Donahue stepped in on her behalf:

Donahue:	At least she is being honest. She is saying, "I don't feel comfortable about this."
Lawyer:	No, she's not being honest!
Donahue:	She is sharing her feelings.
Lawyer:	She's not being honest about it.

In this exchange, Donahue and his guest disagree about whether this woman's communication can be labeled as honest; but they agree, at least implicitly, that she is "sharing her feelings."

This exchange between Donahue, his guest, and an audience member, shows two different ways of speaking that are mentioned as relevant here, one is called "being honest" and the other "sharing feelings." These two native genres for speaking will be described in the second part of the book. But for now, what I am attempting to illustrate is the approach used throughout this study. I take seriously the words people use to discuss speakers and speaking. I am investigating how people organize themselves and their communicative routines through their use. The approach is distinct from, yet complements those who move rather quickly to more abstract analytical frameworks (e.g. Grice, 1975; Sacks, Schegloff, & Jefferson, 1974; Sanders, 1987; Searle, 1976). Because of its sustained interest on native terms, the study is more an ethnographic interpretation of linguistic communication, its common meanings and forms; it is less an abstract investigation of universal patterns of language use, or universal standards for the interpretation of language.

The general approach is guided by the descriptive framework of the ethnography of communication as conceived by Hymes (1962, 1972). The Hymesian framework is used to describe codes or norms for interpreting a cultural ethos of persons and speaking, and as a basis for comparative study by juxtaposing the American patterns herein against other cultural patterns from around the world (Philipsen & Carbaugh, 1986).

I also draw heavily upon Schneider's theory of culture (1976). Since I am focusing the inquiry on symbols and meanings that are spoken, I use Schneider to emphasize that what I am studying is a "*system* of symbols and meanings." I am not interpreting isolated cultural symbols, but *systems* of symbols and their meanings that are spoken. Thus, in the first part of the book I look at a system of symbols that organize senses of personhood for speakers. The system includes a whole array of symbols, including "needs," "rights," and "choice," but can be summarized with three core symbols: "the individual," "self," "social roles," and their interrelations. As Schneider (1976), Carey (1975), and Philipsen (in press), following Burke (1965), make clear, systems of symbols as this one provide people with sensible orientations in the world, and such orientations serve to unite people in communities (Taylor, 1977) as well as form bases for creativity. Thus, when I write of a cultural use of symbol systems, I do not intend that the use oppresses or unduly constrains persons, though for some it may do just that. What I suggest is how the use of symbolic systems engages persons in an effort to render the world intelligible, and as they work to do so, they may signal membership in the American community, and lay groundwork for their subsequent human creations.

A second communicative accomplishment of persons is the organization of human energy into forms, for it is through forms that human energy moves (Burke, 1961, pp. 124–161). I will use the concept of form to identify the cultural sequencing of acts through native genres of speaking (Philips, 1987). Just as Katriel and Philipsen (1981) have identified a ritual form in American communication, so I will attempt to describe other cultural forms that persons use when speaking, such as a vectorial form of "honesty" and a spiralling form of "sharing" (see unit 2).

The focuses of the study then are spoken systems of symbols and symbolic forms that construct cultural views of personhood and speaking. Of particular interest are the meanings they invoke in the talk of the "Donahue" show. A few comments are in order regarding the latter, meanings. Throughout the study I am exploring what could be called *contextual*, rather than intentional, *meaning*. What I have access to are the words that persons are speaking and their common intelligibility within this context. I am writing therefore about the contextual meanings of symbols and symbolic forms, a function of their use in context (Mishler, 1979; Richards, 1936, pp. 23–68; Wittgenstein, 1958). I am, in general, not writing about intentional meanings which actors "shoot" from within their heads, unless such a distinction is useful for unraveling misunderstandings, (e.g., she intended to say, "it is a worthy goal for women to be mothers" but the context could support only the unpopular statement "I like traditional social roles"; see chap. 5).

I will also attempt throughout the study to distinguish the meanings in symbols and symbolic forms that are prominently intelligible, from those that are perhaps hearable but less intelligible to the common ear. One might call the former common meanings or figured meanings that are highlighted in the verbal play of cultural discourses. One might call the latter grounded meanings, since they are hearable in the discourse but generally silenced in favor of the more active figures. For example, throughout chap. 4 we will see how "the self" as a cultural symbol highlights prominent meanings of independence, uniqueness, and expressiveness, that is, its main figured meanings. More silenced is the form of presentation of self that is dependent upon tradition, and constrains expression. This latter is the grounded meaning. What is realized through this interpretation is a characteristic American pattern of communication in which the figured meanings, especially of individualism and self, negate the grounded meanings of communal form. In this symbol system, individualized meanings triumph over and negate the cultural forms which give them a coherent expression. This is itself, of course, a cultural communication accomplishment that figures individualized meanings over cultural performances.

Interpreting American communication patterns this way enables me to discuss three particular aspects of the symbol system: (1) its *common radiants of meanings* (Eastman, 1985) or the paths of meaning that are made available in conversation. Of course at any one time multiple paths are at least possible. Symbolizing is polysemic. What I attempt to indicate are the most salient and coherent meanings brought to the fore in the use of a spoken system of symbols and symbolic forms

(Gumperz, 1982, pp. 130–171). (2) A second aspect is the *reflexiveness of meanings* in the symbol system, as illustrated above where individual meanings negate cultural forms. Interpreting the "talk" this way introduces the reflexivity among levels of symbolic meanings and the sociosemantic loops that sometimes result (Cronen, Johnson, & Lannamann, 1982; Pearce & Cronen, 1980). (3) As paths of meanings are interpreted and relations among them discussed, one can hear "relations of dominance among [the] understandings" (Kirkpatrick, 1983, p. 12). I will not explicate in detail the relations of dominance, but mention them here to suggest this aspect of the symbolic system that becomes more visible and audible as a result of the inquiry. To pursue it in detail would require a more ideologically oriented theory of discourse, or a critical linguistics (Fiske, 1986; Hymes, 1983; Jhally, 1987; McGee, 1980; Montgomery, 1984; Parks, 1982; Thompson, 1984; Weiler, 1984).[1]

One final comment on the general approach. Unlike Schneider (1976), but like Philipsen (in press) and Varenne (1986, esp. pp. 1–9), I am interpreting *spoken* systems of symbols, symbolic forms, and meanings. It is what people are saying and how they are saying it that is my main concern.

Discourses on Personhood and Speaking

The two major units of the book deal with two types of discourse. The first explores utterances in which codes (subsystems of symbols, symbolic forms and their meanings) of personhood are used. Four chapters discuss in turn codes of "the individual," "choice," "self," and "traditional social roles." These symbols were chosen because they met the criteria of being deeply felt, widely accessible (used across many topics by many persons, not to mention their display to millions) and commonly intelligible (used with a forceful coherence) (Carbaugh 1988). One cannot help but notice the prominence given to these symbols as Americans speak. My task in these chapters will be to describe the cultural meanings of these terms and their social use to construct aspects of the American person.

[1] The general approach taken here also complements others that investigate and propose to investigate the interaction of mass communication texts and cultural discourses (e.g., Corcoran, 1983; Fiske, 1982, 1983; Newcomb, 1984; Rushing, 1983), the common consciousness and understanding of the media consumer (e.g., Chesebro, 1984; McGee, 1984), the nexus of cultural code, communal conversation and mass society (Corner, 1980; Hall, 1980) and the interaction of mass communication systems and social structures (e.g., Corrigan & Willis, 1980; Golding & Murdock, 1978; Meyrowitz, 1984).

The second major unit explores utterances in which codes about speaking are used. In each of these chapters, on "sharing," "being honest," and "communicating," I will be exploring both the meanings of these cultural labels for talk, and the verbal enactments that were so labeled. Thus, I am looking here at labels about speech, *and* the verbal performances that were so labeled. My task is to describe how persons conceive of and evaluate these genres of speaking.

Each of these discourses will be introduced in more detail at the beginning of each unit. Each also is intimately linked to the other. How does one get a sense of who one is, if not prominently through what is said? How does one know what to say without a sense of who one is and a sense of the other(s) involved? It is the social union of these two discourses that forms the central thesis of the book: Ways of using language and enacting communication are intimately linked to deeply cultured ways of symbolizing personhood. Abstract theoretical efforts to understand the sociocultural life of language and communication, that do not take into account localized views of human nature (persons), will suffer from deeply implicit culture skewing, and will be of questionable use when attempting to understand communication in its place. For example, it is unclear in powerful writings as diverse as those of Goffman (1959) and Searle (1976) just what is purportedly universal in human action and what is a product of Western concepts of self and speech. Both forces are probably at work but as of now we do not know which features of these theories reflect strictly analytical concerns and which are more descriptions of Western culture (Hymes, 1986a; Rosaldo, 1982).

Three Cases of Culture, Persons, and Speaking

To illustrate the main concerns of the book, that is, talk as a contexted and cultural resource, discourses of personhood, and discourses of speaking, and to add a cross-cultural flavor to these concerns, I will describe three analogous cases.

Case 1: The American Boy Scout. The Boy Scouts of America offer young boys the opportunity to gather together, learn about their natural and social environment, and enjoy being boys (one could say a similar thing about the Girl Scouts). What is it to be a boy in the scouts? What resources of communication give expression to boyness? Perhaps the most prominent place where this youth culture can enact and model their boyness is around the Boy Scout campfire.

Mechling (1980) has described the "magic" of the Boy Scout campfire. His description provides us both a sense of what it means to be a "boy" and an idea of how communication resources are used to express this view of the young person. According to Mechling, the boys in the Scouts are prominently characterized by three main aspects, (1) a preoccupation with the disgusting, (2) hostility to authority, and (3) a degree of anxiety about sexual identity. Because of these socially created aspects of the person, boys are given to talk and song about "greasy grimy gopher guts," and enact skits and chants in order to disdain authority and assert their heterosexual identity. By attending to the union of these aspects of the person and these patterns of communication, that is, song, chants, and skits, Mechling is able to give us a sense not only of a youth culture such as the Boy Scouts, but also of the important and intimate links between the model of the person enacted there, some of the communication resources that (re)produce that model, and the importance of a cultural scene in the performance.

It is the interaction of these features, cultural scenes, views of persons and views of speaking, all of which are constructions in communication, that provides the basic problems for the following study. As a further demonstration of these dynamics, consider another case where views of persons and speaking are locally flavored in a deeply cultured way.

Case 2: The Teamsters of Chicago. On the Near South Side of Chicago is a community which Philipsen has called Teamsterville (1975, 1986a). As Teamsterville persons look out upon their world they see particular places for speaking in it and conduct speaking differently in these places (Philipsen, 1976). More specifically, Teamsterville men congregate with their friends at the corner bar in order to engage in sociable and solidarity conversation. It is this use of place, and the role of a particular kind of speaking within it, that in part creates the Teamsterville role of manliness, and a place for its enactment.

Teamsterville conceptions of personhood are organized along gender lines with different expectations aroused for males and females. To "be a man," the male is expected to defend the honor of women, protect those dependent upon him, especially women and children, and exercise economic and political influence through intermediaries or "connections" (Philipsen, 1976). These criteria are used by "men" to conceive of and evaluate manliness and could be called a code of honor which in part motivates Teamsterville social interaction (Philipsen, 1986a). In Teamsterville culture, the male who leaves his women to fend for themselves, does not defend children especially through nonverbal means, and attempts to exercise control through direct verbal channels, is seen to be ineffectual and risks local accusations of unmanly and nonnormal qualities, for example, of being a "queer" or a "saint" (Philipsen, 1975, p. 17).

In Teamsterville culture, enactments of speaking vary with the gender roles of persons. Hence, for men, speaking is efficacious when he is in a context of symmetrical relations, for example, with like gender, like age, like ethnicity, and like status. In contexts such as the corner bar, symmetrical relations among men preside and are enacted through great amounts of talk. In other social contexts, as when in asymmetrical relations, for example, with a woman, child, or person of different ethnicity or status, less talk is forthcoming. Furthermore, if a man is to exercise power in a manly way in asymmetrical relations, for example, to punish a child or influence a person of higher status, he must exercise other than direct verbal means, such as punishing the child nonverbally or initiating a "rhetoric of connections" (Philipsen, 1975, p. 19). In Teamsterville culture, just as in the Boy Scout case above, views of the persons who are involved and the type of speaking that they are doing are intimately intertwined, as they are also radically influenced by the sociocultural features of context.

Boyness and manness, while obviously related in a psychobiological developmental framework, are not everywhere conceived the same, nor anywhere conceived the same in all social contexts. In fact, it is evermore apparent that today's institutions of education, especially the multicultural classroom, is being bombarded with different forms of discourse that are only natural to the different cultured persons who speak them (Boggs, 1985; Chick, 1985; Michaels, 1981; Philips, 1972). Is it fair to "stack the deck" so that those students who by chance happen to draw a match to the discourse of the teacher become rewarded with higher grades? How can we understand what is being said by those who are speaking? One way to unravel this type of complex issue is to attend seriously to communication in its contexts, be it the neighborhood school or the national talk show, and the cultural views of persons and speaking that come to bear there.

Case 3: The Ilongot of the Philippines. Studies of personhood and speaking among the Ilongot are especially helpful because they bring together native models of personhood with folk conceptions of speech, as they are both played out in a primary social context, "large one-room houses" (Rosaldo, 1982, p. 205). Where other persons social lives are conducted prominently around the campfire, the corner bar, religious contexts (Brenneis, 1978), or streetcorners (Hannerz, 1969), most Ilongot social life takes place in households (Rosaldo, 1982, p. 204).

Rosaldo (1984, p. 146) has described the Ilongot notion of the person as context-dependent, that is, "personal names may change when one contracts disease, moves to a new locale, makes friends, or marries." With such a fluid notion of cultural identity, Ilongot generally do not attribute *intentions* to their own person nor others, but locate the "deepest sense of who they are . . . in a set of actions" (p. 146), and strive to be "the same" as "equal others" (p. 147). By constructing and living this contextual, actional, and "same" conception of person-hood, the Ilongot obviously place lesser salience on the notions of independence, intentionality, and individuality, that is, on cultural aspects of persons that are so deeply ingrained in our Western and American lives—to say nothing of other assumed Western aspects, such as psychological uniqueness and inner sanctity (Rosaldo, 1982, p. 218).

Ilongot views of speech are intimately related to this contextual view of the person. From a Western view, we may think of words pouring from mouths, as an outward manifestation of an inner world. Speaking, from the Ilongot view, is not so much a revealing of inner thoughts, or a revealing of one's intentions. For the Ilongot, it may be more apt to envision speaking as a kind of net that interconnects those present, makes them part of "the same" social cloth, yet with strands that rightly identify the social relations among those present (Rosaldo, 1982). With this view of speaking, the Ilongot maneuver the net, mostly through directives or commands, in a way that gets the things done that need to get done, and does so by prominently preserving the valued "sameness" among persons. It is a relational, more than an intentional, patterning of communication that is used by the Ilongot, and a socially enmeshed conception of persons more than an indivi-duated one that they live and (re)produce.

Rosaldo's work on the Ilongot provides a fine demonstration of how views of persons and speaking are played out in a sociocultural context. Other cases could be given such as the person as a believer who makes prominent use of silence (Bauman, 1970, 1983), the minority person that jokes about his majority consociate (Basso, 1979), and the persons who share a fate and "gripe" in order to publicize their cultural identity (Katriel, 1985). More details on the communicative construction of personhood will be given by way of introducing the first unit of this book. For now, consider how this type of inquiry points to an under-standing of what is culturally variant in constructions of persons and speaking, and lays an empirical base for what might be universal indeed. In order to understand the cultural variations and the universal features, we must pose productive questions, some of which might be: How is personhood symbolized and lived around the world? What is culture-specific and what is general in these accomplishments? How is speaking symbolized? How does it vary cross-culturally? What is the relationship between these models of personhood and speaking? As a contribution to this line of thinking, this study explores the communicative con-struction of personhood and speaking in a prominent American scene. In turn, it will help address these broader ethnological questions.

Methodological Remarks

The communication patterns described below were inferred from multiple sources of data. The primary corpus was the broadcasts of the "Donahue" show from October 1982 to September 1983. The shows were scrutinized in three general phases. First, approximately 60 of the shows were watched and recorded into field notes (412 pages, 300 of which are typed single-spaced, the rest are double-spaced and handwritten). During this first phase of research, transcripts of 28 shows were also procured because of their specific content, for example, a thematic treatment of interpersonal relations, discussions of "America today," or their style, for example, from typical smoothly run shows, to lively contested arguments. These materials, the field notes and the transcripts, formed most of the data for the following analyses.

In addition to the "Donahue" shows, I consulted several commentaries on American life (Berger, Berger, & Keller, 1974; Davis, 1982; Lasch, 1979; Novak, 1982; Schneider, 1980; Sennett, 1978; Tocqueville, 1945; Varenne, 1977; Veroff, Douvan, & Kulka, 1981; Yankelovich, 1981), and Phil Donahue's autobiography (Donahue & Co., 1981). This body of literature was used initially to generate hypotheses. Later, as the communication patterns on "Donahue" came into focus, the literature was used as a base against which my findings were compared. Thus, the genesis of the spoken system of symbols, symbolic forms and their meanings that I describe partly derives from a naïve reading of the "Donahue" text, and partly from this body of literature on American life.

The second phase of research involved a more focused testing of my tentative formulations. All during this process, I returned to *new* instances of the "Donahue" show to test my tentative formulations. In the process, I subjected the posited patterns to the discursive test by asking: Is the hypothesized pattern an adequate description of communication on "Donahue"? If so, it was retained. If not, it was appropriately modified or discarded. In this way, my initial formulations were tested against new data. The process culminated in (1) a reinterpretation of the pattern, leading to further tests, or (2) a validation of the current formulation. This procedure combined with the above to constitute a form of hypothesis generation and testing (Ketner, 1973).

All of the sources described were used in a final phase of research in which the patterns were subjected to various discursive tests. I should emphasize, however, that the ultimate discursive test was always that of communication in the "Donahue" situation. For example, after the patterns were formulated, I recorded six shows for intensive analysis. The inferred patterns were checked against these recordings. Next, I returned to all the recorded data (notes and transcripts) in search of conflicting and validating evidence. Finally, I returned to additional broadcasts (approximately 40) to test the patterns against other new data. Unlike these intratextual tests, and throughout the study, I also tested the patterns in my daily conversation. In what amounted to rather unstructured interviewing, I would sometimes ask: Is this the way you hear people use X (a symbol or symbolic form)? At other times, I would actually use the pattern in an appropriate or inappropriate way—in situations where the symbolic *system* was heard to operate. At still other times, I would explain some observed communication pattern with the interpretations below. The reactions to my speech in these situations proved instructive and provided direction for subsequent inquiry. As mentioned above, however, the ultimate discursive test was always in the spoken text of "Donahue." While the symbolic patterns of other American situations generated useful ideas, it was the speech of "Donahue" that provided the ultimate discursive test. Procedures as these were followed until the patterns gained what was considered to be a high degree of validity. The overall process provided for a type of qualitative convergence among the data of transcripts, field notes, subsequent broadcasts of "Donahue," recordings of the show, and rather innocent native reactions (Campbell, 1975; Smith, 1978).

By responding to the above problems with these methods, I present a view of communication as a spoken system of symbols, symbolic forms, and meanings—both as it is used in cultural contexts and as it uses concepts of personhood and speaking. By examining what people are saying this way, one can understand communication as an activity full of meaning. However, rather than claiming that a people speak the following way, I might be suggesting more as a way of listening to what they say. No person speaks in sole terms of the following symbolic system, yet such a system can be *heard* to operate in the "Donahue" context, and in other scenes of similar design (Coles, 1980). What I present then are cultural discourses that may be heard in a prominent American scene. As such, what follows might offer more as a way of listening to a culture speak to itself, less in a way of speaking it. At one level, the study demonstrates an exercise in "interpretive listening" (Stewart, 1983), a way to hear a playful and integrative type of symbolizing where diverse American horizons are fused. At another, it suggests an analytical framework for interpreting communication by attending to the spoken symbolic systems that are cultural, that is, widely accessible and regnantly intelligible, and by focusing on two fundamental accomplishments within them (constructions of personhood and of speaking).

Unit 1:

DISCOURSE ON PERSONHOOD

If you tell me that an individual and a person are after all really the same thing, I would remind you of the Christian creed. God is three persons; but to say that God is three individuals is to be guilty of a heresy for which humans have been put to death. Yet the failure to distinguish individual and person is not merely a heresy in religion: it is worse than that; it is a source of confusion in science. (Radcliffe–Brown, 1940, p. 194)

Introduction: Personhood and American Communication

As Americans come together to speak, a notion of the person is used to conceive of and evaluate the state of human affairs. What I attempt to do in this unit is explore the notions of personhood that Americans speak on "Donahue." I should, however, make clear that I started this study—as indicated earlier—with an interest in investigating the symbolic system used to render the social world intelligible. I did not start with an explicit interest in symbols of personhood. One of the results of the inquiry was to find that notions of the person received a prominent place within the symbol system used on "Donahue." Thus, I started by asking: What is the nature of this spoken system of symbols, a question that led me subsequently to American symbols of personhood.

The Notion of Personhood

Since Mauss (1938), there has been a convergence of opinion on the concept of person as a useful tool for analysis. In fact, many have claimed that people everywhere have such a notion (Fortes, 1973, p. 288; Geertz, 1976, p. 225; Hallowell, 1955; Hymes, 1961, p. 335; Singer, 1980). But what constitutes the notion has not been altogether clear. Mauss (1938) described how the notion developed from person as "role" through notions of the "individual" to "self" with the latter being a most recent and modern notion. He traced the development by describing the person from what might be called the "outside—in," by exploring the social person from the standpoint of rights, roles and responsibilities, and from the "inside–out," by exploring the outward-looking more intimate and private self (Dumont, 1985). Focusing primarily on the latter, Hallowell (1955) proposed that persons everywhere have some idea of their own personal identity and of what distinguishes one's self as an object from other objects. Geertz (1976) has used the notion as a basis for cross-cultural comparisons of personhood among the Balinese, Javanese, and Moroccan. While these studies converge in their use of the notion of the person and its universal validity, they also reveal distinctive perspectives, namely, the person as a universal category of mind (Mauss, 1938), the person as exhibiting a degree of self-awareness (Hallowell, 1955), and the person as an actor of public cultural models (Geertz, 1976).

There are several issues raised here. Is the notion being used as a representation of mental state (inner), a representation of collective sentiment (outer)? Does the notion rely on a natural boundary (of organismic membrane), or is it a social construction (of native framing)? Is the aspect unique and specific to each individual, common and general to everyone? Is the description from the standpoint of a detached observer in analytical terms, or of a native in folk terms? Is there a developmental sequence involved from minimal to optimal senses of personhood? These are particularly challenging problems for studies of personhood.

I will address these problems by exploring the communicative constructions of personhood that are widely accessible and commonly intelligible within an American scene. It is thus the collective constructions of native frames that are my primary interests. We will see, however, that these Western public frames give shape to privately sensed forms, especially where the cultural symbol of self is concerned. It will also become clear that part of the force in the sayings is the enabling of a simultaneous awareness of self and community, with both caught between imperfect senses of what a person is, and should be. More generally, the study helps meet two longer-term objectives by qualifying some extant claims about personhood, and by providing a needed Western case for cross-cultural studies (see chap. 6).

Cultural Features and Universal Forces of Personhood

In the past few years, interest in the notions presented by Mauss (1938) and Hallowell (1955) has soared. Many recent studies of personhood and self have been conducted all over the world as is evident in several books and collections (e.g., Carrithers, Collins, & Lukes, 1985; Kirk-patrick, 1983; Marsella, Devos, & Hsu, 1985; Shweder & Levine, 1984; White & Kirkpatrick, 1985). Surveying this literature gives one a great sense of the diversity in conceptions of persons in societies, and suggests at least two general types: the holistic notion of persons such as those of the Ilongot and Bali and the individualistic notion of persons, such as those of contemporary America and Paliya (Dumont, 1985; Shweder & Bourne, 1984).

I will not survey this literature here. What I want to do is point to how often these accounts and typologies rely, even if implicitly, upon a rather inchoate Western (often Americanized) notion of the person. Consider for example, the early writing by Hallowell (1955, p. 77):

> a concept of self not only facilitates self-orientation but enables the individual to comprehend the nature of his own being and, by inference, the nature of other selves with whom he interacts. Since concepts of this category define the most typical and permanent attributes of a phenomenal class of objects among which the personal self is included, their importance in any culture is obvious.

Is it? Hallowell (1955, p. 75) describes self as a kind of social residue, or what is considered when the person discriminates one's physical being as an object from all other objects. Notice how this emphasis on self-awareness, one's "own being" and "the personal self" is intended by Hallowell to suggest one instance of a phenomenal category that is part of persons' "awareness" everywhere. Notice also how Hallowell's phrases such as "own being" and "personal self" resonate particularly with the Western mind. But what is the force of all persons everywhere? A self-awareness? An innate ability to distinguish one's biological being from other animate and inanimate objects? If this distinction is ably made, is it salient everywhere? If so, to what degree? Now, some 30 years after Hallowell's essay, it is safe to conclude that such a feature of persons has a prominent currency in the Western world in a way it does not elsewhere (consider the Ilongot above, Rosaldo, 1982).

Descriptions as this one by Hallowell (1955), as productive as they have been, are somewhat ambiguous for we do not know what parts stem from an adequate cross-cultural analytical framework, and what parts reflect the Western turn of mind. One could say the same about the notion of self used by Goffman (1959), the role of "expressed psychological state" within Searle's speech act theory (1976), and the universal standards for interpreting speech offered by Grice (1975). We need an account of the Western conception of personhood to help specify what is Westernized in these frameworks and what applies more generally across cultures. Both are needed, the cultural descriptions and the analytical frameworks, but what is of special importance today is a statement of the salient etic parameters that are necessary and sufficient for interpreting the emic cases. What is especially needed is an understanding of how personhood is variously symbolized so that we can gain perspective on those aspects that are more salient here than elsewhere, and vice versa. It is still too early to provide such a statement. But to work toward that end, I will provide a description of the Western notion of personhood that should make such a statement of etic and emic dynamics easier. Neither level needs to be sacrificed, nor obscured.

Second, there are several points in this literature where other-than-Western notions of persons are compared with a Western notion. Such comparison is inevitable, especially for American audiences, but what is regrettable is the lack of any Western standard of reference for what is compared. Take, for example, Geertz's quick comment (1976, p. 225):

> The Western conception of the person as a bounded, unique, more or less integrated motivational and cognitive universe, a dynamic center of awareness, emotion, judgment, and action organized into a distinctive whole and set contrastively both against other such wholes and against its social and natural background, is, however incorrigible it may seem to us, a rather peculiar idea within the context of the world's cultures.

I could cite other examples (e.g., Rosaldo, 1984, p. 146; Shweder & Bourne, 1984, p. 192). But what is common among this type of statement, I will argue, is a reference to only one aspect of the Western person, the self. Other important aspects of the Western person, as "an individual" and as a player of "roles" are either neglected or explicitly left out (as implied in the quote from Geertz). As Americans speak to one another, they use these aspects thus they should be included in this type of comparative statement. We need a detailed rendering of the Western notion of personhood to help facilitate these cross-cultural analyses.

By providing a systematic study of spoken symbols of personhood then, I hope to help (1) clarify which parts of frameworks are analytical abstractions and which parts are culture loaded and (2) facilitate comparative studies of notions of the person. To move in that direction, I will demonstrate the aspects of personhood that get used in an American symbol system. My thesis about the American system can be stated in three parts: (1) the person is an "individual" with "rights" who makes "choices," (2) the "individual" has a "self" and (3) "self" devalues traditional "social roles." I will develop these three aspects, respectively, as a political code of respect, as a personal code that reflects, and as a polemical code that rejects. Each of these aspects of personhood pervade American speech, with differences apparent among individuals, and different modes being used by individuals at different times. I will devote considerable effort to the use of these aspects in everyday communication. I will eventually show that if, as Geertz (1973, p. 390) claims, the Balinese conception of personhood is "in our terms anyway—depersonalizing," then the American conception of personhood is, from one point of view desocializing, from another, deculturalizing. Where the Bali highlight persons' placement within a never-changing and persistent social order, Americans place personhood over and above senses of social order and highlight ever-changing and resistant personal orders. But this introduces another "cultural loop"— like the individualizing of cultural performances—for it is itself a sociocultural order.

Before I begin the body of the study, a couple of clarifications are in order. First, the cultural terms, "the individual," "self,' and "social roles" are used here as typifications of aspects of persons, as fluid and entitling cultural terms. The meanings of these symbols vary, of course, across discursive contexts. For example, a woman spoke of "the individual inside me," invoking that aspect of the person discussed below as self. Similarly, the use of emphatic particles such as "the real me," or "really who I am," tend to shift discursive emphasis toward self. Thus, I am not drawing a direct correlation between words and meanings. I am, however, using a system of symbols as cultural typifications that give voice to a limited range of common meanings and forms. The range of common meanings expressed through the system is as important to this study as is the particular meaning of a word in a context; the two are obviously related, and both are considered below. Also, I resist tracing the relations of this American system to more abstract analytical frameworks until chapter six, where I draw links to ideas like those of Caughey (1984, pp. 9–30), Shweder and Bourne (1984) and Dumont (1985) as a way of developing a cultural communication theory of personhood.

2

"THE INDIVIDUAL": A POLITICAL CODE OF RESPECT

My initial purpose is to describe a spoken system of symbols that is used on "Donahue" to construct a sense of the person as "an individual." The symbols I will be considering are "the individual," "rights," and "choice." These latter two symbols are necessary to include for they are used along with the individual to form the cultural premises: the individual has rights, the subject of this chapter, and the individual must make choices, the subject in the next. I will argue that this symbolic system is grounded politically and used socially to guarantee a proper respect for persons, that is, as it is used, it provides persons with both the inalienable right to speak, and the freedom to choose. I call this particular system of symbols a political code, since it involves expressions that derive from the principles of the Constitution and the Bill of Rights. I will show how the code operates to create a kind of respect for persons as individuals, and a respect that reaffirms this stature.

My task here is not to treat the individual as an abstract objective construct, but to explore an intersubjective cultural category, the individual, that is used when Americans speak. Thus I am providing a demonstration of the person as a symbol user (Burke, 1966, pp. 3–24), as "both a product and an agent of semiotic communication, and therefore social and public" (Singer, 1980, p. 489). Similarly, I am not describing particular persons or specific individuals. What I am describing are the meanings and forms of speech that provide a cultural model of and for the person.

One final caveat: The interpretations of meanings that follow are not attempts to explicate all the meanings of the code, nor do I claim to capture the meanings of all utterances which use the code. What I claim to interpret are some of the common meanings that recur prominently when Americans use this discourse of personhood. I am all too aware of the polysemy in speech and I am simply trying to work within it. In the process, I will try to describe some of the common symbolic patterns that provide a meaningful resource for the conduct of some everyday discourse.[1]

In this chapter, I am exploring patterns of communication that surround the individual as a symbol. For example, what was getting done when a politician described his tax plan saying: "If you take care of the individual first, then you can take care of the business and corporate taxes. I figure you crawl before you walk"? What did the president of the National Organization of Women accomplish by saying, "some individuals are stronger than some individuals," rather than describing persons in terms of "men" or "women"? Further, how is it that "the individual" warrants, and is given, "respect," as when a male married to a man *and* a woman exclaimed, "I respect your views of morality and I would expect you to respect mine"?

The Person as "An Individual": An Equivocal Affirmation

During one "Donahue" program, audience members began talking about "jobs" in "the military," what "women can do" and what "men can do." After a few comments about the importance of treating women and men equally, giving equal pay for equal work, the discussion turned to "equal work." Can women do all of the military jobs that men do, especially combat duty "up on the front lines"? The question precipitated this exchange among several audience members (AM) and two expert guests, a feminist author (EG1), and the president of the National Organization of Women (EG2):

AM:	Nobody wants to do it [combat duty] but by the same token I think that a woman ain't made to do some of the things a man can do.
Audience:	(I agree . . .)
AM:	Some women are actually—
EG1 [interupting]	—some women are stronger than men.
AM:	That's true.
Audience:	(Applause)
EG2:	Some individuals are stronger than some individuals.

---

[1] The following interpretations are based on multiple instances of symbol use. For "the individual," I have recorded and analyzed 47 instances of use, for "rights," 55, and for "choice," 161. Every effort was made to record as much detail as possible. In all cases a complete utterance containing the term was recorded. In most cases the utterances were recorded within ongoing interactions.

The final word in this exchange implies that persons, as men and women, may be different with regard to their physical strength, but on another level they are alike, for both of these classes of persons are made up of individuals. It is this symbol that allows speakers to transcend the differences that are implied when persons are discussed as members of social groups, be they men or women, Blacks or whites, employed or unemployed, gays or straights, or any other exclusive groups. By defining persons as individuals, speakers can state what is common among all persons and groups, identify that each group is composed of indivisible (i.e., individual) units, with every person at base an individual, and on that level, express what is common to all. With regard to this cultural law, all persons are alike. In the same breath, however, by putting life into terms of the individual, there is recognized a potential distinctiveness to each person, for each is separable from the others as an individual. It is this *equivocal affirmation* of what is common among all people, everyone is an individual, and what is potentially distinctive to each, each is an individual, that makes it such a powerful cultural symbol. Through its use, a definition of persons is constructed which enables meanings of both a common humanity and a separate humanness.

The power of the symbol is audible when ever-present conflicts between social groups are reconciled through its use. In fact, during this same program on feminism, several audience members created a conflict when a few women with unemployed spouses implicitly blamed "the feminists" for crowding others, especially unemployed men, out of the job market. An audience member described her husband's work situation to the political director of the Democratic National Committee, a female (EG3):

AM: Three years unemployed. No compensation, no nothing.
EG3:   That's what's happening throughout this country, especially in the in-
       dustrial heartland. And it's what's happening to families like yours. It
       is happening to men and women. You and I are not opposed to each
       other. We are not on different sides; we are on the same side of
       individuals who are trying to make it.

The politician here attempts to "desex" the issue, and thereby talk over the more special interests of men and the unemployed, by describing the situation in terms of individuals. In her words, she suggests that unemployment, especially in "industrial America," is affecting "families." It is both a male problem and a female problem, a problem that many individuals are facing, and that all might face. She shows her audience a way to describe this problem that does not pit men against women, the employed versus the unemployed, but orients toward a premise of commonality: We are all "individuals who are trying to make it."

I should add here, however, that a few audience members did not agree with the politician's "desexed" portrayal, as was evident when Donahue asked: "If a man and a woman are out of work and there is one job opening and they are both equally qualified, who should get it?" Audience: "The man." (Applause) Thus the conversational meanings *about unemployment* shifted from the inclusive premise: (all unemployed persons are "individuals who are trying to make it") to the stratified premise, (some social groups that are unemployed, i.e., men, have more at risk and thus are more deserving of jobs—if "equally qualified"—than others, i.e., women). Whether or not there is agreement on the issue, and quite aside from the competing premises of personhood that are deemed most salient to the discussion (that is, the inclusive individual or the stratified gender role), it is never questioned that persons are at base individuals.

By expressing a common humanity among all persons and a separate humanness for each, the symbol of individual radiates a forceful equivocation between what is deemed universal for all, and uniquely particular to each. By using the symbol, persons can create a sense of persons as indivisible entities that are distinct from any social group. As such, all persons are spoken as alike, in that all persons are separate and distinct from all others. As is suggested in the above conflict, this sense of personhood is often weighted against others, especially those that consider persons as players of social roles and as a unique self. These, we shall see later, are additional aspects of the American person. Before considering them in greater detail, I will explore how rights and choices elaborate the person as an individual.

"Rights": The Political Guardian of Free Actors

The lot of the Americans is singular; they have derived from the aristocracy of England the notion of private rights and the taste for local freedom. (Tocqueville, 1945, p. 316)

If the private right of an individual is violated at a time when the human mind is fully impressed with the importance and the sanctity of such rights, the injury done is confined to the individual whose right is infringed. (Ibid., p. 345)

The following interpretations revolve around the spoken term, "right," and its two primary radiants of meaning: (1) individuals have "rights," for example, "individual rights," and (2) those "rights" should be distributed equally, for example, "equal rights." First, I will interpret a domain of meaning created by this system of spoken terms, then I will explore how this domain functions in the "Donahue" scene.

The first point to be made as individuals use the term rights is simply this: Persons as individuals have rights. Other people in other places speak of "duties," "obligations," "responsibilities," and so on, but the speakers in this American scene display the premise; individuals *have* rights. Further, not only do individuals, as Americans, have rights, but also Americans, as individuals, preserve and protect their rights through their routine verbal performances.

The central spoken role of rights to the individual was demonstrated during one show on life-support systems. A mother and father described how their son had been disconnected from his life support system, without their consent, because the doctors had considered him to be clinically (brain) dead. The parents believed, however, that the son was still alive because of his continuing circulatory activity. Part of the intense interaction surrounding this drama was expressed as a violation by a doctor of the parents' rights; their right to maintain their son's "life" in any available way. A male guest summarized the position by stating: "In America, and as long as it's the mother-bed of our understanding, I believe the rights of the individuals have to be protected." A human drama was discussed; a drama no less than the life and death of a beloved family member. A central symbol in the drama involved the expression and protection of the individuals', in this case the family members', rights.

Individuals, "in America," are said to have rights, and these constitute a primary sense of what it means to be an individual. Additionally, Americans' rights are preserved and protected in speech where rights for the individual are commonly expressed. The symbol of rights then, creates a shared sense of the individual's capacities, and also creates a communicative context where this shared sense can be accomplished. As individuals speak of rights they create a scene where the individual has rights.

A statement of rights tends to highlight the capacity of the individual to act freely and be respected for it. Because of this, an underprivileged person or group that confronts constraining forces and a lack of respect may forecast violations of rights, and lay claims to them. This dynamic is evident in discussions about public streets and individual's rights to stroll there, in discussions about divorce when fathers' rights and children's rights are mentioned, in discussions about equal pay when women's rights are "violated" and corrections called for, in discussions of parent abuse when parents' rights come to the fore. In cases like these, the symbol of rights is used in order to (re)create persons opportunities for free and respected action. Later I will discuss the role of rights in accomplishing respect. For now, consider how the symbol of rights as an instrument of freedom becomes an unquestioned necessity for all American citizens. When violations of freedoms occur, they are often framed as a violation of rights, a violation against the individual's capacity for relatively free action.

While the symbol of rights may be articulated in the discourses here under study, as a corrective for underprivileged persons or groups, it is the individual that is of primary symbolic concern. This was shown efficiently when a congressman appeared on "Donahue" and described his proposed tax plan saying, "if you take care of the individual first, then you can take care of the business and corporate taxes. I figure you crawl before you walk." It is the rights of individuals that American praxis attends to first. Social groups, institutions, and policies, are moved to the back of discourse, especially if a violation is under discussion. If there is a problem, the individual is cared for first. The state of affairs, as *social* affairs, received little articulate expression, and if the problem(s) is put into social terms, it tends quickly to succumb to "the individual has rights" code.

Important social issues such as medical practices and tax systems, when framed as issues of rights, highlight fundamentally the capacities of individuals, rather than their duties within roles or the responsibilities of institutions. Even matters more intimate, such as sexual satisfaction, are put into these terms, but become especially convoluted. For example, one discussion about male prostitutes and another on sexual matters, demonstrated that both "individuals," when making love, have a right to "equal" sexual pleasure. One psychologist even encouraged masturbating for women since they are so poorly designed, biologically, for pleasure during heterosexual intercourse. Discussing a physical union as a bond of intrinsic worth, over and above individual rights, women's or men's rights, is a difficult theme to sustain when matters of rights prevail.

The dynamics here, where issues become matters of individuals and rights, are captured nicely by Tocqueville's quote that introduces this section. But the "injury done" may be more subtle than an injury to "an individual." There is built into this communication system a cultural capacity to speak of, and for, individuals, a kind of speaking where social matters become individualized, where social praxis becomes articulated in individual terms, and the world speaks over matters of civic virtue, social responsibility, national and international concerns. Through expressions of the individual and rights, speakers mean to preserve and protect their ability to act individually on their own and for their own sake. To have rights, then, is to have individual rights. To express individual rights is to construct a world in terms of the individual.

A second meaning evoked in an utterance of rights is stated in terms as equal rights. Americans say that individuals have equal rights and should have equal opportunity to exercise them. This is a prominent theme in the discourse investigated here, and clearly prominent in the American conversation as the movement for an Equal Rights Amendment demonstrates.[2]

This general theme receives a particular expression on "Donahue" as speakers attempt to apply the valued equal rights to concrete and common cases. For example, a common issue on many shows, and the main topic of at least one whole show, involved the rights of unemployed men and working women (a different show than the one on feminism mentioned earlier). One of the questions asked was: Who should get a job if two applicants are equally qualified, one being a male and the sole financial supporter of his family, the other being a female and a second wage earner in her family? An audience member responded, "I feel that when there are unemployed men with families to support and they are out of jobs and there are women with husbands who are working, I don't think they should have the jobs before the men do." Audience: ("Oooohh.") Another audience member quickly added, "Who says that the men have any more right to have the jobs than the women? If they are equal then everyone has the same right." The main point is stated and embraced: Individuals have rights and those rights should be distributed equally.

The term "equal" is used here as a term of sociality. It modifies a sense of rights so that an evaluation of resources among persons, a social judgment, can be made. Is the relationship between one person, an unemployed male, and another, an unemployed female, or one group, sole family supporters, and another, secondary supporters, equitable? When this type of judgment is made, and both persons fall prey to the equal rights symbol, persons tend to be stripped of their social responsibilities and obligations, and are treated as independent entities outside of groups, regardless of their social circumstances. This is the case above where social concerns of the family succumb to the individual rights of the hypothetical job applicants being compared. For persons to be "equal," judgments of conditions between and among persons must be made, but those judgments tend to occur in individual terms that lead conversational meanings outside of social institutions

---

[2] Related notions on "civil rights" and more broadly "human rights" will not be discussed here since they are not discussed as prominently in this situation.

and contexts. This direction of communication is influenced by the cultural term, "right." Right is a term of individuality. It invokes the freedoms that individual Americans have to pursue their own happiness. Right thus gives license to freedom. But the modifier, "equal," adds social judgment to the exercise of rights. It is in this sense that the phrase, "equal rights," becomes in some Americans discourse a kind of guardian of individual freedom, invoking both social judgment and individual freedom. But equal rights tends to lead decisions into individual terms, with social judgments falling prey to the more fundamental political meanings of *individual* rights.

Note the defeat of the Equal Rights Amendment. Thus goes the dialogue when persons and social issues are expressed through basic cultural terms such as "the individual" and "rights," both cultural symbols that tower over and are balanced—if minimally—by the more socially accountable "equal rights." As cultural terms of the individual, and individual rights, confront those of equality and equal rights, the sense of individuality tends to be figured over social accountability. Through such symbolizing, the American conversation is praxis, with the praxis loudly affirming a common humanity of persons as individuals, a separate humanness for each, while straining to speak in social terms of accountability. When there is a rub or injury done, its sense tends to be heard and resolved in terms of the individual.

Feeling Free and Acting Constrained

If rights should be exercised equally, within an individual domain, then what do such rights enable speakers to do? In other words, how do the cultural symbols of equal and individual rights function socially?

An utterance of "individual rights" *enables individuals to state almost any opinion.* For example, one show featured senior citizens who were currently having, or recently had, postmarital sexual affairs. While some speakers criticized the positions taken by senior guests, others affirmed their right to do so.

AM:	When we get to be senior citizens I think we should have the right to do what we want.
Donahue:	Yeah.
A woman senior guest:	Right!
AM:	And I'm for these people.
Audience:	(Applause)

In particular, the point is stated: Senior citizens should have the right to manage their own affairs, and generally individuals "should have the right to [say and] do what they want."

This general point, on the individual's right to state any opinion, to act freely, has many particular expressions. Donahue asked a woman audience member to react to a group of feminist guests: "How do you feel about these women?" Her response was: "Each woman has their own opinion and if that is what they believe in, fine." The tone of her utterance indicated an implicit disagreement, but she stated explicitly the cultural premise: Everyone has the right to say and do what they want. During a discussion on the government's endorsement of prayer in schools, an audience member said: "We are all paranoid as to whatever it is but the beauty is we all have the right to our own paranoia on our own little cause." Audience: (Applause). Perhaps the most telling example on this theme involved a male guest who was very belligerent and outspoken. He accused Donahue of "asking all the wrong questions"; he associated his fellow guests, police chiefs and officers from America's heartland, with "the KGB . . . in Russia"; he reacted to an elderly woman audience member by saying critically "that's for a different reason, lady." As the show went on, a woman told him (and he happened to be a Black man) that he was "more prejudiced than anyone else in the room," which received cheers and heavy applause. Donahue said to the man, "I don't think that you should be surprised that someone would call to your attention your rather negative personality. Which is still okay. This is America and you are allowed to have one." The man's rather uncooperative actions were rendered commonly intelligible by stating his "right," "in America," to have such a "negative personality."

In each of these examples a person expressed, and was asked to express, his or her own opinion. When an opinion is criticized, rejected, or unduly treated, it may be brought into a coherent frame by acknowledging its speaker's right to say it. This is not to say that all controversial opinions are resolved by stating a speaker's right to hold it. I am only claiming that one meaningful way that varying opinions are made coherent is by recourse to a common verbal code, the individuals' rights to their own opinions.

The utterances of the "Donahue" scene display a particular kind of talk where individuals co-orient to each other's rights to speak and act freely. I would suggest that there is an iconicity between this way of speaking on "Donahue," and the show as a cultural symbol in contemporary American life. For example, the show sometimes features individuals with particular, often peculiar, opinions such as an unrepentant murderer, mothers who gave birth underwater (which in one case was televised), triads who were "married," pornographic film stars, male prostitutes, mothers who have abandoned their families, male go-go dancers (one was a born-again Christian), teen-agers of a "punk" life-style, single mothers who have been artificially inseminated, and so on. As these individuals are displayed for America to see and hear, a shared code is evoked which embraces the expression of individual ingredients; ingredients that are preserved and protected within "Donahue," in its speech of individual rights, and within America, where "Donahue" becomes a prominent and common symbol of, and for, individuals' right to speak what is on their minds.[3]

An important qualification must be added here; there are limits to an individual's rights to speak. Specifically, a speaker does not have a right to any opinion which extends beyond the individual, that is stated for another or is, in a sense, of social concern. Opinions stated as such are heard to violate the rights of others by "imposing" on them. So, speakers have a right to *their own* opinions but not to opinions which "impose" on others. This enactment of individual rights is a type of "negative face want," a cultural rule that one be unimposed upon. Conversely, "positive face wants," the desire to have one's "wants be desirable," become somewhat difficult to hear within this code of individual, since they require explicit social judgments that always risk imposing on others (Brown & Levinson, 1978, p. 67). The conversational rule could be formulated, something like, *when stating a position or opinion, one should speak only for oneself and not impose one's opinions on others.*

This rule is most evident when it is violated, where opinions are heard to extend beyond the individual speaker and impose on others. For example, a mother who had five children by birth and five adoptive children repeatedly spoke against "open adoption," adoption where "open lines of communication" are maintained between the adoptive parents, the biological parents, their sons, and daughters. After repeatedly stating her opinion, "open adoptions sound so good but it's very confusing for kids. . . ." Donahue said to her: "No one is going to deny you your position, but the question is why do you impose it on others?" Her original opinion was an imposition of sorts upon others. She was saying, in effect, open adoption should not be an option for anyone in our society because it "confuses kids." She was not saying, as Donahue and others would have liked for her to say, "open adoption is not an option for me." She was saying, it should not be an option for anyone. That opinion, because it extended beyond her

[3] In fact a 1987 advertisement for "Donahue" says: "America speaks its mind on "Donahue."

person, was heard to impose on others, and thus was called to account. Note, however, that Donahue's prefatory comment, "No one is going to deny you your position . . ." acts, in part, as an affirmation of her right to *her* opinion *as an individual,* but it also does just what he says he will not do, it denies her of her more general position that has explicit social implications. Donahue's speech evokes a common cultural premise of rights by asking, "why are you denying others their right to their own opinion?" By invoking such a question, her more general claim is reduced to an individual's opinion, and that reduction artfully "denies" her of her original societal opinion, contrary to Donahue's prefatory remark. In this scene, utterances as these seem necessary if each individual is to exercise the right to speak.

Another way to state the implicit paradox—speak freely but don't speak impositionally—is in native terms. Donahue often says something like, "Stand up and say what you have to say." The person may do so, but improperly "impose" on others. This motivates the cultural chorus to sing, "I understand that's your position, but why do you impose it on others?" So the person is told to "stand up and say what you have to say," but is best received when they say it the proper way, a way which displays and preserves the rights of all who speak by not imposing on others.

This "nonimpositional" dynamic gets played out for public as well as private issues. One group of speakers was discussing President Reagan's televised endorsement of National Bible Week. An audience member said, "I challenge everybody to name a philosophy that isn't dangerous when it is held by a majority. . . . I don't care what it is, as soon as the majority has the power, it is dangerous." Donahue added, "But it's not about the philosophy; it's about the possibility that the majority will assume the absolute righteousness of that philosophy (and) presume to impose it on other people. . . ." An atheist guest agreed, "The President has no right to endorse this [the Bible] as a moral code of the country because other people are being discriminated against because of it." So, a majority should not have an encompassing "power" that imposes on, and "discriminates against" other people. The only acceptable majority, then, is that majority, in a polity or on a talk show, that co-orients to statements from, of, and for the individual's rights, and does not allow one person's, or one group's rights to impose on others.

There is a native term for those who impose their views on other people, and, therefore, do not allow for others the expression of their rights. These people are said to be "self-righteous." During a discussion about sex, a woman audience member used the Bible to condemn sex outside of marriage. Donahue responded to her by using what he considered to be a superior datum for his claim, a widowed guest who had "intimate relations." He said, "the Bible says it's wrong and you cannot tell that woman (his widowed guest) she's wrong." Another audience member supported Donahue: "There's been other living patterns in the history of the world and what's right for some is not right for others. Maybe it's wrong for her, okay. But maybe it's right for other people and we don't have a right to judge others." Donahue responded, "You have a right to your feeling about the Bible but it's wrong for you to use this book and impose your interpretation of its principles on other people . . . while you're entitled to your beliefs, it may not be right for you to impose them on others." An audience member added: "We don't have a right to be self-righteous. I think that's the worst thing we do to each other." The ultimate paradoxical judgment is made: We/you do not have the right to judge others.[4]

This example brings together several of the above points. First, it illustrates how speakers construct and use a cultural communicative code in which "the individual" has "rights." Next, the symbol evokes the premise that individuals have the "right" to state specific opinions, in this case, opinions about postmarital sex, interpretations of the Bible, and so on. Third, the conversation involves a reduction of an opinion about a social standard to a particular statement from one individual, that is, "Maybe it's wrong for her, okay. But maybe it's right for other people." Finally, the example displays a native definition of a verbal style that is said to impose on others, self-righteous.

These communicational dynamics can be summarized with the following diagram.[5]

Persons are told to "speak freely," to criticize those who (improperly) judge others, and to enact speech "as an individual," which means, contrary to the stated rule, that one should not speak opinions that constrain others or one risks being labeled an improper judge of others, that is, self-righteous. This dynamic enables persons to experience individuality and freedom, while acting in a social and constrained

---

[4] The historical roots of this rule may derive from the norm for communicative conduct implicit in the Epistle of James.

The heart of the matter is communicative conduct. In awaiting that coming [of the Lord], we are not to discriminate, speak against one another, judge . . . for to do so is to usurp the role of the true Judge. . . . Unity of faith and unity of community go together. Division in faith (doubt) and division in conduct (judging) are both to be overcome. We are to avoid communication that discriminates, setting us apart from one another or one above another. (Hymes, 1986b, p. 85)

[5] In the following section I will clarify the relation between respectful and disrespectful judgment illustrated here.

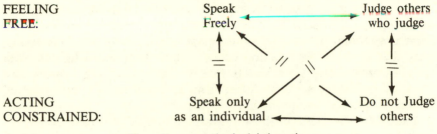

| FEELING FREE: | Speak Freely | | Judge others who judge |

Key: // = paradoxical injunction

2–1. Premises for individualized speaking and respect.

way. This is in part the power of the code of the individual, since it makes respectable the voices of the various individuals who speak while preserving the common humanity who speak this way.

Respect for "The Individual": "Righteous Tolerance"

A preferred climate for speaking is created as individuals talk to one another on "Donahue." Here I will describe that climate by extending the radiants of meaning discussed previously. The demonstration develops as follows: If individuals' rights are to be preserved, then a proper use of speech would "respect" others' rights; if individuals' rights entail the expression of almost any opinion, then speakers should be properly "nonjudgmental" of others' opinions; and if each individual's opinions are to be expressed with minimal imposition, then one must "tolerate a range of views." I will show how these statements function as cultural premises. More specifically, I will discuss the premises as normative features (Schneider, 1976), statements about acting properly that run through the symbolic system that is spoken on "Donahue." These normative premises function to protect the rights of those who speak on "Donahue," and model a proper style of speech for those who gather there. I now turn to these norms that constitute a communicative tone of "righteous tolerance."

The normative premise that epitomizes the rights of individuals— the most central in cultural displays of the individual—is respect. What I am suggesting is that respect is logically superior to the other similar premises, nonjudgment and tolerance. There is a proper way to be judgmental, a proper way to be intolerant, with each being an oral enactment of respect. However, there is no proper way to be disrespectfully tolerant, or disrespectfully nonjudgmental. Thus, the epitomizing normative term, the logically superior symbol in the domain herein described, is respect. Further, I hope to demonstrate how non-judgmental and tolerant speech are instances of this epitomizing type. I am not saying that respect is the most frequently used of the terms, only that it is, in the folk logic herein described, more fundamental to nonjudgment and tolerance. In fact it is my casual observation that much of the speech is accomplished from an oral style of nonjudgmental tolerance, a speculation which I will discuss later.

First, it will be useful to show how respect is used in certain exchanges on "Donahue." During an exchange between Donahue and an audience member, the audience member expressed what is a very unpopular opinion, "A woman's role is a woman's and a man's is a man's." The audience replied with a loud "Oooohhhh!" Donahue then stated the norm, using an educational metaphor, "Class, we will show respect to all of the members." In stating the rule, respect your fellow "members," Donahue restored a coherent order to the classroom. The norm of respect was also stated in the following interaction as an audience member accused three guests—a woman and two men who were "married" to each other—of an "immoral act." One of the guests immediately replied: "There may be some differences in our views of morality. I respect your views of morality and I would expect you to respect mine." As his utterance indicated, respecting another is the proper tone to maintain when communicating. In these and similar exchanges speakers invoke a norm, a norm which demands respect for the speaker. The co-enactment of this respect norm functions as a type of validation; a validation of others by respecting their rights to say their opinions. As a speaker's rights are respected, their opinions are set aside, for one can respect a speaker's right to state an opinion without "accepting" or "agreeing" with the opinion. In other words, the speaker as a rights bearer becomes the fundamental locus of respect, more so than his or her opinions. Speaking this way provides persons with a common meaning of respect, and, as speaking is done this way, the conversation plays a tone where what is said, may or may not be accepted, but the saying of it should be respected.

Of course there are times on "Donahue" when issues become hotly contested, when the tone of respect is threatened. One such charged issue involved an audience member who acknowledged the respect norm, then went on to break it. The audience member was reacting to the "free-form marriage" between two men and one woman when he said: "I'm sorry, Phil, we're supposed to respect your guests and your guests are supposed to respect us but I think it's sick. I really think it's a sick situation." The audience responded with applause. The individuals in the "free-form" triad added fuel to the audience's critical fire by describing several other of their unconventional acts, such as their availability to outside (sexual) relationships. Another audience member said: "You have no standard for your marriage. You have no standard at all. You're degrading even the name of marriage." Unable to take such comments any longer, a male from the triad responded: "Frankly, I didn't come on this show to abuse you and I wish you wouldn't abuse me." The audience applauded.

The audience reaction in this, and other, examples illustrates a shared endorsement of the respect norm. Note how the first applause came after the respect norm was stated, then broken. The second round of applause occurred after a form of the norm was restated, "I wish you wouldn't abuse me." The utterance from the first audience member was applauded because of its acknowledgment of respect, which made it properly critical. Compare that with the second, "you're degrading even the name of marriage," which received no applause, in part because it violated the proper tone of respect rendering it improperly critical. This latter state of affairs was corrected verbally as the male from the freeform triad noted the breach of respect through his comment, "I wish you wouldn't abuse me," a statement applauded by the audience.

This brief little "drama of living" illustrates how some emotionally charged issues are cooperatively discussed. While the differences between opinions are frequently obvious, explicitly stated, and intensely debated, the tone which constitutes proper performance, and the symbolic core which expresses its applaudable feature, radiates from, and is evoked by, an utterance of respect. Speaking respectfully entails a validation of speakers' rights, the intrinsic rights of everyone, by virtue of being a cultural person, to stand up and speak what is on their mind. Thus, proper respect is accessible to everyone for all individuals, by virtue of being an actor in this cultural scene, have a right to speak and be respected, regardless of their particular stance.

There are times when respect involves being nonjudgmental, a type of respect where speakers recognize distinct opinions, do not judge the person who holds them, nor do they judge the opinion which the speaker holds. For example, as is mentioned earlier one show featured several senior citizen guests who had engaged in some form of intimate relationship after their spouses had died. The elderly guests were advocating some form of intimate, often sexual, contact between unmarried senior citizens. After hearing their opinions, and several critical reactions to them, an audience member stood up and asked, "I'd like to know who thinks they can stand in judgment (of these people)?" Similarly, during a show which displayed alternative life-styles, an audience member said, "I would never judge anybody's life." Through this kind of nonjudgmental speech, persons are displaying a proper respect for others. In so many words, they say: Individuals have the right to speak their opinions, a right which should be respected, and, one way of speaking respectfully to others is by being nonjudgmental of them and their opinions.

In the symbol system used on "Donahue," a nonjudgmental norm seemed to have wide application, especially between parents and children. It seemed that great effort was expended to ensure that children's rights would be respected, a point elaborated below. For now, notice how the following typical utterance preserves the personal rights of children and places judgment of others in its proper, unworldly, place. A woman guest (WG) who was married for 51 years explained her current family and intimate life saying:

WG:	In my family we don't give advice. I don't try to run my kids' lives and they don't try to run mine. They want me to be happy. And if I'm happy having an affair, they're all for it.
AM:	I think that's great and, after all, who are we to condemn you people?
EG2:	Right!
AM:	We're not God.
EG3:	That's correct.
Audience:	(Applause)

In this example, the older mother has taken a position, a life-style which her children do not judge, as she does not give "advice" on theirs. The children's and their parent's life-styles are of their own making, and their right to their own style is explicitly not judged. If there is a proper source of judgment on their life-styles, it is not of this situation or even of this symbolic world, but from another world where God is the ultimate and final judge.

Nonjudgmental speech entails a kind of respect which, fundamentally, preserves the rights of individuals to state any opinion; protects the individual from judgment by others; and, helps buffer the individual's opinion from judgment in this world.

Because individuals' intrinsic rights are to be respected discursively, and their rights to specific opinions are not to be judged, persons are implicitly and explicitly asked to tolerate a variety of opinions. For example, during a discussion on homosexuality, an audience member explained his opinion by exploiting this common theme: "We're here and we procreate as God planned for us to do. They (homosexuals) don't, so they're abnormal. That's my opinion. *You're entitled to yours.*" Of course by implication the speaker is entitled to his as well![6] Another

---

[6] Note that to judge an opinion but not the person stating it is to violate a common sense of "nonjudgment" discussed above and below.

show featured film stars from pornographic movies and an audience member said: "I'm not going to argue with anyone's morals, but what about imagination?" He is not willing to argue the merits of other opinions, and thus is willing in public to grant legitimacy to a range of views. These statements demonstrate a type of symbolic tolerance, a willingness of speakers to allow a variety of opinions to be expressed. The preference for and correctness of tolerance is displayed in prefatory comments, "I'm not going to argue with anyone's morals," "If that's what you believe, fine, but . . ." "you have a right to your feeling . . ." and "you have no obligation to conform." In all such speech, a tolerance is displayed as individuals verbally exercise the individual's right to state opinions. As varying opinions are stated, speakers' intrinsic rights to state them are respected—though their specific opinions may not be accepted—and a wide range of views are properly tolerated.

In summary, the following points have been stressed. First, the individual has the right to speak opinions and that right must be respected. Second, opinions which apply to an individual are not to be judged unless the judgment is by God, or preceded by a proper acknowledgment of respect for another's right to speak. Opinions which impose on others may be critically judged if they violate others' rights to speak opinions. Third, and consequently, since individuals have the right to state their own opinions, and these opinions are not generally judged, speakers must tolerate a range of views. The norm could be stated: It is right to be tolerant of others' rights to speak opinions; the proper tone to maintain is a righteous tolerance where it is right to tolerate a range of views.

One implication of the above discussion merits a comment. Consider how nonjudgmental speech involves a noncritical stance toward a speaker *and* his/her opinion. There is an unnecessarily strong sense in being nonjudgmental which disallows criticisms of the person speaking and what they have said. A person in this symbolic web might wonder, how can I be truly nonjudgmental if I criticize this person's opinion? I would argue, based on my observations, that being nonjudgmental in this symbolic domain means, prototypically, neither judging the person's right to their opinion nor the particular opinion which they hold. This sense of being nonjudgmental is accompanied, and necessarily so, by the sense of tolerance. If a person is not to judge a speaker's right to speak, nor his or her stated opinion, then one must tolerate not only that particular speaker and his or her positions, but all speakers and their varying opinions. I have suggested that these meanings, of nonjudgmental and tolerant speech, constitute a type of respect, a climate of righteous tolerance, for those who speak and listen to "Donahue." However, notice that respect as nonjudgmental and tolerant speech is differently articulated than respect as respectful speech. If one is respectful in terms of nonjudgment and tolerance, then one displays a type of respect virtually incapable of criticism, for both imply non-critical discourse about speakers and their opinions. But, if one verbalizes respect for persons and their right to speak, then one has most effectively wrestled the speakers from their position, freeing it for a proper critique. The implication I am observing here is simply this: nonjudgmental and tolerant speech are less effective for properly criticizing opinions than are verbalizations of respect. Thus, the symbols may be used nonevaluatively or critically, but the former seem to be most typical, with discussions assuming an air of righteous tolerance of persons rather than a pointed critique of positions.

Conclusion

Given the symbolizing of the person as an individual with rights, it should be noted that many substantive disputes were elided in favor of cultural premises of the individual. Differences of opinion, such as arguments over moral premises, were sidestepped by a retreat to this common cultural ground. Generally, this involved a verbal reaffirmation of respect and tolerance for individual views. The effect of such conversing was the mutual endorsement of rights which relegated the topic of discussion to a secondary status. Substantive issues therefore were not resolved, but avoided. Issues of culture were not raised, but celebrated.

A point of implicit celebration was the cultural code of the individual. Through its enactment, a powerful force can be heard for it brings together an atomistic and freeing sense of individuality and an enactment of community (Varenne, 1977, pp. 148–149). It takes agreements as these on what a person is, what it can and cannot rightly do, what it should and should not say, for the community to converse cooperatively. As the conversation occurs, the individual symbol enacts common standards of the community, that is, we are each an individual with rights, speak freely but constrain yourself, do not judge but if you must, do so properly. Paradoxes are evident here, but are not something to lament, nor to poke fun, but to try to understand so critical use can follow.

Paradoxes . . . comment on themselves, for what they ultimately refer to is the interpretive process itself. Precisely because in paradox one meaning is not dominant, interpretation not singular, and truth not apparent, paradox operates as a figure of thought which foregrounds the multiplicity of meaning, interpretation, and truth. (Bruner & Gorfain, 1984, p. 64)

So be it. By understanding the paradoxes in communication, we may be better able to appreciate and celebrate their constructive powers, and if necessary, modify their use toward more humane ends.

An American reader of this chapter may well conclude that this all makes a degree of sense, after all, persons are at base individuals; individual Americans exercise rights, most prominent among them perhaps being the right to speak freely. Further, perhaps the reader is already privy to the Batesonian insight that life in society is inherently double-binding. But there are dangers in this ho-hum response. First, note how the individual code makes an articulation of some groups' special interests problematical (e.g., Blacks, the unemployed, women). The social dynamics of racial issues or equal pay become quickly spoken as individual matters, of one and/or all, thereby speaking over the special circumstances of a group that is unlike others. Impatience wells up in the face of such social difference, motivating moments of symbolic identification and empathy through the code of the individual, and hiding matters of distinctive, perhaps deeply important, class differences. Second, this *everyone and/or only one kind of talk* often applies uncritically the celebrated assumption that people are everywhere individuals. As such, a unity in faith and conduct is displayed, rather than a grappling with more distinctive mid-level, other-than-thou, means, meanings, and motives. The inability to symbolize through—or articulate with—another different system was apparent when "Donahue" was broadcast from the Soviet Union, with a Russian audience and guests. That some persons would express positional rather than personal opinions, or virtually not talk at all, violated the assumed cultural premise used on "Donahue" that the individual has something to say and should indeed say it. This premise, especially the person-as-individual, so pervades Western scholarship and life that it seems almost nonsense to question. But a distancing from it is necessary if we are to dialogue with distinctive others, within and without American society, especially when they are symbolized less as individuals, and more as members, representatives, or "dividuals" (see below).[7] If we are to articulate deeply with other persons, patterns, and plights, we must understand from whence we speak.

As a point of contrast, let me describe the Hindu person. While the person, to the Western mind, is an indivisible and bounded unit, an organismic whole, to the Hindu, and it seems to South Asians generally,

---

[7] See the introduction to Unit 1.

the person is a "dividual," consisting in various particles and substances (Marriott, 1976, p. 111). This quality of the Hindu person is described through the cultural symbol, *"rasa,"* or "juice," and is especially apparent upon marriage.

> A woman merges and loses her entire personality into her husband's *substance* at the wedding . . . she actually changes her natal essence for that of her husband's, she merges it with his quite literally—not through sex and childbirth as romantic western readers might be inclined to think, but in a truly material sense. (Bharati, 1985, pp. 220–221)

As important and as powerful as the individual symbol is in American discourse, what is deemed "an actual person" here as opposed to there will vary. This much is clear in societies where spirit persons and relations play a prominent role, and in those features of our own society where parasocial phenomena are evident (Caughey, 1984). Thus, as popular as it is for Americans to espouse the particular universal, everyone is an individual, elsewhere this is not the case, at least as we intend it generally, nor does it apply equally to all situations and communities in American society (Hannerz, 1969; Philipsen, 1975). The person is not symbolized everywhere the same, nor is it in any society symbolized the same in all social contexts. Without realizing as much, we risk endangering human diversity, seeing others solely in terms of our own.

3

THE "RIGHT TO CHOOSE": STRADDLING POLITICAL AND PERSONAL CODES OF PERSONHOOD

In the discourse of personhood here under investigation, choice plays a pivotal role; it has a janus-like character. An utterance of choice at once faces the political code of the individual further specifying its right, and it faces the personal code of self asserting a unique identity. Consider for a moment the variety available in some products, for example, Coca-Cola. Why do we have a New Coke, Classic Coke, Diet Coke, caffeine-free Diet Coke, caffeine-free Classic Coke, Cherry Coke, Diet Cherry Coke, caffeine-free Diet Cherry Coke, and so forth? By making several "options" available, a manufacturer creates a context where choice can be exercised; an individual right asserted; a unique identity enacted.

In this chapter I will explore the symbol choice as it is used within a discourse on personhood. I will begin by interpreting some of the meanings of the symbol, move to identify two of its prominent premises, that is, abundant and tough choices. Then, I will examine a few instances where persons lamented "no choice" and expressed limits to choice. Finally, I will discuss how the symbol functions to assert individual identity, exhibiting personal power and freedom. Throughout, I hope to demonstrate how the symbol of choice invokes meanings of freedom and individuality by enacting cultural premises, a conformity that creates an individualized sense of social actions where each individual is held personally responsible.

The particular sayings of interest in the chapter are exemplified by the woman who, when asked about professional planning, asserted, "we have the power to choose!"; by the mother who locked her son out of her house and explained, "I had my choice"; and by the "Christian" who claimed that he was "ripped off," he "had no choice" in his education because he was forced to learn the "Big Bang theory" and "evolution." What are the communicative meanings, cultural premises, and social uses of this symbol in the American discourse of personhood?

On "Choice," the "Environment," and Responsibility

Frequently Donahue and his guests discuss leisure activities and places where people go to socialize, such as "religious functions," "social activities," and "bars." During one such discussion an audience member said,

> A lot of it has to do with choice. You talk about a *Playboy* and *Playgirl* and all of these things. You have a choice of whether or not you want to buy a magazine and certainly people can talk about the merits or whether something is good or bad but you have a choice of where you want to go, whether it's for a drink or whatever and you're not going to change the environments if people want to go to a pick-up place because if that is what they want they can find it. . . . It would be too easy to make the people who don't like the environments they are in to think they are victims of their environments rather than saying they have a choice of where they want to go or where they want to be.

Donahue responded: "So, in other words, the culture did this to me so therefore I can't do anything about it. Therefore, I don't have to do anything." She said: "No. That's not true. . . . It's her choice of what she wants to do." A male expert guest added: "Exactly."

This brief exchange nicely summarizes and illustrates three meanings which radiate from uses of the term, choice. First, a person, by virtue of being a person in this culture, is said to be a self-activated, choice-making agent. Each person, when fully functioning, has the capacity to choose what one will do, when and where one will do it, with whom, and why. Making such choices grants each person a wide degree of latitude in constructing a life; each person has, as many speakers in this situation are wont to say, "the right to choose." As the speaker above said: "A lot of it has to do with choice . . . you have a choice"; she later repeated, "you have a choice. . . . They have a choice. . . . It's her choice." The expert guest agreed: "Exactly." In this kind of speaking, it is not only that a person has choices to make, but also that a person, as a person in this culture, is said to be a choice-making agent, an agent whose freedom and identity is in part constructed by the choices that are made.[1]

---

[1] For a critical interpretation of this theme see Berger, Berger, and Kellner, 1974, pp. 181–200.

A second meaning of choice is a type of assertion over the environment. A choice displays an assertion over situational constraints. As a person moves about and speaks in the world, endless "environments" are confronted, such as "religious activities" and "bars." Each of these is discussed as places where certain types of persons choose to go. Being in a particular environment, therefore, says more about the person who is there, by virtue of choice, than it does about the environment by virtue of its constraints. Persons are discussed then not as "victims of their environments" or "culture," but as having "a choice of where they want to go or where they want to be." For instance, "playboys" and "playgirls" are the people who "go to a pick-up place because . . . that is what they want." This is an individual's choice of environment. A person is said to support a particular environment through their choices rather than the environment's supporting a particular kind of person through its constraints. In short, as the individual articulates his or her choices, each is shown to be an active agent over the environment; statements of choice forecast free acts of the person, not constraints of an environment.

A third meaning is frequently evoked; through choice the individual becomes the hub of responsibility, of social accountability. The person, not the environment, culture, their parents, peers, or so on, is responsible for choosing what they do, and subsequently who they are. The above utterance nicely illustrates this meaning as Donahue prods, "the culture did this to me so, therefore, I can't do anything about it. . . . I don't have to do anything." The audience member reacted: "It's her choice . . . with the expert guest responding, "exactly." What point is unquestioned and endorsed? The culture or environment is not responsible for what a person is; it is the individual who is responsible, and held accountable, since fundamentally, actions are discussed as individualized, as matters of choice.

These cultural meanings create a sense of human lives and actions that highlights the individual as a free agent of choices, who has an active role over the environment, and is held accountable for actions. But how prevalent are choices? What is it like to make them? I now respond to these questions as a way of elaborating the meanings of choice as they are used and heard on "Donahue."

Premises of "Choice": Abundance and Difficulty

A first premise of choice involves a common moral imperative: individuals should talk as if to maximize an abundance of choices; the more choices displayed, the greater the assurance that individuals are free and responsible. This premise is invoked in situations where there are abundant choices and in situations where there are not. Whichever the case, persons talk as if to maximize the number of choices. If one says there is no choice, discussion turns to the choices that were unknowingly exercised, or could have been exercised, especially when stereotypical roles are topics for discussion. During one show, the stereotype of the teen-age girl was being discussed. An expert guest representing the Equity Institute—which "trains people on equity themes"—said:

> If we don't help girls to at least know that choice is there, many of them won't even take it. If we can all just let each other do what we want to do, I think that would be a blessing. But we have to help girls understand that there is that choice there.

A woman audience member added:

> I feel the feminists are doing a good job because they are giving the girls a choice. If a girl wants to stay home and raise a family that is fine. If that is what my little girl decides to do that is perfectly fine because that is what she wants to do. But if she wants to go out and be a doctor, a lawyer or anything else, I think we should be able to give her the support that she needs to make that decision on her own whether she is male or female. I don't care if the kid is a male or female, if they want to be something then support them. Don't say, "oh, you can't do that because you are a girl, you can't be a truck driver because you're a girl." Baloney! If she wants to drive a truck she can.

The woman from the Equity Institute added,

> [we are] providing girls opportunities to make decisions. They could be in very traditional areas in sewing and cooking and learning new math [and] metrics through the lessons we have at the club. But we also are letting girls have a chance to know that there is more than one kind of wrench and hammer and how to fix things. They can make the decisions after that. But what girls clubs do in communities across the country is expose girls to choices and to help them make them.

By talking this way, a cultural premise is displayed and reaffirmed: Individuals, especially young girls, must have an abundance of choices, such as staying home and raising a family, being a doctor, a lawyer, or a truck driver, learning traditional skills such as sewing and cooking, or less traditional skills such as metrics or the use of a wrench and hammer. Discourse such as this creates and manifests the premise:

Individuals should speak as if to maximize an abundance of choice. When speech reveals an abundant pool of choices, individuals are said to be able to exercise a prominent right; that is, their right, their freedom to choose *their own* position. In speech which reveals this choosing, one's status as an individual is reaffirmed.

Also, note the social consequence of choice. *Individual persons* must assume responsibility for whatever they have done; *individuals* are held accountable for the actions they have performed. Whether required by environmental constraints or not, individuals are held accountable for their actions of choice.

Speaking of abundant choice is necessary for the individual's optimal expression and development; as individuals are said to have a greater opportunity for choice, their potential for freedom and growth is enhanced, their responsibility increased. Notice how the "traditional areas in sewing and cooking" are not heard as full-fledged voluntary choices, but as stereotypical role constraints on a girl's future opportunities. These options fail to convey the full sense that free and responsible action has been exercised. Why? Unlike the imperative to choose freely, traditional actions smack of constraint. They exude a degree of conformity to social expectations rather than a degree of individuality. Thus, if the person wants to express a fully fledged individual, she is put in the position where she must exercise other less traditional, more novel, choices. These choices become necessary in order to provide the individual with an insurance, and listeners with an assurance, that the choice is truly one's own, rather than one prescribed by societal role. This is one of the reasons why a continual display of creative and new choices appears on "Donahue" for they extend, and at times transform, the wide range of actions available to those who gather there. Symbolic displays which reveal this abundance of choice guarantees both an ample opportunity for voluntary choice, and a communicative context in which the person is maximally free so to choose. When the premise is reaffirmed, free expression is maximized and the potential for freedom and growth, for responsible action, is assured.[2]

By speaking this way, there is created and revealed a moral premise: Individuals should have an abundance of choice. As broad ranges of choices are discussed, persons preserve a cultural capacity of the individual (1) to make choices, (2) to act freely over the environment in order to change and grow, and (3) to assume responsibility for any and all actions that are subject to choice. These cultural messages are

---

[2] The particular premise here can be interpreted as a realization of Habermas's ideal speech situation as wide-ranging actions enter the dialogue, are comprehensible, and are accurately, sincerely, and truthfully portrayed (Habermas, 1976).

sensed as liberating, thus negating their status as constraining moral imperatives.

A second premise of choice assumes that many acts of choosing are difficult. There are several reasons why many choices are said to be difficult. One of them, resulting from the above premise, involves the sheer number of choices that one must make—or realizes in retrospect that one has made. Since this moral premise grounds one's discursive life in an abundance of choices, one is duty-bound not only to make one choice after another, but also to reconstruct one's life's experiences on the basis of choices. This everyday act of building one's life on the basis of one's choices places a great burden of responsibility on the individual as a maker of abundant choices. Someone has said that "life is one damn choice after another." Under the sheer weight of the numerous choices, and the sole responsibility one must take in making them, the act of choosing is difficult.

A second reason that choices are said to be difficult is because the act of choice is sometimes assumed to decrease the abundance of one's future choices. Making a choice is sometimes heard to imply fewer future choices, and having fewer choices violates the abundant choice premise described above. In other words, if one has a choice to make, and makes it, then one will have fewer choices to make. But having fewer choices violates a cultural prescription that "there should be an abundance of choices." So one is put in the rather difficult position of trying to make a choice, while preserving an abundance of choices, at one and the same time.

This feature of difficult choice is evidenced at several levels as individuals talk about important topics such as marriage, sexual relationships, family, career, parenting, and so on. At one level, the difficulty involves an individual in an exclusive choice, a choice which results in abandoning future possible choices. For example, a mother described her decision to leave her son in a detention center for 2 months—a decision that was a part of a Toughlove program for parents of "unruly teen-agers":

> Let me say that I had my choice. I could have bailed him out within 24 hours and spent thousands of dollars on an attorney protecting and actually rewarding him. I did not. I made that choice and it was the toughest choice that I ever had to make in my entire life.

The mother made her "toughest choice," a choice which disallowed other choices. It is the abandoning of the other possible choices which, in part, made this choice her "toughest."

Because of the need to consider the implications of one's choice on other possible choices, individuals sometimes choose only those options that maximize their choices. Consider the show that featured a "free-form triad," two men and one woman who claimed to be married. Throughout the program it became clear that their choice of marriage was attractive to them partly because they all agreed on one thing, that was, they should maximize their choices. They each had their own bedrooms, but could share each other's if they so chose. The men had available to them sexual relations with a man, and/or a woman, whichever they chose. Also, they permitted sexual relationships between their partners and others from outside the triad. Their positions on these sexual issues symbolized their attempt to preserve a feature of "free choice" within their choice of the immediate "marital" relationship. Their choice of a triad was said to be attractive to them, in part, because of its preservation of such abundant choices. So, what may have been considered a difficult choice of marriage—because of its exclusivity—was articulated as less difficult because it preserved an abundance of choices: a choice of choices. As the triad members spoke of their arrangement, they displayed their difficult choice of "marriage" while preserving an abundant sense of individual choice, at one and the same time.

In addition to preserving one's own choices, the difficulty in choosing may also involve the attempt to preserve the choices of others. This difficulty is expressed most clearly in the following example as a parent discussed "toughlove" and the "tough choices" that a parent and kid must make as a result of a kid's unruly behavior. A woman described how the program might be presented to a kid: "Here are the other alternatives for you [the kid]. Here are the other houses; here are rehabs; here is the halfway house if you have that in your community." A toughlove mother said: "The kids make the choices." A cofounder of the Toughlove program added: "We give them choices." A toughlove father explained that "the basic premise comes down to putting . . . the crisis back on the kids instead of saying it's our crisis. It's their choice whether or not they're going to beat it [the problem]."

The parents here are faced with a difficult choice in what to do with an "unruly kid." They must make a choice. They described what they did as a choice not to tell the kid what to do, for that risks being heard as imposing on the kid, displaying intolerance and disrespect. They described what they did as a presentation of alternatives from which the kid can choose. Specifically, the parents' choice involved placing a card on their front door which informed their kid of his available alternatives, such as going to other houses, to rehabs, or to the halfway house. The kid, then, could choose from these alternatives.

As parents and cofounders of Toughlove described the program, they displayed the tough choices that were made, such as not letting the kid come home. They attempted to preserve a degree of choice for the kid by supplying the kid with a list of appropriate alternatives. As a result, the parents' choice was discussed as a difficult one since it involved ruling out the kid's choice to come home, but preserved his right to choose from among other alternatives.

In addition to the effects of choice on the processes of one's and others' choosing, choices also assume a difficulty because they display a moral stance. For example, a father who chose a career of building nuclear missiles suffered through his children's criticisms of his career. The parents who chose a toughlove style of parenting discussed the unforeseen and troubling results, such as those who criticized their difficult decisions. In these and similar cases, one's choices are attributed great difficulty because of the sometimes implicit moral stance that may provoke unknown, and sometimes unknowable, reactions from others. After choosing, persons may react variously, and the individual choice-maker must assume responsibility for the action done. But there are not only the reactions of others to anticipate, but also the consequences on the choice-maker's identity. In acts displayed as matters of choice, one is making a moral statement about who one is. When one discusses the choices which one has made, one marks one's speech with forecasts of one's identity, a personal moral order. One's choices then are heard both as they influence others' future actions, and as they display an individual as one who would so choose. These consequences, on others, and on one's own public identity, help create and reveal a climate of difficulty in which individuals speak about abundant and difficult choices and are, as were the parents above, held publicly accountable.

Taken together, the premises of choice impose both a sense of liberation by asserting a wealth of abundant choices, and a sense of burden by acknowledging the difficulty (and accountability) involved. While these meanings and premises tend to highlight choice as liberation, they tend to overshadow other constraints. What gets overlooked, what is talked over and silenced, is the sense of burden that may oppress the individual as each is held publicly accountable—in individual terms. This is especially troubling where one's actions are constrained by institutional and role requirements but are expressed in terms of individual choice. A conformity to role constraints tends to be made commonly intelligible in terms of the individual's choice. The rhetoric of being duty-bound to roles is not preferred as much as the symbols of individual choice. But what is overlooked is this: The cultural preferrence for choice itself requires conformity, conformity to a code of the individual where life is put into individual terms, thereby silencing the sociocultural forces in the making. This is at base the dynamic I hope to have captured when I write: The cultural person in America is spoken as an individual with the right and freedom to choose, a person that is symbolized prominently over the institution, culture and/or environment. The premise is spoken and sensed individually, thus giving the community an individual shape, but hiding the necessary conformity of persons to its great symbolic force.

"No Choice": The Individual is "Ripped Off"

Situations said to involve "no choice" generally involved some force or institution which acted over an individual. While the force may have been some disease or accident, the examples I will discuss here are of the institutional sort. For example, a Christian audience member discussed his lack of choice in certain educational matters:

> In school we were taught the Big Bang theory; we were taught evolution. I am a Christian and I don't believe in some of these things. We were tested on them and I had to take the test on them. It was a matter of passing the grade. There I as a Christian was ripped off because I had no choice.

The educational institution is spoken of as it "rips off" the individual, since it denies him or her of choice. Since one was denied the choice one could not fully realize his or her potential as a Christian. In this context, the individual could not act over the educational environment, he or she could not be a fully responsible Christian. Since one had no abundant choices, one's activity was constrained and dissatisfying because it was largely, as far as these matters were concerned, involuntary. He or she *had* to learn "the Big Bang theory" and "evolution." As a result, one was in a context of no choice, which disallowed a sense of alternatives and freedom. Since choice was denied they said that they had been "ripped off."

In another example, a mother and father described the side-effects that their daughter had suffered as a result of a DPT vaccination. The mother explained that she and her husband

> were uninformed . . . knew nothing about the possible side-effects and we didn't have the option of making the decision as parents pro and con. We would like to have had the facts and made the decision as the

parents of our daughter and lived with the consequences then. If we had decided on the vaccine, we would live with the consequences.

In this situation, they could not make a choice. Not being aware of choices resulted in a terrible consequence of a daughter who suffered episodic seizures, a consequence which they could not assume full responsibility for because the consequence was the result of an action in which they had no choice. This hindrance on their choice making meant that their ability to act adequately on the environment was impaired, and their opportunity for responsible action was denied. They wanted parents to become aware of the possibility for choice in such matters. They proposed a state of affairs which would remedy the situation through an affirmation of the code of choice, through educating parents' on their rights and abilities to make a choice about such matters. By acting this way, the couple could then reaffirm their status as responsible actors by acting retrospectively over the flawed DPT environment.

As DPT was discussed, an expert mentioned that the vaccination is often a legal requirement for children prior to formal schooling. This aroused a major controversy centered on the wisdom of requiring a vaccination that has possible negative side-effects for children, although the side-effects were said to be rare. During the discussion, Great Britain was raised as an example where "they give you an option." A medical expert restated the point: "They give you an option." The point elicited a high degree of intense reaction as persons wondered; if we are the land of freedom where individuals have the right to choose, how is it that the British have an option and we do not? This query was later addressed as the use of DT vaccinations (without the P which seems to create most of the possible problems) was discussed. Donahue asked: "Is that [DT] an option?" A medical expert responded: "That is an option, yes." Another medical expert added: "That's an option but the government admits that the DT vaccine is probably no good."

An option is introduced but is said to "probably [be] no good." Why have an ineffective option? One way to approach an explanation is by examining the role of options as prerequisites for choice. An introduction of an option creates a symbolic environment where the individual can function as a choice-maker. Without options there can be no choice. Without a choice, one can not claim to have acted responsibly over the environment. With an option, even if it is ineffective, the individual can symbolize a valued sense of choice. Regardless of the difficulty in choosing, a difficulty fostered by the prolonged discussion of rare side-effects, the option introduced a necessary element for choice, an element which avoids allegations of being "ripped off" and preserves the people's sense of the person who can act freely and responsibly over the environment.

Note how educational and political institutions were conceived in terms of choice and criticized for constraining this freedom, that is, the student had been "ripped off," and the citizen-parent had been improperly imposed upon. In one sense, these cases exemplify how the normative law of choice shapes institutions by forcing them to respond to the demands of individual choice. But what happens when the verbalized normative law confronts representatives of the positive law?

Consider the case of "the California stroller," a young Black man with very long hair, who expressed pleasure in walking through white suburban neighborhoods. Over a period of 15 months, the "stroller" was picked up by police officers 18 times, and arrested 15 times for "failing to identify himself." At the time of the show, the "stroller" was suing the state of California and the United States government—the case went to the Supreme Court—for a breach of the Fourth Amendment: "The right of the people to be secure in their persons, houses, papers, and effects against unreasonable searches and seizures shall not be violated."

This show can be seen as a part of a social drama in America. The "stroller" explained how he had made a free choice and he had decided to exercise his right to walk in suburban neighborhoods. But, his choice was violated by, as he angrily put it, "conservative police officers" (who were present during the show) who hold to "a religious belief that the darkie in the dark in the park is out to get you." He claimed his right as a choice-maker had been violated; he could not adequately act over his environment; he no longer had an abundance of choices regarding his personal activities. By describing his infringed capacity to choose, he revealed an inability to accomplish a central feature of his identity, being a "stroller." Since his identity was continually called to account by police officers, its social definition was rendered problematical and practically indefinable through the police officers' enforcement of certain legal codes. Thus, he could no longer choose to be the individual he wanted to be. Also, he could no longer exercise his freedom since he was subjected to continuous searches and seizures, a procedure alleged to impose on his rights adding to the difficulty of his choice to stroll. The individual "stroller" had become powerless in the face of the law; the individual choice-maker had become a helpless pawn in the face of an ominous environmental force. Rather than acting over the environment, the environment was acting over him. This breach was said and heard to be an imposition on his rights to define who he was, to act freely, and to exercise his rights as an American.

This violation aroused an anger, a hostility from him and others in the audience, a sense where the person was said to be "ripped off." The "stroller" was shown to an American audience and discussed by reference to a breach in a cultural code; the individual could not be a full-fledged person, since for individuals to be who they are, they must make choices, which are sometimes very difficult to exercise over their environments. But this breach of a cultural code, like any similar breach, required some redressive action which would restore the code to its unmolested form. In part this was accomplished by the "stroller's" appearance on "Donahue," publicizing the incident and giving an individual a powerful voice over an institutional environment. Further, within 4 months of this televised showing, a legal redress from the Supreme Court was granted as the "stroller" won his case. Thus, the mediated forum helped redress allegations of an individual being "ripped off," and reaffirmed the "stroller's" and all Americans' right to choose freely who and where they will be a cultural person.

Limits of "Choice"

There are some infrequent, but notable, utterances where a cultural mandate for "choice" is said to be somehow inappropriate. For example, one show examined an injectable birth control drug which is effective for 3 months. A doctor who was president of Family Health explained the biochemistry of the drug and its physiological effects. He also took a noncommittal—nonimpositional?—position toward the drug saying: "I'm for open and free information so you can make a choice." Upon hearing this an audience member exclaimed: "I took (the drug) and ended with (some unintelligible disease). I can't make a choice. You as a doctor need to make the choice for me."

The doctor expressed his opinion by acknowledging the individuals' rights to choose the drug if they so desired. But, the audience member had made the choice, a difficult choice that resulted in her contracting a disease. She did not want—for herself or others—the burden of choosing on her own. She could not choose in a way that was well informed and aware of the full implications of her choice. She did not want to bear full responsibility for a choice which she was being asked to make. She wanted the doctor to advise her of a choice. He was seen as better informed about the drug and aware of its possible effects. So, the woman was asking the doctor to choose, as the doctor invited the audience to make their own choice. The issue was not resolved, but the discursive puzzlement is clarified by interpreting the code of choice as a matter for the individual, and a choice for others as an imposition or violation. The question is raised: How can persons speak about choices that are best made by others for themselves? An adequate response requires a trip beyond the domain of choice herein described, beyond individual action and personal responsiblity, a trip which these speakers did not make, perhaps could not make, as their spoken code articulates the individual's choice-making capacity above the actions which others do for them—or they do for others.[3]

Some Americans sense a second general limitation of choice. It involves an inevitable realization; as individuals make different choices, coordinating their lives becomes problematical. For example, the woman in the "free-form triad" with two other men expressed a desire "to have another woman around." An audience member asked: "what if the woman he (one of the men in the triad) chose, you didn't like? Then what happens?" The woman replied: "If that would happen, that would be a problem but that might happen in any marriage."

The expressed problem here results as individuals make different choices. When choices are made, there are inevitable problems as one person's choice interferes with others'. This sense of choice, and the resulting problem, is widely intelligible, just as the woman's description of the problem went unchallenged. What is discursively unproblematical is the articulation of individuals' choices which results in a problem of cooperation. The common problem enters as individuals try to coordinate their independent choices. A woman in the audience wondered: "Then what happens?" When one moves from a code of individual choice, to an arena of relational coordination, problems ensue, problems which require working out in order to reach some decision. The unanswered question, "what happens?", involves some act of combining individual choices which is not, in this case, verbalized. As a result, individual choice can be easily articulated and widely understood. A problem that results as individual choices interfere with each other is easily articulable and widely understood. But what it is that happens when individual choices must be coordinated and combined is left unsaid. The unsaid extends beyond the meanings of choice here described. But the code itself is left intact for its common meaning is used to express the common problem of coordination.

Individual Identity, Frailty of Choices, Freedom, and Power

So far, we have moved from various meanings of choice that create a sense of the cultural individual, to two premises of choice, to some

---

[3] This emphasis on choice overshadows other possible symbols such as duty, honor, or obligation. For a related comment on the rise of dignity and a fall of honor see Berger, Berger, and Kellner, 1974, esp. pp. 83–96.

violations and limits of choice. We now turn from these meanings, premises, and uses, to a more explicit linking of choice to enactments of individual identity.

Identity management. If it is the case that the individual is responsible for making choices over the environment, and, the individual has a right to choose any opinion so long as it does not impose on others, then one symbolic way of discovering another's identity is by listening to the choices that the other has made. In other words, as the speaker states choices, individual identity is displayed. For example, a woman caller described some of her past choices as follows, ". . . when I got out of high school I worked. I didn't have a career but I worked and then I got married and what did I do? I chose my career. I got married and I chose to have a family." The woman chose her career, and her career is her family. She intended to say that this is something she took responsibility for herself, not something which she was obliged or duty-bound to do. To put her life into terms of choosing a career, rather than the traditional and dispreferred "being a housewife," she at once attempted to legitimate her traditional choice. This dynamic, a conversational wrestling of the individual with traditional social roles will be discussed later. For now, notice how the woman attempted to articulate a traditional role in terms of the liberated choice, a saying that could not attain a "full-fledged female identity" the way a non-traditional option would, for example, company vice-president. But what she does try to indicate, by describing her choice of career, is a public definition of who she is, a free individual that chose her family as her career. This statement of her identity gains clarity when placed against those other individuals who did not explicitly state their choices, and were thus heard to have conformed to the felt societal obligation for the woman to raise a family. This is one way an utterance of choice accomplishes a public statement of identity, in this case and countless others, by claiming an identity distinct from societally prescribed roles.

A speaker can indicate not only one's own identity by referencing choices, but also the identities of others by expressing the choices they have made. Parents were most notable for speaking this way about their children. During a show on "parenting for peace," Donahue told a story about a 12-year-old guest who had found a Nestles candy bar in his bag of Halloween candy. The boy took the candy bar out of his bag, threw it on the ground, and smashed it. He said, on the show, that he did this since Nestles sells an infant formula to third world countries which has "no effect on the babies." The boy's father was asked about the incident by an audience member:

AM: Don't you think that is a little too much for the child to handle? I mean smashing it. When I got a candy bar I was so excited that I couldn't get the wrapper off fast enough to eat it.

The boy's father: I was hoping he would give me the candy and he would send the candy bar wrapper back [to Nestles]. But, no, that was his choice. It wasn't our idea.

Another AM: The fact remains that as parents no matter how much love and effort we put into raising our children as well as we can, we have created unique individuals who when they reach maturity will decide for themselves.

The discourse here accomplishes, in part, the definition—and a creation—of the boy's identity. The speech displays "his choice," a choice to smash a candy bar and send it back to Nestles, and defines the boy as a choice-making individual who has responsibly acted over his environment. The boy's life is discussed through his choice, as a unique individual to become actively involved in a campaign against Nestles. His father helped clarify the independence of the boy as he made a child-like statement: "I was hoping he would give me the candy." When the father introduced the child-like response, a type of status reversal ensued, where the child's choice is heard as responsibly made, as contrasted to the father's comment, which was artfully played. The father thus elevates the child's choice to one of a responsible expression of an individual. By discussing the boy's actions as a matter of choice, the speakers define the boy as a responsible individual who had acted on his own.

The symbol of choice seems necessary in this situation in order to display the identities of children—in fact, the symbol marks a rite of passage from childhood to adulthood, and is a sign of growth generally. That children make choices is seen as necessary for their developing and, for their transition from childhood to adulthood. Heard this way, speech of choice marks—for persons—both development and adult-like behavior. Consider the utterance from an audience member who responded to a discussion on male and female roles by claiming: "Let our sons and daughters have their own choice. We made ours and let them make theirs. That's the bottom line." Statements as this preserve a necessary choice for children so they can express who they are and develop from children to adults. These comments were endorsed by another: "I think as soon as they [the kids] can make their own decisions, the better off they will be . . ." Why would they be better off? Because as they make and articulate their own choices, they verbally accomplish acts of individual identity and its development. These accomplishments are not only timely for children but also timeless for all generations. In the words of an audience member: "What we're giving to the future generations, I hope, is inspiration, and choice." When future generations inherit a symbolic domain of choice, they are provided the discursive opportunity to define and develop who each is; who they are.

Frailty of choices. I mentioned that choices are heard to be difficult because of their possible implications on one's identity. Because there are potentially terrible implications of a wrong choice on one's identity, and others' future actions, it is necessary to be able to change choices. For example, a woman had to "shed" her married life because it did not allow her to be her self. She had made a choice which she found necessary to change because of its negative implications on her identity. She pursued other options and other alternatives which enabled her to change her original choice. Such options and alternatives become necessary safety valves because of the cultural imperative to grow and change, thus always rendering past decisions reconsiderable.

If one makes a difficult choice while aware of other options and alternatives, then one is comforted in knowing that one can change the choice and opt for another alternative. This logical chaining renders the making of a particular choice somewhat easier because one has other options and alternatives, but it also makes the continued commitment to a choice more difficult as one may conveniently opt for another. In other words, speech accomplished this way makes the act of choosing less difficult, and the continued commitment to a choice more difficult. The act of choosing is easier because the original choice is said to be changeable. The commitment to the choice is harder because one is continually reminded of possible changes through symbols of options and alternatives. Further, the commitment to a choice (or decision) is made even more difficult as one's unchanged choices reflect a stifled self, which never can be fully developed, but must continually develop and grow. In order to do so, one must exercise abundant choices. So, to maintain a lengthy commitment to one choice, for example, of mate or job, is to risk a common fear of "stagnation" (rather than stability or security), a lack of personal growth and other similar sentiments (rather than a firm character), which makes the continued commitment to such choices most difficult.

Personal freedom. An accomplishment of choice aligned with individual identity is the expression of personal freedom. In some spoken enactments of choice, one hears not only the individual's particular identity as a choice-maker who acted responsibly over the environment, but also that one has done so freely, voluntarily, independent of other influences. This semantic of choice is often articulated as a "free choice." For example, Donahue and guests were discussing postmarital sexual relationships when he asked a grandmother: "You'd like to be able to make a free choice . . ." She interrupted: "Right. Right. And also I have two living parents. I feel I would give each of them their own choice (to begin another intimate relationship)." The audience applauded.

These and similar statements of free choice are commonly intelligible as accomplishments of personal freedom, as exercises of one's own will independent of other influences. There are, however, more dramatic ways of articulating and displaying one's freedom to choose. In fact, the more unusual one's choice, the more effective it is at conveying a message of freedom. The "Donahue" show is perhaps famous for displaying such "personal freedoms" as transvestites, male go-go dancers, punk rockers, mothers who divorce families, single mothers, and so on. Each of these individuals, as they discuss the choices they have made, meaningfully display a personal freedom, that is, the freedom of each individual so to choose.

Personal power. A third, and related, semantic accomplishment radiates from the cultural symbol, choice, and displays an element of personal power or control. As individuals express their choices, they mean, in part, to exercise a degree of control over their physical and social environment. A woman stated the point here most succinctly when she exclaimed: "We've got the power to choose!" A similar theme was revealed when a female customer of male prostitutes was questioned by Donahue: "So you're saying, look, make a contract, pay for it and it's your choice regarding where you want the evening to go, right?" The woman replied: "It leaves me in control." A female author forecasting a "Coming Matriarchy" (the topic of her recent book) explained that "more and more women are going to be making more decisions, going to assume more positions of power, and have more money, and all the tools that men play the game with . . ." In each case a choice or decision is said to supply the choice-maker with a sense of personal power and control over one's environment.

Choosing and Individual Responsibility

Since choice is the prominent mode of enactment for the individual, it is put to various social uses, to negotiate the locus of motives in medical matters, to render marital problems commonly intelligible, and to preserve—through the introduction of an ineffective option—a polity's sense of voluntary action. These uses demonstrate some of the explicit conversational tasks which cultural symbols—like choice—perform, that is, enactments of identity, freedom, and power.

As I have mentioned throughout, these various uses of choice highlight a sense of freedom, the freedom to choose, while also subverting the tremendous burden of individual responsibility that is required for the performance. Thus as actions are described as a matter of choice, what is foregrounded is the individual will, the free actor over environments. Backgrounded are the following constraints: (1) each individual choice constrains one's self and others, (2) each individual must assume a burden of responsibility for all of his or her actions, and (3) at another more basic level, persons in public must conceive of their lives and actions as individual matters of rights and choice. The sense of individual freedom is foregrounded and praised; the collective actions and points of conformity that enable the performance are backgrounded. Thus, persons tend to speak as agents of free choice and overlook the constraints and conformity in their actions. (See Diagram 3–1.)

I am not claiming that these dynamics are consciously endorsed or happily displayed. It is more that some things are publicly expressed, are matters for communication, while others are sensed but left unstated. Both features, the said and the unsaid, may have mutual coherence, but one gets featured, the other not. Both may also be experienced by the situated ensemble of speakers. In the orchestrated performance of the oral score, a tune is heard; a tune whose harmony is felt and melody recognized as each musician plays not only their instrument of choice, but also a common and familiar cultural tune. Perhaps some hear only the solo performances and the unusual songs from fringe bands. I listen to these too, but with an ear to the repercussions which they have on the familiar cultural symphony, a symphony whose tune of choice is played. But in order to create the tune, collective restraints are required. By leaving these unstated, unexplored, and without expression, we risk being exploited by them. This is hardly a matter of choice.

The above is a rather shorthand way of making an important point: the communication patterns used on "Donahue" are creating a common

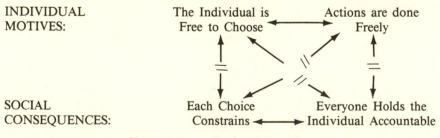

INDIVIDUAL
MOTIVES:

The Individual is
Free to Choose

Actions are done
Freely

SOCIAL
CONSEQUENCES:

Each Choice
Constrains

Everyone Holds the
Individual Accountable

Key: // = paradoxical injunction

3–1. Premises of choice and responsibility.

sense of the person as an individual. We all at times put the person into such terms, into symbols that are systemically and functionally interrelated, that is, the individual is not much without rights and choices. By attending to this system of terms, their meanings, premises, and social use, I have attempted to capture what is widely intelligible when the individual, rights and choice are naturally expressed. I have also attempted to capture some features that are highlighted and hidden in the performance. Through these interpretations, one code in an overall discourse of personhood has surfaced, a political code where the individual has rights, thereby gaining expression and respect. The symbol choice was interpreted as a pivotal term with political and personal features, as a fundamental right of the individual *and* as an assertion of individual identity. I now turn to this more personal side, the part of the American person which is said to be unique, and which the individual *has,* the self.

4

"SELF": A PERSONAL CODE

Modern society . . . confronts the individual with an ever-changing kaleidoscope of social experiences and meanings. It forces him to make decisions and plans. By the same token, it forces him into reflection. Modern consciousness is therefore peculiarly aware, tense, "rationalizing." It follows that this reflectiveness pertains not only to the outside world but also to the subjectivity of the individual and especially his identity. Not only the world but the self becomes an object of deliberate attention and sometimes anguished scrutiny. (Berger, Berger, & Kellner, 1974, pp. 78–79).

Learning to love your self is the greatest love of all.
-Whitney Houston

The public discourses of Americans is replete with "self" expression. In fact, my corpus of "Donahue" communication includes more than 315 "self" sayings, including all pronominal derivatives, for example, "yourself," "myself," "himself," "herself," and seemingly endless hyphenated terms, for example: "self-esteem," "self-respect," "self-image," "self-actualization," "sense-of-self," "self-worth," "self-help," "self-confident," "self-justification," "self-approval," "self-support," "self-consciousness," "self-fulfillment," "self-attitude," "self-centered," "self-assured," "self-interest," "self-abortion," and so forth.

These terms and tropes of self were put to various uses. For example, a woman discussed what she considered to be the fundamental requisite for high-quality education by claiming that the student must first "feel good about himself." Her creed displays the mission for educational institutions as one of creating a place where self can feel good. On another topic, and on several showings, divorced persons justified their divorces in terms of self, for example, "self-fulfillment," "self-esteem," and so forth. A critic of this trend has written: "there's no doubt that without the word *self*, and the values and concepts it currently brings with it, the divorce rate would be considerably lower than it is" (Rosenthal, 1984, p. 5). What role is self playing in our discourse of personhood? In common senses of education, of marriage and the family, of religious and political issues? What is meant as the person puts the world into terms of self? What does this cultural symbol accomplish in the American system of communication?

My purpose in this chapter is to interpret how self constructs a code of American personhood. In particular, I will show how the symbol self is considered something that the individual *has*. It is claimed as the personal part of the person that is played—in conversation—over the more political individual and as demonstrated later, against its polemical "traditional social role." It is this conversational playing that accounts for some of the modern tenseness, the isolation and alienation, that warrants "deliberate attention and sometimes anguished scrutiny" (as is mentioned in the quote that introduces the chapter). It is also these dynamics that help motivate one—very popular—solution to the "anguish" of American modernity: "love your self," a solution that further perpetuates the modern trend.

In the first part of the chapter I will develop three dimensions of meaning that differentiate self from social role. Each dimension provides a "two-valued set that is used to conceive of and evaluate" the self (Seitel, 1974, p. 51). After defining the semantic dimensions, their use will be demonstrated in a typical personal story, in episodes of conflict, and in a prominent American myth.[1]

The second part of the chapter will examine metaphorical statements in speech which treat self as a container. The metaphor will be shown to express self as a "thing" in physical and spatial terms. The analysis reveals a cultural evaluation of self as an internal arrangement that has or lacks substance, and can be "lost" and/or "found."

Throughout the chapter, I am working toward two general goals: to show how semantic dimensions can be used to interpret speech patterns; and to show how three oral forms, personal stories, myths and metaphors, form "an interrelated semantic system" (Seitel, 1974, p. 51).

Spoken Meanings of "Self"

As people talk on "Donahue" they use two clusters of terms that compete as aspects of the individual. One cluster includes self, its pronominal derivatives and certain adjectival uses listed above. The other includes "traditional social roles" and other terms, such as "housewife, macho men, sex symbols, atheists, and gays" or almost any term referring to groups of individuals. Self and social role are differentiated along three semantic dimensions: independent–dependent,

---

[1] Semantic dimensions can be understood as indigenous code rules, or norms, of interpretation (see Carbaugh, 1987; Hymes, 1972, p. 64; Sigman, 1980).

aware–unaware, and communicative–closed.[2] In this chapter, I will define, analyze into finer discriminations, and illustrate the self poles of the dimensions.[3]

Independent-dependent. Speakers of "Donahue" use the dimension *independent-dependent* to conceive of and evaluate a common sense of self.[4] The dimension is heard to operate in speech as individuals differentiate an independent self from a more dependent social role, as they conceive of self as relatively stable across contexts, and as they express self as a unique arrangement of personal qualities.

The dimension is used as speakers express their choices, which are made on their own and demonstrate their responsible ability to act independently—outside any social role. For example, a woman stated her position as independent from other women and the whole ERA movement saying: "Well, they [ERA supporters] go and say you've got to have this, you've got to be for ERA because it's going to help you as a woman. I've done what I've done as my own person." She expresses an independence from the movement. Her expression defines her actions as independently done, on her own, outside her social role as a woman and ERA supporter.

To speak independently is to act on one's own, outside one's socially prescribed roles. A rhetoric of independence is displayed as speakers articulate the free choices they have made, as they take sole responsibility for their choices, as they preserve their right to choose through a norm of (individual) respect, and as they criticize those who violate this independence as being self-righteous. This is the domain of independence, the symbolic arena of free, voluntary, and unimposed choice. As speakers discuss varying topics of varying importance, they artfully display and preserve their own, and others', independence.

There are at least two additional radiants of independence that are used. One is the core quality or stable features of self; it is spoken as somewhat unaffected by temporal or spatial location. Each self is said to have a stable center that remains relatively uninfluenced by a social situation, particular environment, or context. This quality is spoken of as rather enduring, ubiquitous and is sometimes used as an account when speakers co-orient to untoward conduct. For example, one guest

---

[2] The dimensions were inductively derived from speakers' discourse. I tried to make sense of the ways "self" and "social role" were used by subjecting them to a type of distinctive feature analysis. Upon formulating the dimensions, I returned to the situated discourse to test my hypotheses. After several "trips to the data" I was able to confirm my hypotheses and obtain speakers' terminology for the semantic dimensions.

[3] In the next chapter, I will develop the poles of "traditional social roles."

[4] I follow closely here the wording and method of analysis suggested by Peter Seitel (1974), and used in Katriel and Philipsen (1981).

made several derogatory remarks to Donahue, other guests, and members of the audience. His verbal violations of proper respect were rendered intelligible by reference to his "negative personality" which, as was said, in "America . . . you are allowed to have." By attributing his actions to his personality, speakers could understand his comments as "the way he is," as an assortment of stable features that were brought into the speech situation and unaffected by it. So a more refined sense of independence refers to those aspects of self that are said to be relatively stable across time and place.[5]

A second radiant of independence evokes a quality of psychological uniqueness that cannot be equated with any other. A self may be said to be stable across time and space, and like others. But the sense of self here contributing to a broader meaning of independence refers to the personal uniqueness which every self is said to have, that differentiates one self from all others—and all others from one's self.[6]

The verbal expression of uniqueness can be heard as speakers co-orient to personal "needs." One person's needs are said and felt to be different from all others'. A need might be common, such as sexual expression, but the particular means, the desired frequency, the place, the relational context and so on of its satisfaction are all expressed as features of the particularly unique self. As needs are expressed, and means toward their satisfaction are negotiated, one hears a degree of independence through the presentation of self as unique from all others.

When individuals speak of self they mean to say that they are independent; they are free to choose, choose they must, and they do so on their own. To speak of self this way is to refer to the core feature of the person which is disclosed across varying places and times. Presentations of self as these are heard as distinct combinations of qualities unique *in toto* from all others. Thus, self is symbolized as independent, a stable core of uniqueness.

Aware-unaware. A second dimension used in conceiving and evaluating self is *aware-unaware.* There are at least two types of awareness that radiate from self. One is primarily an act of self-awareness, a personal recognition that reflects one's sense of who one is, one's self-concept. In particular, this dimension was used as speakers were admonished to acknowledge responsibility for the choices they will make and have made. By recognizing choices, speakers could display a fully functioning self, aware of its unique qualities and circumstances.

---

[5] Note, however, that this stable core of "self" is also supposed to develop over time, show "true colors" and grow, thus demonstrating degrees of both permanence and change.

[6] The analysis of "self" here corroborates Hevvé Varenne's (1977) analysis of individualism as personal identity, voluntary choice, and personal uniqueness.

To act fully over the environment, self is expected to be "in touch" with various issues and problems. Through expressing an awareness of the issues—which are thematically treated on "Donahue"—self is said to be better able to cope with the complexities of everyday life. For self to address the issues most appropriately, a verbal display is required, a display of awareness where one's own attitudes and actions are revealed.

However, speaking in a way that demonstrates only an awareness of self and problematical issues is not enough. Recall those who verbally imposed positions on others. Acts like these may be performed with a degree of awareness, but they also presume to know what is best/ right/good for others. Speech which reveals a full-blown awareness of self exudes an awareness of one's own self, of social issues, and an awareness of the self of others. Those who do not adequately communicate a proper awareness of other's self are said to be self-righteous or selfish.

The ways in which proper awareness of other's self is discursively performed merits a comment here. A communicative event which demonstrates such awareness is initiated with several prefatory acts like: "I'm sure you are a wonderful wife and a good mother who takes good care of your kids, but . . ." In these opening lines, a respectful awareness of another self is expressed; a speaker reaffirms a set of valued qualities, such as "wonderful wife" which an addressee is said to emulate. In spoken acts as these, an awareness of another self is discursively displayed. The statements may contain references to social roles—mother, wife, and so forth—in fact must contain references to more than one social role if the verbal address is to refer explicitly to self, that is, a unique person beyond roles. So one discursive means of showing an awareness of another's self is by referring to some unique combination of common values and roles which an addressee is said to embody uniquely.

In another example, Donahue asked a group of young boys if they "would like to lead the lives that their fathers led?" A young boy responded: "No, because my father would lead me every step of the way. Then he would tell me what he did and I'd have to do what he did." The boy's statement was heard to be inappropriately unaware: it was heard as an inadequate self-expression on two counts; it did not reveal an awareness of the child's self; and, it was improperly unaware—somewhat disrespectful—of the father by evaluating his implicit flaws (i.e., he was not nurturing the boy's independence and he was not allowing the boy to become aware of his own choices). Donahue rescued the father's interactional identity, and educated the boy who rather innocently criticized his father by repeating the "obvious": "obviously your dad is smart enough to know that you are a talented individual who is going to make your own decision about what you want to do with your life. But just generally, would you like to lead the same lifestyle?" The boy: "Yeah." So the father's awareness of his son—as an independent other—was (re)affirmed, while the boy's awareness of his father as a respectful and respectable person was displayed. Shown as well was the son's "obvious" potential for independent decision making. Thus, awareness and independence give meaning to these demonstrations of the cultural self.

In these and similar utterances a semantic dimension of awareness is used. As persons conceive and evaluate the actions of one another, the negotiation turns to self. As a result, an awareness is preferred not only of self, one's choices, one's needs, and important issues, but also of another's self, which shows them a proper tolerance and respect. The interactional accomplishment attends to all identities as unique, thus displaying an awareness of the unique self that each individual has.

Communicative-closed. A third semantic dimension used in the conception and evaluation of self is that of *communicative-closed.*[7] The dimension is synonymous with several native terms related to communicativeness such as openness, expressiveness, talkativeness, and so on. I have chosen communicativeness as a convenient label for the dimension because of its empirical prominence and its grounding in related literature (Katriel & Philipsen, 1981). The semantic feature referred to, regardless of the label, arises from statements which evoke a common value of, and normative injunction for, self to be expressive and communicate. For example, Donahue asked a wife about a problem with her husband:

Donahue: Do you talk to your husband about this?
Wife: We try.
Donahue: We have no remedy here except to say your husband has a responsibility to be more verbal.

During another program a guest stated similarly, "you're supposed to express your feelings." In a similar situation, another wife asked what she could do to help her "father face the situation":

---

[7] The dimension of communicativeness described here refers to the conception and evaluation of the cultural individual or "self." It is an interpretation of "communication" from the standpoint of the symbol "self." Thus, the norm may be stated, it is preferred that the "self" be "communicative." For a complementary interpretation of "communication" as a cultural category, see Katriel and Philipsen, 1981, and chaps. 9 and 10 below.

Donahue: Talk to him.

Wife 2: [I've tried but] he is constantly evading the subject. He will change the subject constantly; he just avoids it.

Donahue: I assume that you have to respect that, huh. You can't force feed someone the opportunity to express themselves.

Note that the wife must "respect" her husband's wishes not "to talk." Thus, it is *preferred* that one be communicative about self, but *prescribed* that one *respect* the choices of the individual.

These utterances illustrate a plea for self to be communicative, expressive, and verbally open. When speech is seen to fulfill this plea properly, a common moral good is displayed. However, when self is said not to be communicative, the individual might receive tolerance and respect, but at the same time fail to meet a valued preference for self to communicate. When this occurs, speakers frequently publicize the problem. For example, a stepmother disclosed how she and her husband "fight over disciplining the kids." Donahue asked: "Do you have conversations about this at home?" She replied: "That's one of the problems." A lack of communicativeness, therefore, is a problem. The problem with being noncommunicative or closed is at least twofold since (1) an individual is not making his self available to others, which is heard as a problem that (2) negatively affects not only relationships with others but also his wife's sense of self. In situations where non-communicativeness is widely present, social action is rendered most difficult since, as is sometimes said, there is "a conspiracy of silence" where those who are silent are suspect. Being silent or closed is said to help create a common problem which is variously called a "lack of communication," "a communication problem," or "a breakdown in communication." Problems as these indicate an inability or unwillingness to make self available to others which renders cooperative social actions problematical.

Expressions as the above illustrate the value and common use of *communicativeness* in conceiving and evaluating self. To be communicative is to meet a shared moral imperative for self to communicate. Not to communicate, or to suggest not to communicate, is to open self to a wrath of speech in search of expressive remedy. Yet the function of communicativeness in the symbolic domain of self goes deeper than this.

The communicative dimension can be seen first of all to operate in speech as a means of self creation and display. This is done as individuals express a sense of independence through their choices, define who they are, and display their personal freedom and power. Participants may discuss their stable qualities and their unique features, which are said to be relatively stable across contexts. They might discuss and reveal a unique combination of qualities that distinguish them from all others. Communicating this way functions to create and display a sense of independence for self. In this way, a communicativeness is necessary for self to be presented socially as independent, thus accomplishing satisfactorily a cultural feature of the person.

Another way the communicative dimension is used involves the creation and display of awareness. In communicating, speakers sometimes reveal an awareness of personal needs and the choices made in their satisfaction. Speakers are also expected to show an awareness of others as they respectfully discuss their needs, help them in making choices, and in facing issues. By verbally displaying a proper awareness of one and another's self, one is showing a preferred ingredient which is necessary for one to be properly in command of the cultural self.

Both these uses of the communicative dimension treat speech as a means to valued cultural ends, such as the independence and awareness of self. To state the logic implied in the dimensions: Independence and awareness are valued cultural goals of self while communicativeness is a valued means toward their creation and achievment. However, communicativeness is not only a means, but also an end. Speakers not only use the dimension of communicativeness as an avenue to independence and awareness, but also demand communication as a common goal toward which cultural self should move. I am pointing here to a coalescing of communicativeness, as an analytical dimension, and really communicating as a cultural symbol. Communicativeness within the domain of self not only refers to the means of creating and revealing self as aware and independent, but also to the culturally identifiable act of doing so; and this act represents a shared and shareable goal of the cultural self that is evoked with the regnant term, communication. To refine the logic of the system: independence, awareness, and communicativeness are spoken goals for self, while communicativeness is also a cultural means toward their creation, evaluation, and achievement. This characteristic of communicativeness gives it a powerful and compelling force for self in this cultural system. For it is not only a valued means but also a valued state of sociation.[8]

In summary, a set of semantic dimensions are used to produce and judge a cultural sense of self in everyday American life. The dimensions help distinguish the individual, the prescribed code of the person, from the self, the preferred code that the individual has and should display verbally. Thus, everyone is an individual and everyone should show

---

[8] From the standpoint of "self" however, the semantic dimension of communicativeness does not exhaust the cultural meaning of "communication." See unit two.

their self. The dimensions also demonstrate how persons distinguish self from social role with three poles defining the optimal self as *independent, aware, and communicative.* The discussion lays an analytical and empirical base for the complex hypothesis: self is expressed through a personal code of unique independence, awareness, and expressiveness that is socially preferred; self is a part of and distinct from the more encompassing individual, a political code of rights and choice that is prescribed. The hyothesis applies to a general field of discourse which can be identified empirically and semantically; empirically through the co-occurrence of certain terms, the individual, rights, self, needs, and choice; and semantically as persons are defined as common and separate entities that are uniquely independent, aware, and expressive. The hypothesis helps define the patterned and regularly occurring discourse in which self is a prominent ingredient. The discourse works through a practical communicative force which is culturally constructed in the common symbols and meanings of the "Donahue" scene (Cushman & Pearce, 1977, pp. 344–353). As a result one aspect of the individual, the quintessential cultural self, is discursively conceived and evaluated along dimensions of independence, awareness, and communicativeness; independent of social role, stable across contexts, and unique; aware of one and another's self, in touch with important issues; and able to create communicatively and reveal an independence, awareness, and expressiveness by engaging in communication.

Displaying the Cultural "Self": A Personal Story

Self and the individual are unquestionables in this discourse. That is, both are assumed to be aspects of the person. But, as the husband described above, the person may choose not to disclose self. More prevalent, however, are the valued displays of self. Consider the following exchange between Donahue and an audience member. The two were discussing an anger clinic which the audience member, a middle-aged nun, had attended. She explained why she went:

(1) Nun: I was not really doing my best for the girls for the simple reason that instead of really putting my mind and attention to what they are saying and listening to their feelings, mine were getting in the way. I thought one thing I can do is find a place where

(2) I can get in touch with my own feelings, see how to handle it, and then I was able to deal with the girls because I was able to listen to them.

(3) Donahue: So you found yourself tempted to be angry with these girls for having these problems?
Nun: Correct.
Donahue: (later) How have you changed?
(4) Nun: I've excused myself for being angry. That was one of the first things I was able to tell myself.
Donahue: You don't feel guilty now?
Nun: Not one bit. I can get angry and I don't feel
(5) guilty about it and I can tell the other person, "hey, I really don't like what you're doing." To
(6) me that was very freeing. . . . Before that I was a people pleaser. I grew up being a people pleaser. I'm fourth in the family and that made a lot of difference. The only way I could get along is really by pleasing my parents all the time. I learned I don't have to please anybody else, I can please my self. And once I became really convinced I can please myself, I don't have to do what you're telling me to do, then I became
(7) free and I was able to tell them "hey, I don't want to do that."
Donahue (later): They admired you for this?
Nun: Right.
Donahue: Thanks a lot Sister; you obviously care a lot for those girls.
Audience: (applause)

This conversation gives a particular expression and weighting to the dimensions developed above. By interpreting the conversation, using the dimensions, we can understand that part of the nun's speech which displays a cultural sense of self and its development.

At point (1) the nun expressed an imbalance in awareness. Her awareness of her feelings were interfering with her awareness of "the girls." This imbalance made it difficult for her to function optimally as a self, and in her role as counselor.

She described her way of managing the imbalance at point (2). Here, an act of recognition of self was expressed; she articulated a newly formed awareness that put her in touch with her own feelings, and those of "the girls." By being in touch the nun was better able to "deal with the girls." Thus, getting in touch meant that she was now not only aware of her feelings, but also more able to listen to others and become aware of them.

At (3) Donahue referred to this acquired awareness as an act in which the nun "found [her] self," a common metaphor for a renewed awareness of self. At (4), the nun expressed comfort in her newly found awareness, a comfort which she took solace in, and used to explain her improved ability to listen.

At (5) the nun explicitly displayed her communicativeness through a metacommunicative act. She expressed how she was not only more aware of her feelings of anger, but also more able to communicate them without guilt. Through her act of (meta)communication, she conveyed a sense of being aware of who she was and of how to talk, while creating and displaying a sense of independence from others' coercive influences. Acts of communication like the one she suggested display an awareness of who one is, of how one feels, and establish an independence of self from others.

At (6), she defined her newly found sense of independence as "freeing" and described her self-evolution from a dependent "people pleaser" to a person who is now free to please herself. She concluded, at (7), by emphasizing her communicativeness and independence through her ability to tell others, presumably her parents, just how she feels. Her presentation of self, coming from one in a visible social role of service to others, was enthusiastically applauded.

Through her speech the nun accomplished a cultural sense of self, a self that was dependent but now is free and independent; a self that is aware of her feelings and those of others; a self that is endowed with the communicative ability to show awareness and independence through her communication.

All speech which exudes expression of self will not, of course, use all three semantic dimensions. In fact, many speakers on "Donahue" reveal self using only a dimension of independence and applying it to several relational contexts such as family, marriage, work, and so on. Their expressions of who they are display independence across all social settings. Others, the more intellectual types, express their self as not only aware of who they are, and who others are, but also aware of a variety of issues, the many facets of the issues, and the endless opinions on each. This type of self was observed prominently in expert guests whose multifaceted awareness of the issues made decisive (impositional?) communication, or the statement of unqualified opinions, most difficult to hear. The available choices were made clear, the reasons for making each choice were somewhat clear, but the evaluation of one choice as better than another was frustratingly elided. Also, and not surprising for a talk show, "Donahue" attracts self-defined talkers ready to speak at length at any moment.

As these semantics are played out in talk, they display persons with unique senses of self, but with each given a degree of coherence through the cultural and personal code.[9] The general point is: persons jointly produce through their talk a cultural sense of self. This plurivocal sense is interpretable along the semantic dimensions of unique independence, awareness, and communicativeness. While each dimension is not always relevant, all are salient in hearing the communal dialogue—a dialogue that is used prominently to construct and evaluate a common sense of self. This performance of self highlights the meanings of unique independence as *the American community* converses through their separate, but common, identity.

A Conflict Between "Self" and the Traditional Woman

Generally, audience members express agreement in their use of the above dimensions. However, there is at least one recurring dispute which can be heard as the semantics of "self" are differently assessed. The main dispute can be heard in response to questions such as: Who am I (are you) as an individual? A woman? A mother? A wife? In these discussions, speakers use the above dimensions, especially independence–dependence, to evaluate the self differently as, for example, career woman, mother, and/or wife.

One commonly endorsed position is a kind of *personal declaration of independence.* The liberation is enacted through statements that display the woman's independence from others, or movement toward that independence. The assertion is stated prominently as women discuss entering the workforce. These narratives often display how work helps the self assert a valued independence which transforms her into a more complete, subsistent entity. As a woman guest said:

the woman . . . out there in the workforce, she is treated like a colleague by her coworkers. She begins to think of herself as something in addition

---

[9] The dimensions posited here are abstractions and, of course, coalesce empirically. However, for analytical purposes, they suggest a typology of spoken cultural "selves" as independent, intellectually aware, and talkative or commnicative. Thus, the speech of this situation can be heard as differently embodied in these general types. These types articulate nicely with the concepts of "noble selves" and "rhetorical reflectors" as originally presented by Darnell and Brockreide (1976), and developed by Hart, Carlson, and Eadie (1980).

For those of a constructivist orientation, the types suggest a measurement of individuals' abilities to express their "self" along the various dimensions and their subfeatures. Listening for such culturally grounded dimensions would reveal individuals' differing levels of disursive complexity in conceiving and evaluating "self" (Delia, 1976; Delia, Clark, & Switzer, 1974; Delia, O'Keefe, and O'Keefe, 1982), and "self" in "relationship" (Delia, 1980).

to other than solely a member of some family unit. And the changes, the interactions are quite profound.

Similarly, a woman guest responded to a question on why women "are marrying later, and when having children, having children later and having fewer children": "I think women are obviously doing it because they don't want the enormous burden . . . because [there are] more economic opportunities, more desire to live one's own life as a full female human being." While the expressed reasons for "having fewer children" may be disputed, their assertion of independence is generally not. As a result, the woman's self is expressed as achieving, or moving toward, an independence that is consciously sought and prominently expressed. The independence is communicated by defining a woman's self as "something in addition to . . . a member of some family unit," and "a full female human being." These terms do not rely explicitly on a relational feature for their definition. As a result, a sense of self as independent is spoken. A valued dependence may be privately held, but it is not, from this position, a matter for speech.

There is another position which many expressive women, generally audience members, assert. It involves speaking of self as dependent on a family context for its satisfactory definition. For example, an audience member explained, "[I] raised children by myself. I remember my grandmother going to school and working so that my grandfather could go to chiropractic school." In the example, the persons as "mother," and "grandmother," are partly defined in reference to others, that is, children, and husband. Subsequently, the woman speaks of her grandmother's work *for* her husband, and her own, *for* her children. Expressing their lives in this way kindles a sense of dependence with others, children and husbands, which is less aligned with a semantic of self and more aligned with an enactment of a traditional social role. These personal stories contrast to those above where the woman was said to be "something in addition to . . . a member of some family unit." However, the above utterance also includes a hint of independence where the woman made it clear that she raised children by herself. Though subtle, the mention points to a valuing of speech which displays independence (and dependence), and suggests the discursive rule: one should speak of self as independent (of role obligations), even if one often and happily enacts traditional social roles.

Disputes like this one tend to lean toward favoring independence as is indicated by the woman's statement of raising children by herself. Yet, the debate is nurtured as participants differently disclose their life's work as, on the one hand, comfortably dependent on their children (e.g., as mothers and grandmothers) and husband (e.g., as wives), or on the other, as needing an emotional and psychological independence from them (e.g., as women, as women who divorce their families, and as a "full female human being"). Undoubtedly there are elements of both these extremes within the *experiences* of the women (and men) who speak here. Yet, the dilemma results as persons negotiate which elements are to be spoken: How does one conceive, negotiate, and evaluate a proper cultural sense of the female person in America today?

One might expect at this point that the above disputes could easily be resolved by resorting to some sense of interdependence. But a sense of interdependence seems to imply, to many of these speakers, a mutual dependence which the assertions of independence are designed to attack. In other words, speech of interdependence is likely to be heard as a type of dependence; and when a self is heard to be dependent, as in this type of dispute, assertions of independence are commonly made.

What this brief analysis suggests is a way to hear a recurring dispute on "Donahue," and in the contemporary American scene. The dispute consists of speech, on the one hand, that defines the person as a self, as independent of a relational context, aware of its definition, and willing to be expressive about it; and, on the other, speech that defines the person as dependent on a relational context, aware of its definition, and willing to be expressive about it. The former is heard to assert an independent self, as woman, over a relational environment. The latter to assert a self that is dependent on a relational environment and constrained by a social role, for example, wife or mother. The differing views are expressed on "Donahue" as both use, but differently evaluate, the dimension of independence–dependence. The net outcome of such discussion is a variant conception and evaluation of the female person, one spoken as an independent self, the other as a self who happily displays features of a traditional social role.[10]

The "Negative Personality"

Another notable act of talk which the dimensions render intelligible is the use of "personality" as a cultural account (Buttny, 1985; Scott & Lyman, 1968). As mentioned before, some verbal displays of self are heard as offensive, derogatory, and so on. Consider the guest who told Donahue he was "asking all the wrong questions," talked while Donahue

---

[10] The declaration of independence noted here was celebrated in a recent *McCall's* survey. Readers selected Katharine Hepburn as most admirable "because she dared to be different: she had no children and loved a married man." The survey is reported in a national newspaper (Verve . . ., 1983) and features Hepburn's picture with the bold title: Independent: "Hepburn dared to be different."

" personality "

was talking, referred to police officers represented on the show as like the "KGB . . . in Russia," and belittled an older lady in the audience by exclaiming: "That's for a different reason, lady!" In the final moments of the show, his untoward behavior was held socially accountable through an applauded reference to his "negative personality."

This redressive use of the term, personality, as an account, can be explained along the dimensions developed above. The account was effective as it defined the offender's self as independent of others, presumably stable across contexts, and certainly unique in this situation. By modifying personality with the adjective, negative, his particular communicativeness was devalued and negatively sanctioned as offensive and tactless. However, there was a potential for saving his face in using the term, personality. In its use, a common meaning was evoked, which referred to those aspects of his self which were heard to be stable and potentially out of his awareness. This use of personality placed his intentionality in question, defining him as perhaps unaware of what he was doing and, therefore, not fully accountable. The outcome of the account is powerful because it is equivocal; there is blame (for his acts) and not blame (of his self) at the same time! While his actions were rather directly criticized, social judgment about his self could be suspended, and responsibility for his personality could remain in question, since certain of its features were heard to be matters not of his choice. Yet, even if he had deliberately chosen his negative personality, that is the individual's right since, "in America," he is "allowed to have one."

This use of negative personality, as a cultural account, suggests a cultural definition of self heard to be *independent* (stable across contexts and unique), inappropriately *communicative,* and perhaps *unaware* of what he was doing, of how he was speaking. By using the term personality this way, the dimensions of independence–dependence, and communicative–closed are activated, while artfully suspending consideration of the third, awareness–unaware. As a result, personality is used to account for untoward behavior while minimizing the threat to the speaker's self, or public face (Goffman, 1967; Scott & Lyman, 1968). Concepts and principles such as personality, rights, and so forth, provide fodder for accounts, and, when understood, can help unravel their cultural and discursive force.

George Washington and the Cherry Tree: A Myth

Another use of the dimensions occurs in a popular and timeless oral form, a myth of George Washington and the cherry tree. This myth about the "Father of the American Country" is told to schoolchildren in most educational settings around the United States. The myth is not a datum on "Donahue" but is a prominent oral form within America and probably intelligible, reportable, and repeatable, to most all of those who speak there.

I have two major reasons for discussing the myth. First, it illustrates the dimensions described here and second, it provides a historical sense of these dimensions. Through a myth as this, one can hear both a sense of a person in the past, and a sense of the cultural person in the present. Through this cultural myth, persons share a verbal resource, a resource which is accessible to them in their efforts to conceive and evaluate a public and historically grounded sense of who they are.

The myth is recorded by a historian as follows:

> George Washington, as a little boy, was given a hatchet for his birthday. Tempted by his shiny new tool, George went out and practiced chopping on one of his father's cherry trees. When the tree was found dead . . . George was asked by his father if he had done it. "I can't tell a lie, Pa; you know I can't tell a lie. I did cut it with my hatchet." "Run to my arms you dearest boy", cried his father in transports. (Robertson, 1980, p. 11)

The myth is part of an American oral heritage which tells Americans something about The Father of their Country. In the story, an independence is acted out, an independence which is both individual, in the cutting of the tree, and national, the cutting, in the original version, was of an English cherry tree. His independent act was of an individual over and against his physical and sociosymbolic environment. The child of George set out to chop the tree, to test and assert his powerful skills over his physical environment, just as the father of George set out to establish an independent nation. These are acts of independence, in the former done innocently and in the latter done with conscious power and skill. The child's awareness of his act is displayed in a culturally valued way where he admits, "I can't tell a lie. I did cut it with my hatchet." He is fully aware of what he has done, and he is able to convey these things in a valued and honest act of communication. The act displays an individual who is able to acknowledge his discreditable behavior in the properly honest way. A reason the act is heard as an acceptable assertion of self is because of its honesty, as a properly aware and truthful disclosure of what was wrongly done.[11]

---

[11] The communicative form of "honest" speech is discussed further in unit 2.

This tale of George Washington, as the honest child and the Father of the Country, displays those public dimensions which each American individual has access to in developing a sense of who he or she is. It is not only that Americans use the myth, but also that its form embodies a coherent and timeless tale; a tale of a man/child who struck out on his own, aware of his task, able to acknowledge honestly and responsibly what he had done, even when his acts were discreditable. As a result, the myth informs its listeners about the person, George Washington, as an American, while telling a shared moral to Americans, about persons, who strive for a proper *independence, awareness,* and *expressiveness* (Robertson, 1980, esp. pp. 11–15). So the telling of the tale provides not only a model of a great American person—in George Washington—but also a model for the personal American, whose symbolic chopping is still being done.

Thus, a set of dimensions run through the American discourse, from a modern story of finding one's self to a traditional tale of the nation's father. The semantic dimensions in the discourse provide the common resources from which the person may purchase in creating and evaluating a proper sense of who they are. From the tales of long ago to the stories of today, a coherent and common concept of the person is spoken, a person who exudes an independence, an awareness, and an ability to say properly what needs to be said.

"Self" As Container: Metaphorical Speech of Personhood

When persons talk on "Donahue," they create a sense of self as a separate, or at least separable, entity. This common-sense notion, emblazoned in the communal conversation, is complemented by several metaphorical utterances which reaffirm the independent status of self. In this section, I will demonstrate how the above semantic dimensions are put to use in metaphorical speech and how such speech involves a system of semantic relations. In particular, I will examine speech which treats self as a container, analyze its physical and spatial entailments, and note those aspects that are highlighted in the talk (e.g., being separate and unique) and those that are hidden (e.g., being connected and common).

Several clarifications are necessary before describing this metaphorical speech. First, in their essay, "Conceptual Metaphor in Everyday Language," George Lakoff and Mark Johnson (1980, p. 477) claimed that "we experience ourselves as entities, separate from the rest of the world—containers with an inside and an outside" (emphasis in original). However, they ground the container metaphor in the experience of persons (an "experientialist perspective," p. 453), thus treating everyday language as *manifesting* experience. Their explanatory level is the experience of individuals, where mine is the talk of individuals and its cultural meaning. Thus, their analysis is of human experience as revealed in metaphorical language, where mine is of communication patterns as enacted through metaphorical speech. Both, of course, are related yet each has its particular focus.

It may also be helpful to retrace the logic which I am assuming in the following analyses. The case description began with an empirical fact: The talk of "Donahue" is flavored with models of personhood. I examined the speech of "Donahue" and argued that a fundamental sense of the cultural person is expressed through the political code of the individual, who has rights and makes choices. A more specific sense of the cultural person was expressed through a personal code of self, a "thing," which the individual *has*. This spoken sense of the person was interpreted along three semantic dimensions of unique independence, awareness, and communicativeness. So the descriptive tide has taken us from symbols of the individual to the self. Now, I will include one cultural trope, a metaphor, where the self (like the individual) is expressed as a container (more precisely, a container within the indivisible individual, a container within a container).

Another more specific clarification is in order before beginning. I am not saying that the term, container, is a native metaphor, only that individuals speak as if the self were such a thing. I use it as a general metaphor because it helps in interpreting and organizing the way persons speak. For example, speakers do not say, "I am a container," nor do they say, "my self is a container"; however, they have said, "I am relatively self-contained," "I have got my self together," "I am trying to put the pieces back together again," you might "reveal a piece of yourself," and "it's in my head," all to a degree metaphorical statements which treat self as a container. So, I have discussed speech of the individual as self, the self as a semantic system, and now turn to speech where the self is discussed metaphorically as a container with physical and spatial entailments.

Metaphorical speech of self as a container invokes a physical metaphor which Lakoff and Johnson have defined as

> the projection of entity or substance status upon something that does not have that status inherently. . . . (With them) we understand either nonphysical or not clearly bounded things as entities. In most cases such metaphors involve the use of a concept from the physical domain to structure a concept from the cultural or intellectual domains. (1980, p. 461)

The concept from the physical domain under analysis here is that of the container, and the one from the cultural domain is self.

The metaphorical speech which reveals a container metaphor of, and for, self is expressed with phrases from "Donahue" speakers such as:

1. The person inside me;
2. I filled myself up with drugs;
3. When you elect a president, you elect a package deal;
4. There is nothing wrong with getting angry. It's just how you handle it . . . keeping it inside is no good;
5. To be angry with a stranger or someone who only knows you a little bit is to reveal a piece of yourself that you don't want that other person to see;
6. She has a fight with her brother and she gets that out of her system;
7. Now that I have a part-time job I feel much more secure within myself;
8. The problem is that we never learn who we are before we try to give ourselves away to somebody in marriage;
9. If I cannot entertain myself without calling a male prostitute then I know it's in my head.

In metaphorical speech like this a sense of self is expressed as contained, packaged, and discursively located somewhere "within" or "inside." Sometimes the container is said to reveal parts of itself in anger or "give" itself "in marriage." In others, the contents are said to be "shared" (e.g., "she is sharing her feelings").[12]

In this speech, the prime features of self are placed within the person. Through this discursive placement, self becomes commonly intelligible as a container exuding a physical status aligned with a physical body, an object, or an entity. By speaking of self this way, interlocutors reinforce its independent cultural character as a bounded or packaged object. We shall plunge into this cultural construction of the container self and try to figure out what is being said.

As a bounded and unique container, the self is said to contain many things, most notable among them are needs, desires, thoughts, and feelings. These things are said to be personal and internal resources which in part constitute self and from which it draws. Sometimes these are "given"; sometimes they are "revealed"; sometimes they are "shared."

---

[12] The intimate link between the container metaphor discussed here and the "conduit metaphor" discussed by Reddy (1979) demonstrate once again the reciprocal role that personhood and speaking must play in theories of communication.

However the resources are said to be distributed, it requires some act of opening the container so that others may hear and see. This can be done either from one's self, for example, "being honest," or with others, for example, "really communicating." Other native terms for this act of opening are "sharing," "being open," "really talking," and so on.[13] At times these acts become a type of personal show and tell. To be successful at the show, self must act independently by having some commonly important and/or unique resource to share; must be aware of those personal resources which all individuals are said to have within; and, must be open in the sharing of them. These acts are imbued with great moral value—and frequent apprehension—as they provide symbolic occasions in which the packaged self is unwrapped, and one's resources which are said and felt to be personal and internal, are displayed.

As a result of the above communicative patterning, metaphorical speech informs interlocutors about who each is (e.g., a contained self with uniquely personal and internal features), how to be who one is (e.g., share, be aware, communicate) and how to feel (e.g., if one is composed of internally unique qualities, then the sharing of them may involve a degree of apprehension, embarrassment, pride (Scruton, 1979).

If it is the case that metaphorical speech creates and reveals a sense of self that is contained, and is composed of shareable resources within, then such speech should also reveal a sense of the arrangement of those internal resources. Speech of self as container reveals such a pattern as it constructs and evaluates the packaged ingredients as a matter of substance or lack of substance.

The self which exudes substance is said to be a "solid person," one who has "really got it together" or who has, after more trying times, "pulled oneself together." Also, the substantial self may be said to be one who is "clear headed," has thoughts, emotions, and desires which reflect a specifiable and bounded organization. This is the valued self who is in his or her proper—cultural and personal—space. The self who is said to "lack substance," however, is said to be "falling apart," "spread too thin," or "scatter brained." This is the self who is hard to place, who is not properly—culturally and personally—contained. All such speech depends on a metaphor of self as a container or package which has ingredients that are more (as substantial) or less (as lacking substance) bounded.

So far, metaphorical speech has been seen to reveal a bounded sense of self which has certain internal resources that are said to be given or shared. The general sense of such speech creates a notion of self as

---

[13] See unit 2.

a container. A similar metaphor, which builds on this notion and is a metaphor within the container metaphor, occurs when the self, like a container, is said to be lost and found.

A self may be lost, as in the "poor lost soul," when it is not fully aware of what it is saying or doing. In these moments, a person is said to have "lost his self" or to be "out of control." A person may lose parts of his or her self, "I've lost the ability to have fun," or all of her self, "when a mother loses her self and needs to get out, she shouldn't be looked down on any more than a man who does the same thing."

A guest who conducted "anger clinics" used the metaphor in this way:

> What we very often do as parents is we invalidate that child's anger. We say things like you have no right to be angry at me, I'm your mother. Well, we succeed in making the child feel guilty, we make him feel as if he is invalid for having this invalid emotion. And after you do that about 2,000 times the child as a 17-year-old doesn't know who he is anymore. Then we say our children have to go out and find themselves. They shouldn't have lost themselves in the first place.

The child's self is said to include an emotional resource of anger of which he or she is potentially aware, but of which one must remain unaware because of a parental imposition. The result is said to be a "lost child," a child who becomes less aware of anger (in this case a valued emotion) and more aware of guilt (a devalued emotion). A parent who denies a child's rights to his or her feelings is said to be a parent who contributes to a child's being lost. In this case, if a child has "no right to be angry," then he or she is easily lost. The speaker says, part of being lost is the subverting of emotions like anger which are labeled invalid.

When a person is said to be lost, he or she must have access to a means of discovery, a way of being found, as in a "search" for self.[14] As some speakers on "Donahue" have said, "I'm still in search of myself"; "I thought it was a lifelong process in search of myself." So the self spoken of here is never fully found because, to mix metaphors, it is always growing; the contents of the package are never fully discoverable, for they are always changing and marked by growth. Speech like this gives testimony to the infinite uniqueness that is available within all selves, and the endless search for the identifiable and natural resources therein.

---

[14] This "search" is the topical theme of a recent commentary on contemporary American life (Yankelovich, 1981).

The full set of resources within a self may not be findable, but some of its features may be. The act of finding is said to be a moment of recognition, of awareness, in which self discovers one of its knowable parts. The newly found awareness is said to imbue self with a potential for control over the environment which went previously unrecognized. For example, one female guest, a recovered (a newly found) anorexic, was asked, "What did you find out about yourself?" She explained:

> Well, through the course of dealing with the anorexia and ultimately through the therapy too, I came to grips with the fact that I had confused my self-worth with what I did and how I performed instead of who I was as a person. That is very easy to do. . . . I also felt that there was much of my life that wasn't really my own. So when I finally found myself at 140 pounds at 16 years old, I felt there was much of life I didn't have control over, including my weight at the time. . . . So I decided one day when I felt really literally out of control—I was sobbing on the couch in our den and said I'm going to lose this weight if it's the last thing I do. I've got to get control over this thing.

What she eventually found was a sense of her self-worth, a sense of who she was as a person. Through this discovery, she became more fully aware of the resources she had within, which were not to be confused with what she did nor how she performed. Her speech revealed an awareness of her self and of her worth which—as contained within— was something only she could find. She reaffirmed her status as a more fully functioning self by communicating an awareness of her ability to control herself and her environment. Her story aligns her worth with internal resources and contrasts worth to external performance. Thus, worth becomes entirely a matter and manner of self-control.

Personal searches designed to discover self-worth were said to be enhanced when they occurred within a particular physical and psychological environment. An optimal environment in which the self can be found, in which it can maintain a maximum level of awareness, was one with optimal time and personal space. As speakers on "Donahue" have said, "you have to have some time and space . . . for yourself"; or when Donahue asked a mother, "what do you do for yourself?" She replied, "not much now but in a short while I'll have the time to do some things." The self, then, as an independent entity, is discussed as in need of an environment in which it has space and time. Personal space and time are discussed as a type of symbolic mote, a social buffer zone, which operate to facilitate the identification of that which is contained within and to preserve certain internal resources from forces on the outside.

When one's personal space is said to be violated, when one recognizes a threat to one's independent self, then some type of redressive action must be initiated for this is a breach of a cultural code; a code which endows self with its proper space. Consider the following comments about family life in terms of space: "We have to learn how to unhook ourselves . . . from the child's behavior"; a daughter described how she "disengaged" from her well-intentioned father; the development of a boy was discussed as he "emancipates himself from the mother." In metaphorical speech like this, a symbolic and often times physical, space is created around self. The space serves to nurture self—or to signal a development toward it—by separating it from others and by preserving the uniqueness which is said to be contained within. Metaphorical speech like this produces a sense of self that is separate and isolatable. Because each self is said to inhabit personal space, a communication of communicativeness is required if self is to be available to others. If so, one must open and share one's space and resources with others. Thus, metaphorical speech of self motivates a native genre of sharing, just as acts of sharing (and openness) motivate metaphorical speech of self.[15]

In summary, the container metaphor takes the cultural term, self, and renders it intelligible with physical terms, for example, package. The self as a package is heard to contain certain internal resources, that is, needs, desires, feelings, thoughts which are assessed according to their substance or lack of substance. One entailment of the self as a container is its capacity to be lost and found. The losing of the self involves a decreased sense of awareness which is devalued, and when lost, results in searches which result, when successful, in a renewed awareness. The success of such a search is facilitated by the allocation of time and space for one's self. Having such time and space is said to enhance the finding of self, enhance its awareness of its own resources, and establish its distinctness from others.

In terms of the semantic dimensions, a sense of self as *independent* is symbolically created and maintained by using container metaphors, for example, by treating self as a substantial package of resources that need space. A sense of self as *aware* is articulated and sought as it is said to be lost and found. As a sense of self is coconstructed which is separate from others, and aware of its separateness as well as its own resources, a common imperative to *communicate* is heard: Be open and share the resources that are contained within. As a result, the metaphorical speech sketched here helps create a cultural orientation

---

[15] Suggested here again are the reciprocal formative properties of native genres of speaking, symbols of personhood, and metaphorical speech.

from which self feels compelled to communicate, strives to stay in touch, or be aware of its natural and personal resources, and independently assess its own worth.

A Note on "Self" and Other Cultural Persons

The American self then is constructed as something that the individual *has*. The code of self is personal because it is composed of a unique set of resources that are within each person and accessible only to that individual. It is an internal uniqueness that one should come to know and share. Because of this preference for sharing and being open the exemplary acts for self are reflective, a way of "getting in touch," and assertive, making one's self heard. Taken together, these radiants of the person are interpretable along three dimensions of meaning for the person, the appropriate poles being uniquely independent, aware, and communicative. These are played out in various oral forms from personal stories and cultural myths to metaphorical speech.

The cultural sense of personhood produced in this discourse stands in contrast to those of other places. For example, Geertz (1976) has described expressions of personhood in Bali:

> anything idiosyncratic, anything characteristic of the individual merely because he is who he is physically, psychologically, or biographically, is muted in favor of his assigned place in the continuing and, so it is thought, neverchanging pageant that is Balinese life. It is dramatis personae, not actors, that endure; indeed, it is dramatis personae, not actors, that in the proper sense really exist. Physically men come and go, mere incidents in the happenstance of history, of no genuine importance even to themselves. But the masks they wear, the stage they occupy, the parts they play, and, most important, the spectacle they mount remain, and comprise not the facade but the substance of things . . . of course players perish, but the play doesn't, and it is the latter, the performed rather than the performer, that really matters. (p. 228)

To be a person in Bali is to be a player of roles on a cultural stage. The play endures, regardless of the particular set of actors in the scene. Rosaldo's (1982, p. 218) interpretation of Ilongot speech and life provides a similar case:

> what Ilongots lack from a perspective such as ours is something like our notion of an inner self continuous through time, a self whose actions can be *judged* in terms of sincerity, integrity, and commitment. . . . Ilongots do not see their inmost "hearts" as constant causes, independent

of their acts . . . what matters is the act itself and not the personal statement it purportedly involves.

The Balinese and the Ilongot senses of the person is contrasted with that coenacted by a situated group of Americans. It is this American discourse which shuns the masks, stages, and roles, eschews the identifiable social ground upon which others so persistently play. But this renunciation is done while playing the cultural drama of self. To symbolize the preferred person in this American scene is to symbolize a self, to state who one is as distinct from the common masks, roles, and stages of everyday life. To be such a person is to express the unique characteristics and personal qualities of which the cultural person strives to become aware. But to do so is to act in the proper cultural way. It is this dynamic, the voice of self that sounds uniquely independent and the voice of the collective that demands the performance, that demonstrates the power in the cultural discourse. In this symbol system, independence is at once conferred and taken away, but the semantics of self negate the sense of "taking away," as both presuppose the collective drama (See Diagram 4–1).

Lakoff and Johnson (1980, pp. 458–460) have discussed everyday metaphor as it highlights that which we readily comprehend and hides that which easily escapes our attention.[16] The features highlighted in the above discourse are those of personalness, separateness, uniqueness, and personality. Those features mostly hidden are those of connectedness, commonality, and sociality. The patterning of the discourse itself makes it difficult for persons to speak, hear, and feel connected as cultural members, or united. More specifically, if one wants to continue tradition, for example, "be a naturalist because my dad's a

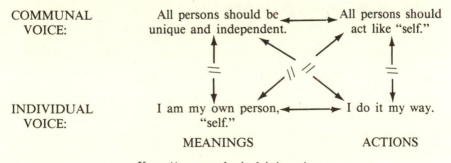

COMMUNAL VOICE: All persons should be ———→ All persons should act like "self."
                  unique and independent.

INDIVIDUAL VOICE: I am my own person, ←———→ I do it my way.
                    "self."

                  MEANINGS   ACTIONS

Key: // = paradoxical injunction

4–1. Cultural enactment of "self."

---

[16] Recall Burke's (1965, pp. 5–18) discussion of "orientation," that involves—borrowing Veblen's concept—a "trained incapacity."

naturalist," one must—if one is to enact a full self—put the act into more individual terms, emphasize one's own desires, unique interests, and personal choices. For those who do not sense this dynamic, an endless search may ensue, a continual search for self that is unlike others. (Note the portrayals of unusual persons on "Donahue" that reflects and accentuates this trend). In this scene, because of the criterion of unique independence, acting like another is simply not enough. Similarly, if one is put into situations of cooperative action, for example, family, work, school, government, that may not allow for one's full uniqueness, then one feels—from the standpoint of self—oppressed (rather than a loyal member). But is this popularly sensed oppression better or worse than the more implicit tyranny of uniqueness? The price for the latter are feelings of isolation, alienation, and instability and are linked to social trends as varied as divorce, jogging, and bilingual education (Rodriguez, 1982). One way to bring the complexity into focus is to create a way of listening to ourselves, to self, for dimensions of meanings along with its spatial and physical entailments. Such a hearing could help unravel native models of personhood, what they bring to the foreground, what they place in the background, and what they place out of bounds. In the process, we can understand the common meanings which render the models regnantly intelligible, as well as the other dynamics which are more hidden, but if speakable may enhance the performance.

One as yet untapped resource for constructing common senses of the person are explicit symbols of group identity. Within this discourse, are there symbolic expressions of groups of persons? Symbols that extend the common meaning of the person beyond the individual level? To classes of persons? What place do symbols of social groups have in this American discourse of personhood?

5

"TRADITIONAL SOCIAL ROLES": A POLEMICAL CODE

In this chapter I write of "a polemical code" of personhood.[1] What I attempt to capture with this phrase is a deep dilemma that is built into this symbolic system. The fractionating force inheres in an agony between the cultural symbols of self and traditional social roles, between symbols of the unique person in the here and now, and those about a group of persons constrained by historical forces. The latter, the code of roles, functions mainly through a renunciative voice, a rejection on the one hand of communal expectations that one conform, and on the other, of society in general (Dumont, 1985). Symbolizing persons in these terms leads to feelings of oppression that constrain yet motivates free expressions and reflections of self. Because this conversational interplay acquires the status of what Burke (1961) might call a devil-term and good-term drama, I write of polemical forces, dramatistic dilemma, and symbolic agony.

Of special concern in this chapter are utterances that contrast institutions of society, especially traditional social roles, to self. For example, a woman guest said, "one of the things [the women's movement] would like to see more women do is make a decision *all by themselves* without regard to what *society or somebody else* says"; a mother described her daughter's anorexia saying, "she was reinforced by our society that says, boy, you look good if you don't have a little fat on you"; a man explained his wife abuse by exclaiming, "it's society," then went on to describe "the macho man" roles of John Wayne and Humphrey Bogart; and an elderly woman said, "the female is the victim

---

[1] The code of "traditional social role" is related polemically to the personal code of "self." Because I want to emphasize the *relation* between the codes in a *system* of spoken symbols, I write of a polemical code, the polemic consisting in a tension between self and role. The "traditional social role" code, when considered by itself, is a positional code emphasizing as it does identifiable positions or roles in various social institutions. When wanting to emphasize the intimate relation of the two in this discourse, I write of the *polemical code*. When emphasizing aspects of the "role" code by itself, I write of a *positional code*.

of society that has programmed us . . . to accept this [secondary] role."
What meanings and motives are enacted in the symbolic agony of self
and social roles? How is this polemical code enacted communicatively?

I will begin by pointing to the historical grounding of the polemical
pattern, move to a description of four communicative strategies that
invoke its features, explore the contrastive semantics and rhetorics of
self and traditional roles through the native trope, "a nation of lemmings," then discuss some ironic consequences of the polemical code.
My main purposes in the chapter are: to show how speech can be
interpreted through a historically grounded polemical code; to demonstrate how such a pattern operates within a limited semantic and
rhetorical field; and to illustrate the diverse sociocultural functions
served by the code.

A Short History of the Polemical Code

In *The Social Contract and Discourses,* Jean–Jacques Rousseau (1762/
1978) wrote about "The Civil State": "man acquires in the civil state,
moral liberty, which alone makes him truly master of himself; for the
mere impulse of appetite is slavery, while obedience to a law which
we prescribe to ourselves is liberty." Rousseau wrote for the French
during the Enlightenment and enunciated his doctrine of the "social
contract." Through it, he enabled a movement from a Lockeian individualism to expressions of a people's general will. If Rousseau were
an ethnographer of the contemporary American scene, he may well
have written; "man says he, in spite of society, has his own rights, his
own choices, which alone make him truly master of himself; for the
mere obedience of law is slavery, while the impulse of all appetite is
individual freedom." The general forces may be conceived similarly,
but their valence has changed. The contemporary American—at least
those of "Donahue"—has ready access to a discourse that enunciates
a general movement from "social constraints" to specific assertions of
individual will.

Several observers of the American scene have noted and used this
historically grounded discourse. Through it is expressed a felt opposition
between the freedoms of self and the commonly felt constraints, or
"yoke," of "society." One of the earliest commentaries on the theme
appeared in Tocqueville's classic essay, ***Democracy in America*** (1838/
1945, p. 11):

> When the inhabitant of a democratic country . . . comes to survey the
> totality of his fellows and to place himself in contrast with so huge a

body, he is instantly overwhelmed by the sense of his own insignificance and weakness. The same equality that renders him independent of each of his fellow citizens, taken severally, exposes him alone and unprotected to the influence of the greater number. The public, therefore, among a democratic people, has a singular power . . . a sort of enormous pressure of the mind of all upon the individual intelligence.[2]

More recently, Victor Turner (1974, p. 54) has commented:

Society is what some of them [i.e., existentialists] term the "seat of objectivity" and therefore antagonistic to the subjective existence of the individual. To find and become himself, the individual must struggle to liberate himself from the yoke of society. Society is seen by existentialism as the captor of the individual, very much in the same way as Greek religious thought, particularly in the mystery cults, viewed the body as the captor of the soul.

The observations by Tocqueville and Turner help in making two important points about the polemical code under discussion here. First, although its valence varies from the Enlightenment, to colonial America of the early 1800s, to its contemporary expression on "Donahue," and although not generally recognized as such by present-day Americans, the polemical pattern is an historical one. Through it, persons have wrestled symbolically with the common definitions of who each is, of who they "taken severally" are, and the common ways in which their lives are motivated together. Second, the expression includes the key polemic between two codes of personhood, a personal code of self and its polemical counterpart, in this case society and one of its prominent radiants of meaning, traditional social roles.[3]

---

[2] Echoing Tocqueville, a contemporary historian of American myth has written:

The independence of the individual—from other individuals, from society, from government and regimentation especially—has been the long-stated aim of all American individuals. As individuals, Americans are therefore revolutionary, and opposed to, in conflict with, and contradictory to, government, established authority, social imperatives . . . individual rights are in contrast to the rights of society and state (but the presence of a society and a state to be independent of is necessary to the dynamic of the myth). Government, legal, social, and economic institutions are, in the logic of individual independence, always threatening to overwhelm individual life, liberty, and the pursuit of happiness. (Robertson, 1980, p. 133).

[3] The following interpretations are based on approximately 150 uses of the terms, "social roles," "society," and "this country."

"Self" Versus "Traditional Social Roles"

> The generations of Americans who grew up after the Revolution were and are impatient with the remnants or existence of dependence, inequality, and restrictions on individual freedom which they found and find in their lives. Since the Revolution, Americans have not known the oppression of colonial life, but they intended and tend to destroy any structures within their society which try to teach people their place and keep them there. Americans do not believe that individuals ought to stay in one place. And they do not intend that their nation keep to its place, either; for individuals and for the nation, there is a manifest destiny to fulfill. (Robertson, 1980, p. 147)

Social roles may be defined as features in, and of, discourse that teach people their proper place(s) and its meanings. They are constituted *in* discourse when (1) a symbol defines a social position(s) and its meanings, (2) that includes certain normative forces, that is, actions that are appropriate or inappropriate for enacting the position (Schneider 1976). For example, one interpretation of communication might examine uses of "professor" as a code of personhood within an American discourse of education. As a cultural symbol, professor may suggest a role with common meanings of "sophisticated, learned, reasonable, and intelligent." The normative properties of the role may prescribe certain behaviors, such as "researching, teaching, attending professional meetings, committee work, and community service." Through symbolizing a social role, persons identify some commonly recognizable social position, ignite a range of intelligible meanings for the position, including normative standards for its public enactment.[4]

On "Donahue," a use of the generic term, social roles, is prominently heard as an imposition for it inappropriately puts self in a historically constraining place. Consequently, the symbol motivates feelings of oppression by imposing a relatively fixed, therefore inadequate and harmful social order. In the process, the valued personal code of self becomes underheard and overlooked, making social roles objects of attack. For example, since women are highly visible in, and to, the audience, womens' traditional roles in society, especially as "homemaker, wife, mother, and sex object," are continually negotiated and criticized. Audience members frequently refer to media images such as "Marilyn Monroe" and "Mrs. Olsen" as the traditional roles for women. As these are discussed, the prominent features of sex symbol and housewife, respectively, are criticized. These images are said to victimize

---

[4] The definition of role here adds a cultural dimension to that proposed by George Herbert Mead and adapted by Cushman and Craig (1976, pp. 49–54).

women as they confine self enactments in devalued ways. An elderly woman stated, "I think society has programmed the female to accept the secondary role . . . as the decades went along there was progress made but I think we are the victims, the women, the female is the victim of society who has programmed us . . . to accept this role." Thus, society and roles identify the forces that victimize individuals by displaying symbols of an historically conforming force, and are thus said to be oppressive, inadequate, and harmful.

An analogous example about men occurred in a show on wife abuse. Several audience members wondered how any man could bring himself to beat his wife. A wife abuser explained his behavior by referring to his past, his father's abuse of his mother, then went on to exclaim "it's society!" He referred to the common social role for men as "macho men." The models which made him into such a man were evoked by referring to the tough guy media images of John Wayne and Humphrey Bogart. The man explained his problematical behavior by reference to a society that provides such harmful social roles. As a result, his actions were said (and felt) to be motivated not solely by this person in the present, but by those prominent impersonal forces from the background that individuals—like this wife beater—constantly combat. Through this explanation, self can be somewhat absolved from responsibility since its agonistic historical counterpart is expressed as a primary motivator of the problematical action.

Since interlocutors speak of society and social roles as major forces of oppression, they must face combat with them. The battle is fought in at least four distinctive ways. One involved direct *polemical symbolizing,* verbalizations that contrasted societal roles to the more valued features of self. Donahue, adept at this kind of thing, said: "the Marilyn Monroe figure, although we all know now what a very complicated and also talented, sightful, and creative person that she was—her image was that of dumb, and empty, and blonde, and pretty." In a statement, Donahue affirms the "person" of Marilyn Monroe, her self, over and against the image or role that society gave to her, and which she now symbolizes. Her "complicated, talented, sightful, and creative" person is held over and against her—and symbolically all women's, especially blondes'—impersonal image as "dumb, empty, and pretty." This type of polemical contrast is a prominent way to hold self over roles and enables Donahue to state what "we all know now," Marilyn Monroe was a person whose tragic death symbolizes the fate of those who succumb to life in a social role.

A further way this discourse combats society and social role is through an *explicit devaluing* of the symbols which are implicit in the polemical symbolizing. For example, some utterances boldly criticize any type of conformity to shared social standards. A woman said: "One of the points that the women's movement makes is that for too long women have been too influenced by what other people think and one of the things they would like to see more women do is make a decision all by themselves without regard to what society or somebody else says." Displayed in the woman's speech is a common disdain for doing things as most others might expect them to be done, traditionally, through the enactment of some social role. Celebrated is the ability of each person's self to act independently, to make their rightful choices, "without regard to what society or somebody else says."

The general premise supporting these sayings is: society and social roles are semantic loci of oppressive historical forces that constrain self. However, my point is not that all societal roles are said to be harmful, oppressive, and so on. Rather, that oppressive forces are said to act over the person and are stated in terms of society and traditional roles. Furthermore, the oppressive roles are not only said and shed for persons as self, but also for any member of any group (or class) that risks being prejudged by some impositional standard. For example, children are discussed properly not as helpless (nor with any such image that does not allow for their independent thinking and acting), politicians not as dishonest, erotic film stars not as sexually permissive, and so on. In all such discourse, common societal roles (their meanings and expected behaviors), that rely on a majority view that is somewhat impersonal and historically grounded, are discursively devalued and set aside as the personal uniqueness of the present self is displayed.

An additional and pervasive way that self is highlighted over and against social roles occurs in a class of *reflexive utterances*. In these sayings, a statement of a general social role, for example, father, housewife, women, mothers, males, is followed by a derivative of self, resulting in statements such as "a father myself," "the housewife herself," "the women themselves," "working mothers themselves," and "males . . . themselves." Through this type of utterance, the self becomes the figure of discursive concern with a diffuse social role as its symbolic ground.[5]

This same polemical dynamic is invoked when persons *address each other*. The trend appears on "Donahue"—and in many settings outside of "Donahue"—as individuals refuse to use social roles. Consider the popular introduction of persons by their first names, rather than by

---

[5] For these same reasons, it is more sensible, through this discourse field, to talk about the "self" of a mother or the "mother herself" and less coherent to talk about the mother of a "self" or the "self mother." In other words, the "self" requires social role as background, devalues the role, and is, therefore, motivated to act against it.

their titles and/or social roles.[6] Lovers and sometimes spouses will introduce each other euphemistically as a "friend." More specifically, since beginning this project I have heard several utterances where a person has said: "Hello, this is Bob," and consciously not said, "Hello, this is my husband, Bob." I have heard the rule explicitly stated; "We do not refer to each other as 'my wife' or 'my husband'." Similar uses are illustrated where maiden names are retained, and various hyphenated forms of names are created to ensure that self is not consumed by implicitly constraining societal roles.[7] In discourse accomplished this way, utterances highlight the person's self as something valued over common societal roles. In Burkeian language, a grammar of self and social role provides a rhetoric that motivates the voice of the personal minority in the present, over and against the impersonal majority forces from the past.

Yet, what semantic forces animate the polemical code? Which rhetorical forces capture the collective sentiment? In what follows, I will discuss further the limited set of semantic dimensions introduced in chapter 4, and introduce the rhetorical forces that help explain this

---

[6] This form of address enacts a valuing of intimacy and equality, over that of authority and status difference. Yet, what sometimes occurs in such address is a verbal act of equality, accompanied by nonverbal acts of inequality: Parents may talk equality and act inequality, just as Donahue and others may address equally, but enact power relations more subtly. For a treatment of address forms in American discourse, see Brown and Gilman (1960), Brown and Ford (1961), and for a bibliography of empirical studies of personal address see Philipsen and Huspek (1985).

[7] The polemical code is used not only within utterances, but also gets played out processually. Consider the following story about a 40-year-old woman, Cecilia, who was first meeting a female colleague of her husbands,

a woman of their age, who told Cecilia that having heard good things about her from her husband, she was eager to learn more about her. Cecilia says that she began, "I have four children . . ." but the woman persisted, saying, "Wait just a minute. I didn't ask about your children, I asked about you. Where are *you* coming from?" At this Cecilia was stunned. "I mean, my role was a housewife and I didn't quite grasp what she was really talking about." But the woman told her: "I'm not talking about your identity as Greg's wife. I'm concerned with your identity as a human being, as a person, and as an individual, and as a woman." She invited Cecilia to join a consciousness-raising group, "a turning point in my life, a real change for me." (Bellah et al. 1985, p. 159)

That such a discourse functions to redefine traditional roles is testament to its great ideological force. Other examples, perhaps less popular, could be offered in the other direction as when the woman said she "chose" her "family" over a "career," thus rendering her role as more a "wife and mother" and less a full-fledged "woman." In either case, the discourse involves a deep agony between the person and the forces of society, be they "traditional" or "liberated."

polemic between codes. My major purposes are: to show how metaphorical speech enacts and resolves the agony, to demonstrate how the polemical code coheres along the semantic dimensions introduced earlier, and to refine a sense of the dimensional contrasts by examining the rhetorical force of each.

Donahue, and others of the show, have referred to "our society," "this country," and so on as "a nation of lemmings." The image is one of persons succumbing to external forces that sweep one up and move one along. The metaphor summarizes the effect, derogatorily, of living through social roles. As I understand it, a lemming is a small, furry rodent endowed with an unusual genetic code. Periodically whole lemming colonies, with each mindlessly following the other, will migrate into the sea, resulting in a type of mass, colonial suicide. On "Donahue" the phrase, "a nation of lemmings," is used as a cultural code which identifies deeply rooted (historical?) and tragic actions of a majority that "swims with the tide" and neglects the opportunity for individual expression. In terms of the dimensions, social role evokes problematical actions that are heard to be dependent, conforming, and closed. The associated images are toward not contained orderliness, growth, and change, but apparent chaos, death, and decay.

If symbols of self are commonly intelligible as *uniquely independent,* then symbols of social role are *dependent.* When considered "a nation of lemmings," individuals are placed in a semantic field where their actions depend on everyone else, where they must do as everyone else does. A male guest, speaking on ethics, said: "we live in a 'designer jeans culture' where everyone buys designer jeans because everyone buys designer jeans." He evokes an image of social subjection, of mindless conformity, an image of lemming-like behavior. This type of symbolizing invokes a felt dependence of individuals on what a majority says and does.

Through symbols of society and social roles a cultural imperative is expressed: "follow the rules." "That's what society is, rules," said an audience member. Rules are heard to constrain expressions of self by devaluing one's uniquenesses, power, and freedom. The dependencies invoked elicit a *rhetoric of slavery,* a way of speaking that is heard and felt to constrain the free acts of self. Contrasted to such rule and role rhetoric, is the self's *rhetoric of individual freedom.* If self is said to have rights which guarantee and choices which enact freedom, then society, through all of its rules, laws, and roles, is felt to invoke a type of slavery. Through symbols of society there is enacted a sense more of rules than of rights. When action is symbolized through role, the unique self is molded into the impersonal group. Further, when a person dared to be unique—a senior citizen talked about sex—an

Will The Real You Please Stand Up?

Submit to
pressure
from peers
and you move
down to their
level.
Speak up
for your own
beliefs
and you invite
them up to your
level.
If you move
with the crowd,
you'll get
no further than
the crowd.
When 40 million
people believe in
a dumb idea,
it's still a
dumb idea.
Simply swimming
with the tide
leaves you
nowhere.
So if you
believe in
something
that's good,
honest and bright—
stand up for it.
Maybe your peers
will get smart
and drift
your way.

A message as published in the *Wall Street Journal* by United Technologies Corporation, Hartford, Connecticut 06101 audience member lamented: "Society makes fun of them." The senior's personal opinion was allegedly judged improperly by imposing impersonal societal standards, that is, a judgment of a group (i.e., "them") by a group (i.e., "society"). The judgment by society was considered inappropriate because it held society's roles over this self. The speaker's judgment was considered appropriate, however, because it implicitly (and paradoxically) publicized the nonjudgmental rule (judge so to be not judged). In other similar cases, society was criticized for protecting a common role (e.g., the elderly symbolize a puritan ethic and sexual taboos), rather than tolerating the uniquely expressed present self (e.g., the elder speaks out in favor of sex). This rhetoric enacts social roles as an oppressive type of slavery, dependence on others, against which the free self must be asserted.

Along the second dimension, symbols of self mark actions of which one is personally *aware,* which one has initiated and done on one's own. This contrasts to symbols of social roles, which refer to certain actions of individuals that *conform unthinkingly* with external standards, or to actions in which individuals are, at best, aware of the impersonal nature of such standards. Through symbols of social roles, the preferred awareness of self has succumbed to the blind or impersonal enactments of social imperatives. Through "a nation of lemmings," interlocutors describe a social scene in which each mindlessly follows the other around, without any awareness of where each is going, nor any awareness of where the others are going. Thus, the symbols of society and roles express a person whose unreflective awareness has conformed with impersonal and constraining social forces, where those of self reveal a more personal awareness of one's own motives and choices.

Public role enactments and obvious symbols of society are, consequently, associated with obligatory constraints, or in native parlance, "a choice of no choice." Sometimes these symbols implicate a class of choices of which individuals are unaware or to which they are duty-bound to conform.[8] This view was stated most clearly by an expert guest on governmental actions, himself a symbol of society:

---

[8] Several current political policies on defense, nuclear armament, diplomacy, and so on, are stated as an act "of no choice." As a result, these policies are sometimes heard as necessary obligations forced upon the group by external forces, rather than internal commitments, thus diffusing full responsibility, for example, "this *has* to get done." Since such acts are said to involve "no choice," many citizens' motives for political involvement are stifled for they feel enslaved, or somehow obliged to accommodate as political instruments, rather than free to assert their selves. Such use of "no choice," when unexamined, enables the groups espousing such statements to proceed relatively unimpeded. See below.

All the choices are . . . bad. There still is no free lunch. It's going to be necessary to pay more to see a better, stronger, more honest administration which is available or be prepared to suffer a worse standard of living. Those are our choices.
[It is] important to recognize that for both our social needs and our defense needs, the public works—it's not a choice of doing one or the other. We need to do them because we need to underpin our defense capacity and our social capacity.
I think each of us as citizens has got to take a tough choice ahead and face it. Either we must be prepared to spend more money for our roads, our water systems, our sewer systems or be prepared to have further deterioration. . . . Our real choice is how much do we wish to see it decline.

The guest's speech is accomplished with the use of a prominent term, choice. But the choice, within the semantic and rhetoric of society, is heard as a dutiful obligation of "citizens," a social role to which all in the polity must somehow conform. What is heard, therefore, is not a free choice for the self but an "obligatory one" for the citizen; a crown of choice in a kingdom of obligation. It is not that there is no actual voluntary choice in the matter, only that the expressed choices reside in a domain of society, a domain heard as rule-governed, lawful, obligation. So, the speaker was heard to suggest a choice that does not motivate the valued type of voluntary assertions associated with his audience's self; it suggests an act of conformity to a mere citizen role, an obligatory act which lacks a sense of personal freedom.

Because the guest activated an obligatory and enslaving symbolic domain, the audience reaction was predictably passive. For example, a man representing a community action group responded to the speaker by explaining how his group did not need government or politics. He described his group members' independent abilities to do what they needed to do. He explained their choices as ones they could make on their own, not as obligatory ones *for* government or society, but as ones which were independently and freely made.[9] The group member's utterances suggest a preferred way of speaking on such matters through a discourse of voluntary choice, thus affirming the collective identity of the person as a free and independent self; conversely, dispreferred talk defines social actions as dutiful obligations, thus aligning persons' identities with social roles of conformity such as citizens.

[9] While the nature of routine cultural discourse which motivates such voluntary associations has been neglected, the nature of such political associations has been frequently discussed. See for examples, Tocqueville (1838/1945, pp. 304–305), Varenne (1977); Novak (1982, pp. 133, 137–138, 142), and Bellah et al. (1985, esp. pp. 203–207).

These symbols of social roles enact a devalued *rhetoric of obligation,* a rhetoric that gives voice to the impersonal majority, but which fails generally to motivate wide-scale individual and political action. On the other hand, by using codes of the individual or self (which were curiously absent from the official's speech) one displays individual freedoms and invokes a valued *rhetoric of voluntary choice,* a rhetoric in which individuals feel knowingly and freely motivated to choose what they need to do. In this cultural scene, a rhetoric that activates participants' awareness as free and voluntary persons excites more agreeable social passion than a rhetoric that activates the impersonal senses of an enslaving and impersonal role.

The third dimension which helps distinguish speech of self from that of social roles is *communicative-closed.* Using self discursively helps one enact a commonly valued, uniquely independent and openly communicative person. Contrasted to this sense of self are uses of traditional roles and society that represent an interactive system that is closed. As the metaphor, "a nation of lemmings," suggests, Americans are not acting fully human, nor are they interacting creatively enough; they are saying the same old destructive things. In a closed system as this, they are all swimming in a societal sea, doing the American crawl, politely smiling at each other, and uniformly stroking to their mutual tragic end. The semantic of society used here portrays a social life in which individuals know only constraining rules and roles. They speak politely and say only those things that may be said properly. Speaking this way follows restrictions on what is said, where it is said, with whom and so on. As such, the cultural code of roles—just like the genetic codes of lemmings—have Americans doing the same problematical things again and again and again. The playing and replaying of the same closed communicative tune is portrayed prominently through the enslaving symphonies of roles in society.

This dimension suggests a further contrast, on the one hand, between a cultural *rhetoric of self as assertive,* saying what one has to say when one wants to say it, and a *cultural rhetoric of roles, of accommodation,* saying only what should be said given one's role in the social scheme of things. The former highlights the elaborate and unrestrained communicativeness of the self; the latter, the closed and restrained rules of roles.

In summary, three semantic dimensions distinguish the personal code of self from its polemical counterpart, social role. Persons discuss self as uniquely independent, aware and expressive; they discuss role as commonly dependent, less personally aware, and closed. The self is given a voice through a rhetoric of individual freedom, voluntary choice, and self-assertion; social role is given a voice through a rhetoric of slavery, obligatory choice, and accommodation. Where self provides a discursive foreground, which is personal and present, social role provides a background which is impersonal and historically grounded. Where self is aligned with relatively unconstrained symbols of needs, rights, and choice, social role is aligned with coercive symbols of law, rule, and society. Where self radiates the preferred unique humanness of the individual, social role glimmers a dispreferred quality of commonality. In short, the valued self is pitted against and valued over social role, giving the individual a common voice more of separate humanness, than of common humanity (See Diagram 5-1).

Notes on Metaphorical Speech of "Society"

Metaphorical speech on "Donahue" (as discussed in chap. 4) constitutes self as a container, as a package with personal resources, as an entity that can be evaluated regarding its substance or lack of substance, as an object that is commonly said to be lost and found. This metaphorical speech of self coconstructs a sense of the individual as a rather tightly bound and contained package, a sense that stands in stark symbolic contrast to the metaphorical speech of society.

Considering the metaphors of society generally, an image of America is constituted, a nation or country that is not contained or containable, but somewhat out of control and falling to pieces. Such a view defines society as "fractured," "fragmented," "divisive," "divided," and "terribly disorganized." Other descriptors of it were: "a sorry situation," a nation with "no national purpose," and—like an occasional self—as having "lost it." Specific indications of such a fractured, fragmented group were said to be its "inequality," "sexism," and "racism." The societal "disorganization" was described as "rotten," "spoiled," and "troubled," while those victimized by it were said to feel "panic," "fear," and "depression" (Veroff, Douvan, & Kulka 1981). One person summarized the whole social state of affairs by calling it "a mess." Whatever the particular point of focus, society was spoken of meta-

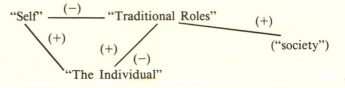

Separate humanness   Common humanity

5-1. Semantics in the codes of personhood.

phorically as a disparate and disorganized conglomeration of things. One is reminded of the individual hiker who stands, for one last bewildering moment, beneath a thundering avalanche, a contained and virtually helpless self amid a dangerous and deadly societal fallout. Similarly, one audience member used the metaphor, reproducing its troubled vision, to critique the scene she sought to remedy:

> While we're talking about men and women, if people would just con-centrate on themselves, and their goals, and being individuals. Society says that you have to earn money [or wash dishes, raise children, be pretty, etc., etc.] to be of any value. I feel that that's very ingrained in men right now. That is what women are fighting. I feel that I am fighting that right now, myself.

The self versus society and its roles.

Related entailments of society generally referred to the moral climate as "sinful," "not pure," "less moral," "amoral," as having a "troubled morality," or as having "no values" at all. Such speech adds an apocalyptical force to an already stormy social climate. Through its use, a stark symbolic contrast is created between the self as a contained and responsible entity, and society as its "disorganized," "messy," and "amoral" environment. In all such metaphorical communication, the cultural self is antagonized by powerful natural forces, be they the conforming animal within, or the messy environment of, society. So conceived, society symbolizes, albeit paradoxically, both the forces of controlling rules and laws, and the images of uncontrollable disorder and chaos. Through the polysemic meanings and motives of this met-aphorical speech, self is said to be constrained and antagonized. Through its discursive forces, society radiates order and disorder, the roles and rules as well as the "chaos," that the contained self must fight in and through.

Discursive Tensions and Unintentional Consequences

One fundamental tension is hearable in this and perhaps any system of cultural communication (McGee, 1984; Philipsen, in press; Rushing, 1983). At one pole, the impulse is toward individualized actions that lack normative constraints, for example, self, at the other, toward communal actions and civilizing restraints, for example, "social role" in "society."[10] Such a tension is felt in any cultural communication system, but is differently conceived and valued within each. Thus, in ancient Greece, an individual's voice of dialectic was silenced in favor of cultural rhetoric (Weaver, 1970); where elsewhen, individual voices were silencing implicitly civilizing forms (Bellah, Madsen, Sullivan, Swidler, & Tipton, 1985; Sennett, 1978). By examining this moment in an American discourse, I have offered a way to hear the tension, a polemical code between self and social role which renders such a discourse intelligible and illuminating. I have found that within a cultural discourse of personhood, as when self and social role co-occur, free assertions of a present self over the enslaving accommodations of a traditional society are motivated. It is through this polemical code that some American interlocutors of "Donahue" display a local solution to a perennial problem; that is, they enact publicly a response to the tension between persons impulses to be free and the constraints of communal life, in this case, through the symbolic interplay of self versus social role. Thus, as "Donahue" strikes a responsive chord in some, a repulsive chord in others, it becomes "perhaps the most important television program" (as advertised), not merely because it educates or entertains viewers, but more because it offers a powerful and popular voice to a deeply pervasive polemic in human lives.

As interlocutors gather around "Donahue," they see displayed a personal code for the person, the self, the enactment of which is said and felt to be relatively unconstrained, unlike, in their words, "traditional social roles." The dialectic is resolved as the freedoms of self are praised over the pitfalls of society. Yet, does not this polemical code communicate another social role, of self? Does this saying place the interlocutor in an unspoken paradox? If Tocqueville were observing here, he might point indeed to the "tyranny of the majority," whose collective voice commands: "be yourself." From this standpoint, the realized self is one who fully complies and conforms with the majority's

---

[10] The nature of this fundamental tension is one between impulses of persons, and restraints of sociality. What is being suggested for future inquiry is a recasting of very old tangles, for example, self/society (McGee, 1984; Western, in press), individual/community (Philipsen, in press; Rushing, 1983), and liberty/equality (Dahrendorf, 1968, pp. 179–214; Ebenstein, 1969, pp. 532–546; Rokeach, 1973, pp. 165–188), into notions of personhood and levels of sociality, discourses that enact each, and dimensions that inhere therein. Consequently, rereadings of these dialectical pairs are suggested with each mediating between identifiable models of personhood, and levels of sociality (social institutions). Such an approach would help unveil the world's various cultural discourses of persons, social relations, and institutions. So conceived, the inquiry applies equally well to democratic and nondemocratic contexts, proposes a rereading of communication systems along a different but distinctive, inclusive, and complementary dimension, thus laying a better base for comparative analyses of cultural communication.

normative injunctions: be independent, be aware, be assertive. So posed, the paradox seems rather obvious: The collective voice is telling each individual to "be your own person." And, the individuals, who use this manner of speaking, are complying. As they speak, they are using the informal and unspoken social pressures that surround self, thus enacting meaningfully a special type of social role.

However, what appears as an irony and paradox to the observer, that is, self as a social role, is not without cultural redress. Self-enactment may be guided by a "tyranny of the majority," but there are two important cultural reasons that qualify self as a special social role, as an antagonist to traditional social roles and as the preferred contemporary social role. First, through a cultural discourse of self, interlocutors enable a wedding of inner and outer form that motivates feelings of authenticity.[11] Through the quintessential self, one's acts are marked socially as individualized and authentic, initiated independently, consciously planned, and genuinely expressive of inner feelings and desires. Conceived this way, acts hold a different message than do those motivated by society, as when traditional roles require acting contrary to inner feelings. Obligatory acts such as these entail inherent feelings of hypocrisy, as when self does not want to do what society demands, and thus creates an asynchronous relation between an inner desire (felt voluntary) and an outer demand (felt obligation). Such an unwanted bind is redressed through this agonistic code, however, as the inner desires of self and the outer expectations for self coalesce. In this very particular sense, there is only an *apparent* paradox, *in this polemical pattern,* since outer expectations for expressive independence are aligned with the inner experiences of self. If everyone is commonly saying this common thing, for example, "be yourself," it is overlooked and does not much matter since each self is heard to speak freely from within. If heard this way, the communal imperative enables (not coerces) the simultaneous experience and expression of community and individuality; that is, interlocutors are saying a common thing but experiencing it uniquely. Thus, self is not felt nor *said to be* a traditional social role but is the preferred model for the free acting person in the here and now, and for this reason is the powerful and popular modern social role.[12] Second, self is unlike other social roles and relics since it is a

---

[11] The distinction used here draws upon Witherspoon (1977, esp. pp. 13–149); and Scruton (1979).

[12] There is an important distinction to be made here between the semantic level and the level of form. The semantics of the discourse highlight common meanings at the level of unique qualities and psychological capacities. So acted, speaking is conceived most coherently as a series of individualized act after individualized act. Speaking and feeling this way renders the communal *forms* used in such discourse as relatively unheard

role without rigid normative constraints.[13] Expectations for the person as self are tremendously broad, providing a type of social license to "do as one pleases." Where a statement of the "professor" role carries normative constraints for teaching, researching, and so on, those for self are felt to embrace a wider possible and proper range for actions.[14] Thus, the discourse creates a distinctive social role (from an analytical, not cultural, point of view) in which (1) inner desires (of self) and outer demands (for self) are united, providing (2) a wide latitude for actions deemed appropriate. As such, the discourse highlights the personal code over its polemical counterpart, activating the common sense of individuality *and* a performance of community, simultaneously.[15]

Note also how this interpretation of American life is distinct from Sennett (1978) and other cultural critics. At one point Sennett (pp. 263–264) writes about a

and unseen. In other words, the semantic level common in such discourse is individualized action, thus hiding its supporting communal forms. It is also noteworthy that common cultural forms (and meanings), such as those enacted in the polemical code examined here, are always translatable into individualized acts since all such discourse, in this scene, assumes persons are, at base, "individuals" with a "self" (Varenne 1977). Such forces make the communal modes and motives for human action difficult to hear, see, and feel. It is precisely this emphasis of individualized semantics over communal forms that makes of "self" not a "social role" (in a native sense) of conformity and obligation but a social role (in the analyst's sense) of assertiveness and freedom.

[13] I am drawing here upon the important distinction between culture and norm made by David Schneider (1976).

[14] One class of examples from "Donahue" includes assertions, such as being a "woman who left her family," that display for participants the possible range of actions that are legitimated as "self." To display this view fully, it is sometimes necessary to show unusual assertions such as male go-go dancers, gay atheists, and a woman married to two men simultaneously, in order to reaffirm fully and publicly the wide-ranging actions that may be necessary for "self" enactments. So conceived, the discourse praises the "positive face" of "self" as long as it is known and asserted, and leaves unimposed its "negative face" through a cultural form of "respect," that is, being righteously tolerant of others actions (Brown & Levinson 1978).

[15] Interlocutors who claim happiness in a traditional role, for example, a "wife," "mother," enact other symbolic forms, and risk accusations of not realizing their "self." As a consequent, several inferences are made such that the "violator" somehow, perhaps unknowingly, contributes to the massive "problem," and so becomes aligned with the problematical "society." But, they may be rendered and redeemed as "individuals" who have the "right" to so be, "after all this is America." Such a conversational move ignites the political code of the person as common symbolic ground. Note that my general hypothesis requires at least a three-tiered analysis of personhood as it is enacted in American cultural communication, that is, the political code of the individual, the personal code of self and its polemical counterpart, social roles. Each has distinctive qualities including lexical items, semantic forces, and symbolic forms. Without understanding the models of personhood coconstructed in systems of communication, we are missing important distinctive principles which some interlocutors have made in practice.

warfare . . . between the demands of social existence and the belief that we develop as human beings only through contrary modes of intimate psychic experience. . . . the quality of the warfare itself can be brought to life by posing two questions. . . . How is society injured by the blanket measurement of social reality in psychological terms? It is robbed of its *civility*. How is the self injured by estrangement from a meaningful impersonal life? It is robbed of the expression of certain creative powers which all human beings possess potentially—the powers of play—but which require a milieu at a distance from the self for their realization.

There are three main points at which my analysis of "Donahue" forces a re-evaluation of Sennett's claims. First, Sennett describes a "warfare" between "social existence" and "intimate psychic experience," a warfare between social life and psychic life, outer form and inner form, the impersonal and the personal. This set of polemics invalidates the symbolic system used on "Donahue." It does so by assuming that public social life is somehow violated if a people speak about psychic, inner, and personal experiences. Perhaps there are disadvantages to this "public-personalness," and Sennett takes great pains to point some of them out. However, in his critique, he overlooks the positive social functions of a civil life where "social existence" and "intimate psychic experience" coalesce. Sennett, perhaps more than anyone, has lamented such scenes and called for a renewed distinction between public and private life. But his critique fails to see any value in symbolic action where unique senses of the individual and enactments of community come together. Heard this way, the *equivocal enactment* of individuality and community, of a separate and common humanness, is a rather ingenious human invention, something to be understood, prior to its critique.

Second, Sennett works with an ideal vision of public man as a playful actor of well-defined roles; a vision which provides persons with an impersonal comfortableness (pp. 313–340). He uses this ideal to critique the Western "fall." He calls it a fall since this vision is no longer played out in Western interactive life. What has replaced it is "the intimate society" which, he claims, hinders both public and intimate life.

The approach in the present study is different. Certainly there are many things that American social action is not. But, there are also many things that it is, and many things that it does—whether one likes them or not. Rather than divide the scene into psychic and social polemics, we have discovered how both, ironically, are used together. On "Donahue," the symbolic enactment unites psychic and social meanings, but values the psychic over the social; conversely, the performance conforms with social constraints for personal freedoms over the more distant concerns of role. In the collective performance, persons are uniquely independent; this is a public and social performance. Put differently, the content may at times be "psychic" or personal, but the enactment is social and public. Public—and sometimes intimate—roles (codes) are played with, used variously, and ground the performance. Perhaps this is not the vision of public life Sennett had in mind. But it is public and civil nonetheless.

Finally, Sennett contends that Western life is "robbed of civility . . . the activity which protects people from each other yet allows them to enjoy each other's company" (p. 264). As I understand it, civility demands politeness, courtesy and respect, all of which are evident at times on "Donahue." Various normative constraints of "respect" are used; one can hear a type of righteous tolerance, a notion of "civility" operating. Thus, this American social action operates to both protect "people from each other," and allows an enjoyment of "each other's company." The American pattern enables both connecting and separating, both are necessary for "intimacy" and "civility," as Sennett implicitly acknowledges. Thus, one cannot claim a blanket statement that Americans are "robbed of civility"; we have a particular—some might say peculiar—form of it, for example, civil individualism.

The American discourse of personhood generally accomplishes a powerfully regnant function (Schneider, 1976). Through the collective recital, in which all may sing and hear the communal song of self and social role, there is a coherent unification. By participating in this scene, even if silently, participants hear a collective will echo across America, a common and redressive plea for *each* person to stand up and confront voluntarily its terrible coercive forces. Through the polemical interplay between self and social role, social actors commiserate communally as a way of realizing their shared identity, a shared destiny. Through such cooperative enactments, they motivate the imagination of their contemporaries, constitute shared sentiments, thereby unite against society, all in a constructive mode for bettering the social scheme of things. The community of sensibilities felt in such collective statement is the cultural function of the message, that is, the simultaneous enactment, affirmation, and union of individual persons in and against society.[16]

There are several premises about communication that support these communal symbols and functions. Four agreements that, when followed, enable the polemical discourse of personhood to occur, and ground the

---

[16] A similar force is enacted in self-help groups, sporting events, some committee meetings, and elsewhere when individuals talk about, and act against, other antagonizing—often institutional—forces.

cultural performance, may be summarized as follows: (1) each person should speak their own unique opinions as a constituent of self; (2) participants must grant the individual the moral right to speak through opinions; (3) the speaking of various opinions should be respected, that is, tolerated as a rightful expression; and (4) societal and institutional standards for conduct that are explicitly transindividual are to be left unsaid since they impose by unduly constraining the preferred presentations of self, infringing upon "individual rights," and thus violate the code of "respect" (Carbaugh, 1987). While the rules are only sketched here, they suggest a system of agreements about communication that is followed commonly and consensually on "Donahue." Such a base supports the collective enactment, is constituted through it, thus provides symbolic motives for social union and division simultaneously (See Diagram 5–2).

Conversational rules as these yield an identifiable form, and consequence, of communication.[17] It has been hypothesized that communication in which solidarity is a primary function occurs in a spiraling form, a cycle of recurring acts (Katriel, 1985), as contrasted to some problem-solving communication that occurs in a more sequential form (Katriel & Philipsen, 1981). Whereas consensus in the former is built upon local and general themes, in the latter it is built upon personal themes. However, the deep polemics described above occur partly in a spiraling form as a recycling of personal themes. In the process, persons are encouraged to speak *their own* opinion, a saying that usually involves some new twist on the matters at hand, a personal and special "openness" that is followed generally in turn by others. This collective "sharing" creates a series of statements of personal concerns about public matters, connected through a relation of "more of the same." As persons freely state their own opinions, they inevitably disagree with others. One consequence results, that is, "dissensus." The communicative event, so produced, constitutes and follows a spiraling form

"Self"	uniquely independent	collective symbol of freedom	Preferred
"Social Role"	collective symbol of constraint	commonly dependent	Dispreferred
	Division	Union	

5–2. **Cultural functions of polemical symbols.**

[17] Introduced here are a set of concerns, that is, actors' rules, forms and functions, for speaking, that are developed in detail in unit 2.

in which (1) topics are introduced and treated as problematical through terms such as social role and society, (2) self is asserted individually, displaying its necessarily unique and dissonant features, against the problems with society and social roles, thus (3) celebrating a unifying sentiment of those gathered through a polemical code, (4) which also results in a degree of dissensus on the topic at hand (that sometimes was stated as the initial "problem"). Thus, unlike some public discourses in Israel (Katriel, 1985) and Australia (Liberman, n.d.) where consensus is praised and preserved through spiraling forms, in this scene a degree of dissensus is aligned with the spiraling form. Such enactment is proper and necessary for the cultural presentation of the person, but also contributes unknowingly to problems of division being addressed (e.g., lack of coordination, misaligned meanings).

This unintentional trend contributes to a silencing of several important concerns: (1) As dissensus on important topics is co-enacted and preserved, it is virtually impossible for this mass public to witness an explicitly stated, collective agreement, and embrace collectively a powerful vision of the public good—unless, of course, the above rules for communication provide such a thing, that is, the process for interacting is agreeable generally, but renders propositions about important sociomoral issues disagreeable (Baskerville, 1980; Halloran, 1982). (2) The powerful motives for sociality in such public discourse are *said to be* matters of individual freedom and personal power. One's actions are heard to be matters of voluntary association as in clubs, committees, and organizations (Novak, 1982, pp. 128–155; Varenne, 1977). Matters of societal responsibility, civic duty, and honor are not addressed clearly, if implicitly (Berger, Berger, & Kellner, 1974; Sennett, 1978). (3) The powerful symbolic meanings of persons, from the standpoint of this discourse, are those which articulate with independence, assertiveness, voluntary action, and personal freedom. Cooperative interdependence, wide-scale collective action, and societal responsibility lurk in the background (Lasch, 1979; Yankelovich, 1981). In sum, the polemical interplay between self and social roles contributes to a dissensual discourse, a discourse linked to individual modes and motives for acting that hides the communal meanings, modes and motives; the interlocutors are speaking as individuals, but are not hearing their collective voice, nor fully appreciating its consequences, that is, renewed dissensus, collective enactment and solidarity.[18]

---

[18] This perspective on mass communication requires that it be understood as something more than acts of individual intention, but as cultural productions of intersubjective convention (fn Bakhtin 1981; Corcoran, 1983; Grossberg, 1982; Newcomb, 1984).

6

CULTURAL SYMBOLS OF PERSONHOOD AND UNDERSTANDING CULTURED PERSONS

I have interpreted the American discourse of personhood that is used on "Donahue" through three cultural codes. First, in this American scene, the person is symbolized as "an individual." This symbol provides for—to follow Durkheim—the collective representation of *the* person. In public speech, it has a prescribed force making it a generally unquestioned premise of personhood. The symbol functions culturally as a partial constituent of American personhood, enabling the equivocal affirmation of separate humanness and common humanity. Socially, the symbol—along with the rights it has—is used prominently to accomplish tolerance of diversity, freedom (mainly to choose and to speak), and equality. Through the combination of its prescribed force, its cultural and social functioning, the symbol supports and helps (re)produce exemplary acts of respect (of persons as individuals).

Second, the individual has a "self." Self symbolizes the collective representation of *a* person, a uniquely independent individual. It is very strongly preferred, in public speech, that self be communicated and made available to others. However, its verbal display is not required, because a person may choose to be silent, unaware of personal acts, dependent on others, or be otherwise untoward. That is the individual's right. But it is strongly preferred that the person present self. Self functions at the cultural level to display the ever-changing and unique identity of the person. It thus elaborates the separate humanness of the individual but does so in the commonly preferred way (through the analytical role of self). Socially, it is used prominently to highlight independent action, conscious awareness and expressiveness. Because of the combination of its strongly preferred force, its cultural and social functions, and its polemical relatedness to roles, self occurs through exemplary acts that are reflective and assertive.

Third, self is symbolized over and against traditional social roles. Social role provides for the collective representation of *a group* of persons. In this public speech, it is generally dispreferred that one sing the praises of role. At the cultural level, the role (and the society) symbol constitutes an identity that blindly conforms with common expectations and displays a devalued dependence and closedness. The symbol is used socially to publicize personal constraints that are felt widely as a kind of slavery. It is thus heard to be a development of the commonness of the individual. Because of its dispreferred force, its cultural and social functions, and because of its polemical relation to self, the symbol is enacted through a renunciative voice that rejects.

Considered together, the individual symbol and its equivocal potential is elaborated personally through self, which is acted polemically against role. These are the essential dynamics in an American discourse of personhood as it is spoken in a contemporary American scene.

Further, however, as noted in Diagram 6–1 and as introduced briefly throughout this unit, each American code of personhood is loosely aligned with native genres of speaking. "Being honest" identifies a kind of truthful and open talk where individual rights are exercised and self is displayed. Likewise, "sharing" is identified as a kind of expressive talk that takes one's own inner resources and makes them available to others in a way that supports and helps them. "Communication" involves—quintessentially—a kind of talk that demonstrates flexibility between openness and supportiveness. But before moving to a description and interpretation of these genres, I want to pose and leave unanswered several questions raised by these American codes, move on to discuss what the codes suggest about some extant claims about symbolizing and personhood, survey some other cultures' patterns, and then conclude by suggesting some implications for a cultural communication theory of personhood.

American Symbols of Personhood	Code	Exemplary Act	Native Genre
"The Individual"	Political	Respect	"Being Honest"
"Self"	Personal	Reflect	"Sharing"
"Traditional Social Role"	Polemical/Positional	Reject	"Communication"

6–1.   Summary of an American discourse on personhood.

A Tyranny of Personal Opinions, Uniqueness, and Openness?

The major purpose of my comments throughout this book—like Baruch Spinoza's—is not to lament the symbolic acts of persons, but to understand them. For a brief moment, however, I wish to strike a more critical chord. I want to raise several questions about the codes described above. I draw upon Tocqueville and Mill, since they link the principles of liberty and equality to the freedom of speech, an approach that suggests limitations to some of these culture patterns in American speech.

As Tocqueville wrote about democracy in America, he struggled to reconcile the forces of individuality and liberty with equality. Of liberty he was most fond, but felt generally unassured about its political implementation; of equality, he waxed more complacent for he believed American democracy had moved it to new heights. But, Tocqueville foresaw some troubling consequences of the newly institutionalized American equality upon individuals' liberty.

To highlight this (among other) concern(s), Tocqueville used the concept, "the tyranny of the majority." He described how a collective's actions, seen through the concept of equality, can constrain individual liberty. One of the consequences he feared was the triumph of the majority opinion (the aggregated sum of equal voices) over unpopular views (the liberty of one). The result? Equality triumphs over liberty.

Tracing these dynamics into the contemporary American scene raises several questions: (1) Have the imperatives supporting unique identity and personalized opinions oppressed others that are more depersonalized?; (2) Have the spoken semantics of the separate and personal person rendered its connected and common features more silent? Perhaps harder to sense and feel?; and (3) Has the majority preference for openness—in personal and separate terms—tyrannized some sayers and sayings that are potentially liberating? Is the contemporary American majority tyrannizing its citizens under the cultural rubrics of personal uniqueness and openness? Is this a pattern of talk that sounds liberating and open, but actually functions to tyrannize persons and close their mind? (a tyranny of openness?). Has contemporary America created a kind of public discourse where each asserts the personal opinion and respects others who do the same, but all are not moving together in any particular nor principled direction? Nor able to?

This line of questioning brings to mind John Stuart Mill's essay *On Liberty,* written in part to respond to concerns raised by Tocqueville. Mill was a great champion of liberal ideals with his writings foregrounding the virtues of individual liberty, but according to Mill, these were only virtues when grounded on the collective's commitment to truth. To Mill, the purpose in freedom of speech was not simply to give people opportunities to express opinions openly, but to commit people to debate, to direct conversation toward a productive outcome, to move the collective toward what is better in word and deed. When persons are symbolized in personal terms, and personal words become the only deeds, then the means to an end—open speech in pursuit of truth—becomes an end unto itself, a tyranny of openness.

Clarifying an American Discourse on Personhood

Several authors have commented about American and Western conceptions of personhood. Three will be discussed here, David Schneider's description of the relative in American culture as a person, and Michelle Rosaldo and Clifford Geertz's comments about the inner-boundedness of the American person.

In *American Kinship,* David Schneider (1980) described the major premise of a relative, being a person, which establishes—at the level of "person"—a "primary identity," "a cultural unit capable of action" (p. 57). This cultural category of primary identity, as Schneider constructs it, amounts to an unique combination of roles:

> A person as a cultural unit is a composite, a compound of a variety of different elements from different symbolic subsystems and domains. The person has either male or female sex as defined by the sex-role system. The person has age attributes as defined by the age-role system. The person has class characteristics as defined by the class system. (pp. 59–60)

Within the American galaxy of kinship, Schneider informs us, the relative is a person with attributes not only of kin, but also of various other "symbolic subsystems and domains." Thus, the American relative is a person whose primary identity derives from a variety of different role systems.

This interpretation of American personhood serves Schneider well in his study of kinship, and the culture perspective that generated his analysis informs in a fundamental way the conceptual framework for the current study. But there are also important differences in these findings and approaches. First, Schneider describes person as a combination of roles. While this description serves to make the point of distinctiveness between and among persons, it obscures another important cultural polemic. Namely, the personal code of self is discussed by Americans as something other than a role. Thus, from the American cultural perspective, the person as self is not a combination of roles, as Schneider describes the relative as a person, but a unique identity separate from them.

There are at least three distinctive positions on the relation between individual identities and social roles. The "authentic self" position is discussed by Berger, Berger, and Kellner (1974), Sennett (1977), and by contemporary Americans. From this perspective self is something unique, separate from, and held over social roles. This position stands rather uneasily beside the "unique role-player" position illustrated by Schneider, and discussed by Goffman (1967), Mead (1934), and Cushman and Cahn (1984). From this perspective, the self is a unique combination of roles, a player of "interaction rituals" that tends to conform to well-defined institutionalized lines. As Mead (1964, p. 357) put it: "The proudest assertion of independent selfhood is but the affirmation of a unique capacity to fill some social role." The third is a more contextualist position articulated by Victor Turner (1969). In contexts of communitas, social roles are suspended and persons meet in liminal union without status differences or role constraints. In contexts of societas, routine social roles are reaffirmed in order to maintain and reinforce existing social structures. In short, the positions might be summarized as two types of enactments, self over roles and self through roles, that constitute the identifiable social contexts of communitas and societas, respectively (Hannerz, 1980, pp. 202–241).

Second, throughout his discussion, Schneider is describing cultural categories in the abstract. He is not attempting to consider their discursive or conversational workings (p. 62). Thus, Schneider moves to relations of logic among folk categories, rather than to conversational functions and forms. Where Schneider makes claims about the distinctive features of cultural categories, I have tried to explore their use in communication.

In sum, Schneider describes the person by analyzing distinctive features of abstractable domains, mainly roles and social institutions, while I have described symbols of the person that are used within an American discourse. Both approaches are guided by systems of symbols and meanings with the former abstracting domains and distinctive features, the latter, discourses and discursive functions. More substantively, Schneider writes of the person as a cultural category of combined roles from the standpoint of the kinship institution. I write of the person as a discourse, a system of communication codes, that distinguishes some aspects, that is, self, from others, traditional social roles. Rather than couching the view of the person within a social institution such as kinship, I have watched from the standpoint of the communal conversation. Both perspectives treat symbols and meanings as focal concerns, but the approaches are also distinctive. Schneider develops an ideational theory of culture through domains; I develop a cultural theory of communication through discourses.

In several ethnographic studies about communication and symbolic action, especially when making cross-cultural comparisons, authors have commented briefly about American and Western notions of personhood. I will consider two such comments which I take to be representative. The first occurs in the writings of Michelle Rosaldo where she contrasts the Ilongot notion of the person to "ours."

> What Ilongots lack from a perspective such as ours is something like our notion of an inner self continuous through time, a self whose actions can be *judged* in terms of the sincerity, integrity, and commitment actually involved in his or her bygone pronouncements. (1982, p. 218)

Similarly, Geertz contrasts "our" notion with the Javanese, Balinese, and Moroccan:

> The Western conception of the person as a bounded, unique, more or less integrated motivational and cognitive universe, a dynamic center of awareness, emotion, judgment, and action organized into a distinctive whole and set constrastively both against other such wholes and against its social and natural background, is, however incorrigible it may seem to us, a rather peculiar idea within the context of the world's cultures. (p. 225)

Both comments are made somewhat in passing, as rather offhand references to something which all in the immediate audience somehow know and take for granted.

Note how both of these comments highlight the one aspect of the American person, self, which is probably most distinctively American. Note how only Geertz points to a notion which pits some features against others. But it is not clear whether the bounded notion of the person that Geertz describes is pitted against attributes of itself or others (i.e., "other such wholes") and/or against its history and culture (i.e., "social and natural background"). Note also how neither Rosaldo nor Geertz comment directly at the level of the person as an individual. Both do implicate such a notion in their subsequent comparative analyses, but the notion itself, as a cultural construction with attendant premises, is not made problematical as a formative feature of American personhood, nor as a departure for the analyses (but see Dumont, 1970, 1985). Further, neither author makes reference to roles as partly constitutive of the American person, nor explores their variation with other cultural patterns including symbols of speaking and action.

Comparative statements are essential for understanding the nature of conceptions of persons and actions, especially if we are to distinguish analytical from the more cultural categories, trace how societies control notions of persons, and identify social forms through which relations of power, intimacy, and exchange are managed. In fact, as much is necessary if we are to further the theoretical points that relate various cultural symbols of personhood to genres of speaking, as both of these construct systems of social relations. But to further that end, we need more refined comparative statements, statements that enter the American case with all of its force into rigorous cross-cultural study. The person is symbolized in America as not only bounded and unique, but as a system of political, personal and polemical codes that is undoubtedly valued variously across various social contexts. Comparative study will further our understanding of these contextual variations, attending both to their nature and use within American society, and to their character across other cultural systems of communication.

Cross-Cultural Study: Implications for Cultural Communication Theory of Personhood

In various ways and in various degrees, the Ilongot (Rosaldo, 1982), the Bali (Geertz, 1976), the Samoans (Shore, 1982), the Hindu (Bharati, 1985), and the Oriyan, Zapotec, and Gahuku–Gama (Shweder & Bourne, 1985) do not communicate notions of the person as self. What is in its place are notions of the person that are more relationally than physiologically based, for example, Samoa, Ilongot, Zapotec, more positionally than personally focused, for example, Bali, Gahuku–Gama, more a dispersable "dividual" than a bounded individual, for example, Hindu. In fact, for the Tallensi (La Fontaine, 1985), the notion of person includes organismic and spiritual aspects such that some animals are considered persons, for example, sacred crocodiles "combine the human spiritual aspects with a living body" (p. 127), where elsewhere, as in Taita, some humans "by virtue of their sex, or specialist roles" are not considered persons at all (p. 131).

Based on this accumulating ethnographic record, several questions can be raised about existing models of personhood and communication. First, the evolutionary feature of Mauss's (1938/1985) statement of the person—if fairly called evolutionary (see Allen, 1985)—can not be supported. Mauss wrote about a progression:

> From a simple masquerade to the mask, from a "role *(personnage)* to a "person" *(personne),* to a name, to an individual; from the latter to a

being possessing metaphysical and moral value; from a moral consciousness to a sacred being; from the latter to a fundamental form of thought
and action—the course is accomplished. (Mauss, 1938/1985, p. 22)

He wrote of the most recent accomplishment, "the notion: the 'person'
(*(personne)* equals the 'self' *(moi)*; the 'self' *(moi)* equals consciousness,
and is its primordial category" (p. 21). The case Mauss develops can
be interpreted at several levels (see Allen, 1985), but risks being heard
in the West at least as a progression of personhood from roles to self.
Perhaps this progression is true within the value system and ideology
of American society, but as a general evolutionary sequence of personhood, it must be held suspect (Shweder & Bourne, 1985). For
example, adult male Ilongot fundamentally value and enact social
"sameness" in their role as a headhunter (Rosaldo, 1985, p. 147). It
is misleading to think of this prominent Ilongot conception as "un-
developed," or "more primitive," for Ilongot can also conceive of the
person "as an individual" (Rosaldo, 1985, pp. 145–146), but simply
do not (yet?) consider that conception particularly pertinent or of much
value. An evolutionary model risks obscuring this kind of structural
and contextual dynamic. One might ask: Under what conditions is one
model of personhood preferred over others? Are the models, when
enacted, associated systematically with components of social settings
and/or consequences? Are there indeed identifiable sequences of development? within contexts? intra- and cross-culturally? If one interprets
Mauss's comments synchronically rather than as evolutionary, and if
one explores the salience and value of cultural categories as well as
their progression, one finds a vocabulary that is suggestive for comparative study.

Second, based on the extant ethnographic record, Hallowell's (1955)
statement must be qualified.[1] Hallowell's admirable objective was to
identify "some of the common functions that all cultures play in building
up and reinforcing self-awareness in the individual through basic orientations, despite wide differences in actual culture patterns" (p. 80).
For his project, the "actual data" included "self-awareness, self-per-
ception, self-reference by means of language, self-conception" (p. 80).
The term self was chosen as central because it "remains closer to the
phenomenological facts that reflect humans' self-awareness as a generic
psychological attribute. It retains the reflexive connotation that is indicated when we say that a human individual becomes an object to
himself" (p. 80). Hallowell asks sensitively: "How do individuals view

---

[1] My specific point is amplified in, but not entirely consistent with, Varenne's general
argument (1984).

other "concepts" of "self"

themselves in terms of the self that they know?" But the avenue of inquiry he proposes is covered with Western concepts, for example, self, self-awareness, self-orientation, and premises, for example, the self-concept develops as the person matures and becomes "the basis for the activities of the individual and the interpretation of his experience" (p. 81). Perhaps the Ilongot, the Bali, and the Samoan can experience as much, but apparently self-awareness and individual reflectiveness are much less salient for them than for us, if present at all. For some, for example, Samoan (Shore, 1982) and Japanese (Takao, 1976), relational awareness is more fundamental to enactments of the person than is self-awareness. To link notions of the person or self to a self-awareness of individual consciousness seems less tenable today, unless one qualifies the claim to apply only to those sociosymbolic systems where such notions are highly salient, or unless the statement is intended metaphorically for purposes of abstract analyses. As the former, the framework is incomplete since it overlooks aspects of the individual and role; as the latter, it is clearly skewed toward the Western frame of mind.

Let us consider a related communication theory, one that is based on the assumption that "the self-concept is the generative mechanism for interpersonal choice" (Cushman & Cahn, 1985, p. 21). On empirical grounds, both within and outside American and Western scenes (Philipsen, 1975, 1976), this assumption is open to serious question. Among peoples for whom self is not a salient cultural category, such as the Teamsters, the Ilongot, the Samoans, the Bali, the Hindu, the Gahuku–Gama, and so forth, in what sense can it be a "generative mechanism"? From the standpoint of these sociosymbolic systems, self-concept is not the primary force in human interpretation and action, nor prominent in message content. These cultural conceptions of the person include, at base, social and relational forces, rather than individual ones. From many such points of view, the person would receive easier verbal articulation if asked the contextual question, where am I, or the relational question, with whom am I? rather than the psychological question: Who am I? These comparisons help in making a more general theoretical point. Self-concept, self-awareness, self-orientation, and so forth, are partly constitutive of an American model that is itself an instance of the cultural construction of personhood. Thus if generative mechanisms operate, they are better conceived—from this point of view—as cultural communicative constructions of personhood, the self-concept becoming one instance in this broader class. Conversely, if communication accomplishes in part the generation, regulation, and validation of self-concepts, it is in large part because this outcome is valued by the common person. It is less because of the general nature of the communication process itself. The self-concept theory of communication may have great currency in much of American life today (Sennett, 1977; Yankelovich, 1979), but it also has clear empirical limits that may be extended if conceptualized at the cultural levels of personhood construction and communal conversation.

Throughout, I have preferred to write at the general level about conceptions of personhood rather than develop a theory of self, individual, or role. Following others (Geertz, 1976; Mauss, 1938/1985; Rosaldo, 1982), I have assumed this convention in an effort to move beyond highly salient Western notions such as self and individual. One might guess that person itself may some day become Westernized. Be that as it may. But for now, at this point in our intellectual history, it seems person is less tainted analytically, thus better adapted for comparative study and better able to offer perspective on statements written in terms closer to home.

Part of the theoretical utility of the concept, personhood, along with its location in communicative enactment, is its heuristic power, its ability to embrace various models of what it means to be person, the various persons it is sensible to be, the things that person should and should not do, what to feel and what not to feel, and what should and should not be said. It is more a sensitizing lens than it is a definitional construct.

But there is more than this. The communicational approach can be further developed by exploring the codes, dimensions, metaphors, and types of personhood.

The *system of spoken codes* or distinct discursive fields of personhood have been discussed by Mauss (1938/1985) and others (Caughey, 1984; White & Kirkpatrick, 1985) and I will not review them here. What I will suggest is that there are probably multiple symbolic codes that co-occur and are available as resources within any society's discourse on personhood, such as the individual, the self, and roles in the American case (which have their analogues in Mauss's analysis). This is an important point not because it is new, but because it has often been overlooked, leaving accounts with only a partial view, often only of valued features, rather than a more holistic and systemic view.

The communication study of personhood would benefit by attending to *semantic dimensions and metaphors*. For example, the American case differentiates aspects of the person along dimensions of independent–dependent, aware–unaware, and expressive–closed. The poles gain a prominent expression through metaphorical speeches of the person as container and lemming. Elsewhere, persons are conceived along dimensions of concrete–abstract (Schweder & Bourne, 1985), material–spiritual (La Fontaine, 1985), and individuated–interrelated

(Bharati, 1985; Geertz, 1976; Rosaldo, 1982). By exploring the various meanings and metaphors about personhood, we may eventually be able to understand their links to broader vocabularies of motives, including native genres and enactments of communication, the nature and form of social relations, and types of social systems. For example, it appears the Ilongot, the Bali, and the Japanese, among others, conceive of and enact communication "from the outside–in," creating personhood prominently as *externally motivated,* with eyes searching social scenes for cues about one's being; whereas contemporary Americans, the Paliyan, and Arapesh enact communication more "from the inside–out," speaking of *internal motivation,* creating one's prominent consciousness as dwelling within. With regard to social relations, the Bali and Navajo (Witherspoon, 1977) symbolize an intricate web of *connectedness,* while Americans and other individualists treat prominently a *separateness.* At the level of social systems, the Bali and Iatmul symbols support institutions that are more *impersonal and positional* while others public discourse supports institutions more *intimate and personal* (Hymes, 1972). My discussion of these dimensions is meant to be suggestive. Inquiring this way should help us understand aspects of persons that are symbolized distinctively within cultures, and through comparative study understand what—if any—analytical levels apply across cultures. Interpretations of native metaphorical speech would enrich such inquiry, especially as metaphors give public voice to persons and speaking (Seitel, 1974).

Finally, the interrelations of symbolic codes, semantic dimensions, and metaphors of personhood would help create an understanding of *cultural types of personhood.* Two productive taxonomies have been developed with both in the form of dichotomies. Shweder and Bourne (1985) have suggested two types, two solutions to the problem of relating "the individual to the group." One is the "egocentric contractual mode," whereby "society becomes the servant of the individual"; who a person is, is a more abstract matter that is symbolized somewhat a-contextually. The other is the "sociocentric organic" model where individual interests are "subordinated to the good of the collectivity" (p. 190); who a person is, is more context-dependent and occasion-bound. Recently, and of great pertinence to this American case, Dumont (1985) has written about the "renouncer" as an "outwardly individual," an "individual-outside-the-world," and the "inwardly individual," an "individual-in-the-world." Combining these types with Dumont's more general thesis provides some provocative leads. Dumont sets out to suggest: "If individualism is to appear in a society of the traditional, holistic type, it will be in opposition to society and as a kind of supplement to it, that is, in the form of the outwardly individual" (p. 96). His types and thesis, along with the American case, suggest the following: (1) individualism appears not only in traditional holistic societies through a renunciative voice, but also in a modern individualist one, for example, the renunciative voice against society, for self, and (2) the "inwardly individual" is aligned both with the "in-the-world" society, *and* enacts prominently his or her place outside it, for example, self in and against society and traditional roles. Do these communicational dynamics enact, through a collective and renunciative voice, both individualism and holism? Does an inward individualism that is focused outwardly through renunciation both replace individualism with a weak holistic voice, for example, self as the collective sacred role, and affirm individualism with a strong individualist voice, for example, self as uniquely separate from all others?

Both Shweder and Bourne (1985) and Dumont (1985) provide typologies of personhood that are highly suggestive in developing an understanding of personhood both intra- and cross-culturally, as well as developing the theoretical links among these models, systems of social relations and institutions.

More generally, by attending to cultural discourses of personhood, systems of symbolic codes, meanings, metaphors, and types, we can enhance the prospects for a cultural communication theory of personhood. Perhaps the above ingredients suggest an early heuristic base. The general project, of course, will require continued empirical work, as well as exploring the intimate links—within and across cultures—among symbols of personhood, systems of social relations, and native genres of communication.

Unit 2:

DISCOURSE ABOUT SPEAKING

> Language as the locus of disclosure is not an activity of the individual primarily, but of the language community. Being a person can not be understood simply as exercising a set of capacities I have as an individual, on all fours with my capacity to breathe, walk, and the like. On the contrary, I only acquire this capacity in conversation, to use this as a term of art for human linguistic interchange in general; I acquire it in a certain form within this conversation, that of my culture; and I only maintain it through continued interchange. (Taylor, 1985, p. 276)

> One good ethnographic technique for getting at speech events . . . is through words which name them. (Hymes, 1962, p. 110)

Introduction

In the first part of this book, I described one feature of the talk used on "Donahue," a discourse on personhood. That discourse was intimately linked to another, native terms about speech and speaking. For example, being an individual was partly symbolized by the freedom to speak and the common premise for speaking honestly; "having a self" was prominently expressed through acts labeled sharing; roles were cast aside by being open and really communicating; and important aspects of the person were conceived and evaluated in part along the dimension of communicative–closed. In this second part of the book, I will examine the latter categories about talk which are used on "Donahue" to label acts and events of speaking.

By attending to this discourse about speaking, I hope to discover a sense of the cultural form of conversation to which Taylor refers. Through being an interlocutor, one uses and (re)produces a sociosymbolic system, one enacts and displays membership in a language community (Taylor, 1977, p. 122). By virtue of acting in community, one engages in some forms of conversation instead of others. Further, by studying the forms which are labeled and enacted by communal members, one can develop an understanding of where and how persons "draw the lines" around their talk, especially through rather routine comments about it. By probing categories about talk this way, one can interpret parts of the disclosure of the community: How do interlocutors give form to the talk that they are witnessing and doing? What symbols are used to comment about talk? Which "currents of conversation" are identified and commented upon? What does this framing of talk accomplish for participants?

Native Categories about Speaking

A general theory of communication—if it is to embrace and illuminate moments of intersubjective meaningfulness and enactments of terms and tropes—must account for the variation of communicative forms (motivated enactments in sequences) and meanings (the common intelligibility of the forms). What persons are saying and how they say it are at the heart of communication. Hymes (1962, p. 105) has put the matter this way:

> The use of a linguistic form identifies a range of meanings. A context can support a range of meanings. When a form is used in a context, it eliminates the meanings possible to that context other than those that form can signal; the context eliminates from consideration the meanings possible to the form other than those that context can support. The effective meaning depends upon the interaction of the two.

One way of investigating these issues is through native categories about speaking: What communicative forms are identified and used? With what meanings?

Since Hymes (1962) early plea for ethnographic investigations of speaking, several studies have been conducted that explore speaking as a cultural category.[1] Philipsen (1986b) has reviewed some of these studies around four themes: (1) the elaboration of speaking in folk taxonomies, (2) semantic dimensions for conceptualizing, evaluating, and differentiating ways of speaking, (3) metaphors for interpreting the domain of speaking, and (4) conceptions of the efficacy of speech.

Folk taxonomies of speaking demonstrate that the form of speaking varies cross-culturally. In particular, degrees of differentiation, enactments, and functions of speaking vary cross-culturally (Abrahams &

---

[1] A related program of study has been initiated recently by Verschueren (1985), who explores native terms about linguistic action, but is distinctive from the present approach since it focuses on "linguistic reflections" about speaking through recall, rather than the actual "talk" about speaking in a native context.

Bauman, 1971; Gossen, 1974a, 1974b; St. George, 1983; Sherzer, 1983; Stross, 1974). For example, among the St. Vincentians, when a person's words are annoying, loud, aggressive, and self-assertive, they may be identified as "getting on rude" (Abrahams & Bauman, 1971, p. 765). This native phrase is of one act within "a folk taxonomy of speech acts" deemed indecorous, bad, or rude. Thus, the St. Vincentians differentiate spoken acts that are deemed indecorous from others, can identify various enactments deemed indecorous and "nonsensible," and have a refined lexicon for those acts that are disapproved, less pleasing stylistically, and unruly. By identifying and enacting these native acts, the St. Vincentians give various shapes to speaking that are unlike others.

To claim that forms for speaking vary cross-culturally is to state a rather obvious empirical fact. What studies of folk taxonomies suggest moreover, are *several paths for comparative studies within and across cultures, leading to more refined statements about native forms of speaking, their salient ranges of meanings, associated social functions and structures, and cultural variation.* An excellent example of this potential appears in Urban (1986).

A second theme in these studies is the use of semantic dimensions to conceive of, evaluate, and differentiate ways of speaking. The St. Vincentians evaluate speaking by using the semantic dimensions sensible–nonsensible, controlled–uncontrolled, and polite–rude (Abrahams & Bauman, 1971). The Haya evaluate speaking along the dimensions of controlled–uncontrolled and substantial–insubstantial (Seitel, 1974). The Fiji Indians evaluate speaking in terms of direct–indirect (Brenneis, 1978) as do the Israeli Sabras (Katriel, 1986). The Kuna evaluate their speaking along the dimension of fixed–flexible (Sherzer, 1983). Of special interest to the present study is the suggestion by Katriel and Philipsen (1981) that some Americans use the dimensions close–distant, supportive–neutral, and flexible–rigid to evaluate speaking. What these dimensions suggest is: *A limited and distinctive semantic system operates within cultures to generate various ways of speaking, some dimensions of some systems may apply cross-culturally, and a metasemantic system may have universal applicability* (Wierzbicka, 1985).

The third theme in studies of cultural categories of speaking explores metaphors used for interpreting speaking. For example, the Haya interpret speaking in terms of "expelling a flatus" (Seitel, 1974); the Chamula in terms of a "heat" metaphor (Gossen, 1974b); and some Americans treat speaking as interpersonal "work" (Katriel & Philipsen, 1981). By using metaphor as an analytical tool—rather than a native term as in those studies cited above—Reddy (1979) claims to account for at least 70% of "English" talk about language. The metaphor he develops is the "conduit metaphor" and he develops it in a way that is "experience near" (Geertz, 1976). He observes that "we" treat ideas and meanings as objects, terms and tropes as containers, and speaking as the sending (along the conduit) of the objects, through the containers, from one person to another. *By studying folk uses of metaphors about speaking, these studies reveal the cultural place of speaking within indigenous symbol systems and suggest a central place for metaphors (about speech) within cultural theories about communication and speaking.*

The fourth theme apparent in studies of cultural categories about speaking is the efficacy of speaking as an action. Seitel (1974) describes how Haya proverbs about speech help interlocutors understand which acts of speech are substantial and which are not. Likewise, Urban (1984) describes how the main theme in a Shokleng myth is "speech about speech," and what the theme speaks about is the efficacy of speech as an action. Its use informs its users when speech is efficacious and why it should be considered as such. Katriel and Philipsen (1981) show how some Americans identify "chit-chat" as less efficacious than "communication." For the Burundi (Albert, 1972), "ubgenge" is valued as a necessary and substantial way to manipulate a hierarchical social order in order to receive requisite goods and services. Conversely, other categories of speaking are considered less substantial than others as is "griping" among Israelis (Katriel, 1985) or "talking shit" among some Black Americans (Bell, 1983). *As speech is identified and labeled through cultural categories, its efficacy as an action—what it is doing, what it should and should not do, what it can and can not do—is displayed.*

Studying communication this way—by describing and interpreting folk categories about speaking, their meanings, metaphors and efficaciousness—is important for several reasons (my discussion here echoes Philips, 1987). First, the categories about speaking are named by natives, identified and performed by them. By investigating native concepts, our understanding of communication will have a context-sensitivity that it cannot otherwise have. As important as universal patterns for the use of speech are (Brown & Levinson, 1978), or universal standards for its interpretation (Grice, 1975), such accounts must be grounded in particulars if they are to be particularly interesting (Hymes, 1986a). Second, native categories about speaking are used socially by situated persons, for their own purposes. If we are to understand communication as meaningful enactment, through local forms, we must attend to the features and functions of local use. Third, focusing on native categories about speaking helps unravel which communicative devices are valued and which devalued, which central and which peripheral in situated verbal performances. This verbal labeling of local resources helps unravel the place of verbal resources in social lives, marking some occasions as occasions where culture is "on display" (Bauman, 1987, p. 9). Attending to cultural categories about speaking, then, enables a bottoms-up kind of theorizing deriving from forms of speech that are named by natives, used for specific social purposes, and related recursively to local patterns of culture.

Ethnographic inquiry into these cultural categories enables movement toward several theoretical goals: (1) investigations of cultural and ideological meanings of speaking, especially if the boundedness of forms is investigated along with theirlinks to social persons, relations, structures, and functions; (2) comparison of native categories about speaking within cases; (3) comparison of native categories across cases; and more generally (4) development of a theory of communication that highlights form-meaning covariation in its sociocultural context.

Of particular importance to this developing program of research is greater attention to more informal speech events that are identified and enacted, especially those used in the contemporary American scene (Sherzer, 1977). As a way of contributing to this general program, I present an analysis of American cultural categories that identify some informal speech events. The symbolic system of American cultural categories is developed from the verbal resources that are used on "Donahue" to organize a common sense of speaking. The system of symbols, symbolic forms and meanings that are of immediate concern consists of the cultural terms, being honest, sharing, and communication.

What enactments of communication do these cultural categories identify? What do these categories mean to participants? What forms do they take? What social and cultural outcomes are achieved by these identifications and enactments?

7

DONAHUE AS NATIONAL SELF-HELP: PROBLEMS AND "BEING HONEST"

The general purpose in this chapter is to present an interpretation of being honest as a cultural category about speaking. Before moving to that category however, it will prove useful to describe a very general cultural sequence—of problem–response—that serves to motivate persons to talk. The chapter will begin with a description of this sequence, then move to the cultural category of being honest. My general purpose is to demonstrate how cultural sequences of speech motivate, and give a more general form to, cultural categories of speaking (Burke, 1968).

The Problem–Response Cycle

An age usually characterizes itself effectively by the manner in which it poses basic problems and by the means which it employs in seeking solutions to them.

(McKeon, 1956, p. 89)

The sense that the present world is in increasing crisis, that the wars and weapons, the waste and pollution, the reforms and revolutions, the exhaustion of resources and the economic crises of contemporary life are signs that today's world is very different from the past, has led to a sense that the ideals and perceptions, the interpretations and explanations of reality, upon which Americans seem always to have depended no longer apply. Yesterday's easy solutions do not solve today's complex, sophisticated, relativistic, insoluble problems: so many of us believe.

(Robertson, 1980, p. 7)

Here's the problem . . . we really are terribly disorganized in every sense in this country. We've got a fragmented country. . . . The problem with you is that when you are not together we hurt more because of the potential damage of not sharing.   (Phil Donahue, 1983)

Those who participate on "Donahue" speak about, listen to, and therefore experience, problems. This discursive fact provides a prominent force which motivates responses. The general performance of talk therefore follows the sequence of problem–response. Through it, interlocutors speak about, listen to, and listen for problems, a listening which invites some verbalized response. Note how the sequence described here does not end with a comment which solves the problems; the sequence is *not* problem–solution, it is problem–response. Normally any response, especially when presented as the solution to a problem, engenders some problematical element to one's interlocutors. Responses to problems, then, entail a problematicity of their own which turns the sequence back on itself, as a pattern of spoken acts offered in response to the problematical feature in others' responses.

Take, for example, the following statements of problems which Donahue has made to open his show:

1. Meet Harry Stein [who writes] a piece almost every month on ethics. And what he discovered, as a result of this, is that maybe we're losing it, friends, here in this country.
2. It is a fact that we seem to be terrified of death in this culture at this time . . .
3. We spend so much time talking about doctors . . . Pressure, all of that, too many patients perhaps, and also availability of drugs to the professional community creates—I think you can all agree—perhaps a bigger temptation to alter moods chemically than might be the case for someone working in a warehouse or factory.
4. Being a man . . . is not easy.

Similarly, during a discussion devoted to "housewivery as a job," a woman inventor described some ways to make the job easier. Her solution took the form of a self-cleaning house which she had designed and built, and she had brought along a scale model for display. The special features of the house included cupboards that washed dishes, drawers that cleaned silverware, closets that cleaned clothes, and windows that were cleaned at a push of a button. After describing her house, the first comment made by another guest was: "The thing wrong with your house is . . ." Similarly, after a barber shop quartet was introduced and merrily sang a happy song, Donahue asked about their travels and the resulting strains upon their marriages. One hears prefatory comments like, "The problem with that is . . ." "That wouldn't work for me because . . ." It is almost as if a rule were being followed within these episodes: The person should notice flaws and criticize. The rule functions prominently to initiate talk about *problems,* and keeps the talk going by eliciting various *responses* to them. (One cannot help but wonder how long the conversation could be sustained if "what's right here?" were the guiding question, rather than "what's wrong?")

As demonstrated in some of the above examples, symbols of society such as "this country" and "this culture," and social roles such as "doctor" and "a man," are sometimes used to identify the locus of problems. As society and roles provide rigid social templates for behavior, the person is said and felt to be constrained (rather than acting from internal dictates), dissatisfied with such influences (since society is felt to oppress individuals), and interactively inflexible (involved in closed, nonsupportive, and rigid communicative styles). Since all persons, as members of this society, are symbolized as experiencing these features, resulting problems are said to be widely spread. In other words, problems are prominently discussed as caused by, or indicative of, society. Thus, problems are discussed as widely distributed across many individuals' lives. For example, problems of women being too accommodating, men being too aggressive, children being too governed, selves being too dependent, relationships being without love, society being "sick," communication breaking down, all involve individuals in problems whose intelligibility is common to all, and corrective responses to which could benefit their common humanity.

Given society and roles as prominent loci of problems, what grounds communal responses? The general social climate deemed proper is one of respect, where the rights of the individual to display and choose a variety of responses is created and maintained. Respect involves the creation of a discursive environment which is righteously tolerant, nonjudgmental, and acceptant in tone (see chap. 2). By speaking this way, a maximum number of responses may be said and heard, since it is right to tolerate a wide range of responses. The climate of respect evokes a maximum number of responses from which an individual may choose; and in so choosing, the independence and awareness of the cultural person is reaffirmed. This general climate for responding is often the irreducible cultural ground upon which the most intensely fought issues are reconciled. The sheer variety of responses serves to guarantee individuality of action. Persons differ in their responses, and the various responses must be respected.[1]

The problem–response sequence provides a form wherein persons communicate and talk. This general pattern was not only enacted on "Donahue," but also attributed to self-help groups. Several of these groups were discussed and displayed on "Donahue": Alcoholics Anon-

---

[1] The description here is a shorthand version of "Donahue" as a ritualized enactment of social drama (Carbaugh, 1984b, pp. 364–394).

ymous, Nurses who Abuse Drugs, Toughlove, Single Mothers by Choice, various community action groups, female and male liberation groups, anger clinics. These cultural scenes were described as places where individuals "sit down and talk," "talk about issues," "talk to each other about problems," "talk out problems," "talk about issues," "talk a lot about everything," and "discuss everything."

The self-help scene is distinctive in part because of the communication or talk that gets done there. The speech of these groups was described as involving individuals in sharing common problems and openly discussing their responses to them.[2] In these groups, open, candid, and serious talk was used to respond to the unique problems of individuals that were shared by others in the group.

This general kind of talk is open and follows a cultural imperative: issues and problems should be discussed and negotiated. The self-help scene is described on "Donahue" as it emphasizes a dimension of openness about one's problems and openness to the problems of others. The performance of this most general task is facilitated since all those who participate in the speech of such groups are assumed to experience various features of the same general problem. In other words, the groups expect unique opinions to revolve around a general problem which they all can share. Resulting is a validation of a personal and a communal experience.

This talk about self-help groups is isomorphic in symbol, meaning, and form, to some speech that occurs on "Donahue." In fact, as mentioned earlier, Donahue proudly states this in his autobiography:

> The fact remains that our show survives on issues. We discuss more issues, more often, more thoroughly than any other show in the business. We also involve the audience in our act more than any other show on the air, period. Without the audience, there's no "Donahue" show. (Donahue and Company, 1981, p. 236)

In the communication of the show, Donahue, audience members, guests, and callers share their thoughts in a collective effort to combat some widely distributed problem. Audience members are especially encouraged to stand up and speak what is on their minds. Donahue approaches them inquisitively: "You are here to say what?" As persons speak about the pressing issue of the day, they not only model a type of communication that is open and honest, but also display support for

---

[2] The phrase "self-help group" is an interesting locution that validates "self" uniqueness, and "group" commonness, simultaneously. The most common medium which brings together the unique and the common, and the most important cooperative act in which the individual-group engage, was said to be one of "talk" and "communication."

others who share. These cultural categories, of being honest, sharing, and communication give forms and meanings to speaking. More specifically, they are used by persons to render speaking intelligible, to give form to the cultural performance, especially as problems are raised and responded to. The purpose aligned with this speech is help for self and group.

"Being Honest": A Cultural Category about Speaking

During a discussion about the problems of drug abuse, a nurse faced the millions in the "Donahue" audience and told of her "addiction with narcotics" that lasted for about 2 years. She described in detail her use of Demerol in injectable form while on the job, and further revealed that she took the drugs for "curiosity more than anything." She went on to explain how her drug abuse also involved alcohol and impaired her "ability to function as a professional person," all symptoms of her self-attributed "addictive personality." After hearing her story, the audience was confronted with another. The second nurse discussed similarly how she received intermuscular injections of Demerol while on the job, how she took patients' drugs and gave them water or saline in exchange, how she felt "very good" and "high" on the drugs, how "she spent at least 6 of [her] 8 hours trying to figure out how [she] could get more," and how these acts "did jeopardize significantly the well-being of the people" in her care. Her motive for the drug abuse was, like the first nurse's, *not* related to stress on the job, but stemmed from a curiosity about how it would feel to be "high."

As persons in the audience heard these personal stories, they grew increasingly restless. Finally, unable to exercise restraint any longer, one participant exclaimed: "These nurses are supposed to be the best nurses available and for them to say curiosity doesn't sound intelligent at all. I mean you could kill somebody." (Applause) Another audience member explained: "I am very angry because I think I was in a situation where I did not get my Demerol. It was after surgery . . . I was crying for 4 hours." A fellow nurse added: "The conscience of doing this to a patient just appalls me. They have their rights!" (Applause) After hearing several accusatory and cathartic exclamations from the audience, the host stepped in and commented about his guests' conduct by saying, "Give them four stars for the honesty of stepping forward and saying they have a problem."

What has just occurred in this discourse? What features of it have been labeled honest by the host? What does this native labeling tell us about this act and event of speaking? And, what does this way of speaking accomplish socially and culturally for those who enact it?[3]

"Being Honest" As An Assertion of Truth

Searle (1976) has suggested a set of dimensions that differentiate five basic types of illocutionary acts. We can use Searle's dimensions initially to classify the force of the nurses' speeches that were labeled honest. This type of speech can be called a truthful assertive (or "representative" in Searle's taxonomy, pp. 10–11). This classification suggests three basic aspects to their speech labeled honest: (1) the basic purpose of such acts is to commit the speaker "to something's being the case" (Searle, 1976, p. 10), in this case that drug abuse occurs among nurses, (2) the acts fit "words to the world" in a way that describes the true state of affairs (cf. Grice's quality maxim, 1975, p. 46), and (3) the acts express a psychological state of belief. Of course, utterances deemed honest will vary in the degree of commitment, truth, and belief expressed, but these qualities nonetheless help characterize being honest initially as an assertive, as a public commitment to a truth that the speaker believes.

During one program about teen-agers and the problem of stereotypes, Donahue asked several young boys if they "would like to lead the lives that their fathers led." The first three responded:

Boy 1:   No, because my father would lead me every step of the way. Then he would tell me what he did and then I would have to do what he did . . .

Boy 2:   No, I wouldn't. I think he worked too hard. He came from Ireland and I think he worked too hard. It would be too hard for me.

Donahue: (prodding the third boy with raising intonation) Yes.

Boy 3:   No, I wouldn't want to be exactly like my father because he left my mother when I was 5.

Donahue: (somewhat surprised that none of the boys answered affirmatively) Okay, that's honest.

Audience: (Applause)

The responses of these boys to Donahue's question demonstrate a way of speaking that is identified by Donahue as honest.[4] Note that

---

[3] The following interpretations are based on 54 instances in my corpus where speech was identified as "honest."

[4] Some readers might hear Donahue's comment as referring only to the comment from Boy No. 3, especially his disclosure about his father leaving his mother. Note how the boy's statement is forceful as a public commitment about this (father leaving mother) being the case, is heard to be true and believed (by the boy). Statements from Boys No.

Donahue said, "*that's* honest," not "*he's* honest." The demonstrative pronoun, "that," is significant here because it refers explicitly not to a person, nor a quality of a person, but to a way of speaking just conducted, and that way is not without common form or meaning, but identified through a prominent cultural category as honest. Donahue's comment, therefore, frames the prior utterances; he has identified them as honest, subsuming the prior acts within the common category of speaking called honest. He is not speaking explicitly about personal qualities, but is saying a word about words; he is saying a word about the boys' prior communicative acts, organizing a sense of the discourse by calling this one part of it honest. In short, by using his word to comment on theirs, he has enacted a cultural category about speaking.

As Donahue framed their way of speaking as honest, the audience praised it through applause. Consequently, the boys' utterances were not only identified as honest, but also applauded as valued acts of speaking. As the prior acts were placed within this cultural frame, a common way of speaking was identified *and applauded*. Thus, at one level, the boys uttered responses to a question, saying something to Donahue and fellow interlocutors, and at another, their responses were talked about, saying something about their sayings as honest. The latter, as a cultural category about speaking, was used as a comment about comments; a frame for responses. Through precisely this use, a kind of metacommunication has occurred, thus creating a sense of the boys' prior acts that moved the audience to applause.[5]

Consider another comment, about "being a man," made as an assistant professor of history from Harvard University disclosed his self to an audience predominantly of women: "It's tough to wake up at 5 in the morning with a baby; it's tough to change diapers, tough

---

1 & No. 2, however, carry slightly different weight on these dimensions. Their comments commit them to something's being the case (i.e., father as overbearing, and working too hard respectively), but entail conventional judgments of quality rather than verifiable acts. But like the proposition from Boy No. 3, the earlier two are stated as true, and believed (by the boys respectively). Thus, the propositions from the boys about their fathers vary; from Boy No. 3 about a verifiable past event (leaving his mother), from Boy No. 2 about a quality of work (working too hard), and from Boy No. 3 about an alleged style of parenting (overbearing), but all are assertives in that they publicly commit speakers to a truth that the speaker believes. This interpretation works, however, only if one takes general implicatures (i.e., father is overbearing, father worked too hard), as well as verifiable events (i.e., father left mother) as the assessable propositions (see Sanders, 1987, especially pp. 43–77).

[5] That "honesty" is uttered after these acts and the ones above suggests its role as a justification for potentially discreditable conduct, for example, criticizing one's father, taking illegal drugs. Both examples display its use to legitimately say generally unsayable things, priveleging access to information over face-work. See below.

to clean up the house." The audience applauded heartily, then Donahue said: "He's being honest." Donahue and the audience then praised the professor for "this kind of honesty," and for being "candid" about his "marital problems." Later, the professor spoke for himself, about men and their speaking:

> Many of us are ready to change, are ready to have two careers: The wife has one and we have one. But still some place we're still traditional. We still want those kinds of things. [e.g., "the coffee ready when you get up"] I think it's important to be honest about that, to talk about it and not to try to hide it and not to try to resist it either.

As the professor discussed what were referred to as his "marital problems," and his "tough" situation, he implies that he is being honest, and he was praised by others for being honest. Again, like the boys' utterances above, his way of speaking was identified and praised as honest. But more than that, and to the apparent approval of all of those present, he implores his audience to be honest, especially in those situations where one's thoughts (e.g., traditional expectations) run counter to one's present actions (e.g., attempts at liberation). Through his comments, he helps interlocutors hear how being honest is a preferred way of publicly aligning one's words to the (one's) world.[6]

Before further interpreting being honest, let me summarize: (1) terms such as "honesty," "that's honest," and "being honest" are native terms that identify a way of speaking; (2) that way of speaking includes acts and events that are praised and promoted in public discourse; and (3) labeling speech this way co-orients interlocutors to an aspect of speech deemed truthful, a verbal performance where words were allegedly aligned with thoughts, feelings, and/or actions.

Motives and Meanings of "Being Honest"

What motivates enactments deemed honest? What are the common meanings of discourse enacted this way? What gets accomplished socially through this way of speaking?

A powerful exigence for being honest occurs in situations where important information has not been forthcoming, and participants commonly sense a dispreferred aura of uncertainty, ambiguity, or stra-

---

[6] The moral enacted here is a most powerful one that has been used to criticize the president and his staff (Bohmer, 1986; Shanahan, 1986), to align community actions (Davis, 1982), and is at the heart of any performance of the timeless American myth, "George Washington and the Cherry Tree."

tegic manipulation. In these situations, being honest is warranted and preferred so that a higher quality of information can be made available, that is, a more accurate and truthful alignment of words to the world is to be preferred. As participants witness puzzling and problematical issues, such as nurses who abuse drugs, troubling sex roles in American society, or the "double-speak" of politicians, there arise moments that warrant "candid" talk which is "open," talk that was defined by interlocutors as "not hiding," "telling what you're doing," "being available," "not resisting," "really talking," "really meaning." By identifying and calling for this kind of discourse, participants help remedy the alleged deficiencies of "silence" or "poor information," and when they do so appropriately, are praised for their acts. Thus, a felt degree of closedness, ambiguity or deceitfulness, creates an exigence where one should reveal the truth, "be open and honest," and if deemed appropriate, like the nurses, professor, or boys, receive praise.[7]

One recent problematical situation involving an economics professor and the President of the United States was apparently corrected through an honest act (Bohmer, 1986). To some Americans, like the professor, some foreign policy activities had seemed manipulatively covert, and even subversive. In fact, the professor wrote about President Reagan's policies on Latin America as a kind of "terrorism." The professor claimed that the President, after hearing so many of these accusations, admitted to so acting. The professor told it this way:

> We don't read that the United States is at war against Nicaragua and El Salvador, but it is. In Nicaragua, we hear there are two contending forces: the Sandinistas, backed by Cuba and the Soviet Union, and the Contras, backed by the United States. But the reality is that U. S. military advisers and the CIA determine strategy, recruit and organize the Contras, pick their leaders, package them, and select targets for attack. For once, Reagan was honest when he said, "I am a Contra": He is their commander-in-chief. (Bohmer, 1986)

Through the alleged statement, "I am a Contra" the President is portrayed as aligning his speech with his other actions—much as the young George Washington when he said, "Father, I did it"; he has corrected a sensed deficiency in available public information, thus

---

[7] Speech that might be labeled "honest" is of course not always valued or appropriate as is the case for example in "white lies." However, if improper "honesty" occurs, the speaker might attempt to justify the improper act as an "honest" one. This is what occurred among some of my friends after former President Carter disclosed his "lust" in a *Playboy* interview. This type of justification suggests that one suspend evaluations about the value or appropriateness of the information disclosed, and value the ("honest") act of speaking it.

making the truth of the matter explicit. By describing the President's speech this way, the professor has highlighted a movement from a problematical state where the President is not "coming clear with the facts," to a better public state where he is being honest.

Through these few examples is demonstrated a particular kind of enactment that responds to social exigencies. Topics come up; information is sensed to be somehow lacking; a person responds by disclosing truthful information; the disclosures may be labeled honest and if the act, as honest, is not challenged, assumes a degree of accuracy and appropriateness as well as suggests a common value in what was disclosed (making needed information available); such labeling may prompt praise for the speakers since they helped remedy the situation by addressing the truth of things, thereby correcting the motivating deficiencies.

When being honest is performed appropriately, it is intelligible generally as a kind of speech that is *open,* where the persons have revealed their own thoughts, actions, and/or objects. More specifically, and as a refinement in our sense of openness, being honest enacts a *truthfulness* that brings one's words into alignment with one's thoughts, feelings, and actions, or with the world of objects. It also involves a sense of being *direct,* of "telling it like it is," of "laying it on the line," through a mode of discourse that is "frank," "straight," and "to the point." Together, these dimensions forground the *referential* or representational function of honest discourse, where speech is connected to and is heard to map accurately the reality of thoughts, feelings, actions, and objects. In each case above, as when the nurses described their drug abuse, when the boys expressed an unwillingness to be like their fathers, when the professor discussed his role and marital problems, and when the President allegedly admitted that he was "a Contra," and in all instances of my field materials, being honest was rendered commonly intelligible as a relatively open, truthful and direct way of speaking. By speaking this way, and identifying speaking this way, participants created a way of speaking that was praised and promoted, and through which the reality of thoughts, feelings, actions, and things is expressed.[8]

Saying Improper Things Properly: Social Functions of "Being Honest"

Since honest (open, truthful, and direct) speaking is identified, praised, and promoted, it is sometimes used as the proper way of saying the

---

[8] The semantic dimensions posited here help not only to refine the senses of "being honest," but also to suggest, by way of contrast, other metacommunicative forms, other cultural symbols about symbolic acts and events, that are more closed, deceitful, and indirect, such as "lying" and "empty words."

wrong things. By speaking this way, a speaker can reveal information that may seem untoward and thus bring discredit to one's self, community, or country, yet do so in a way that is redeemable socially. Take, for example, the boys' responses that they would not prefer to be like their fathers. In their responses are disclosures about their fathers, such as being overbearing, working too hard, and abandoning a wife that are potentially face-threatening to their fathers, as well as to the boys, since such disclosures may constitute acts of impoliteness, lack in appreciativeness, or some other improper conduct. But at this point the boys are not negatively sanctioned for the content of their disclosures, but praised with a public ovation that co-orients all interlocutors to their honest way of stating the truth. Likewise, as the nurses spoke about being "high" for the sake of curiosity, their disclosures violated common standards of responsibility but were said to be honest, thus highlighting the form of the acts, somewhat mitigating the discredit in their assertions because they were stated in the proper form. Disclosures of discreditable information as these are sometimes mitigated socially by orienting interlocutors to the honest form of expression.[9]

Organizing public enactments this way often involves larger "streams of discourse" than individual acts, especially where the human matters are convoluted and variously experienced. To unravel such circumstances one must go beyond being honest as a label for a communicative act, to its use as a label for a broader form, a communicative *event* with some albeit unintentional consequences. While the form is loosely bounded and easily interruptable with other embedded sequences, it is identifiable by natives as an event where social actors are being honest. The general form can span only a few moments, as with the boys above, or much longer, as when the nurses disclosed repeatedly and at length the extent of their drug-abuse problems. The sequence can be conceived as unfolding in four general phases: (1) Initiation: An exigence is created in the communication situation such that uncertainty, ambiguity, a sense of manipulation, or a low quality of information is sensed. Full discussion of issues is therefore deemed problematical, for example, the undisclosed problem of nurses abusing drugs, President Reagan's being quiet about political policies in Latin America, or men being generally inexpressive about parenting. (2) Assertions: Participants speak openly, truthfully, and directly about the topics, often involving some degree of socially discreditable behavior or information, for example, President Reagan admits that he is a Contra, the professor admits difficulty in parenting and house cleaning. The discreditable information may be softened through disclaimers such as

---

[9] Framing acts this way may also suggest that new information is the focus of interactional concerns more so than "face." See below.

"well, to be honest . . ." "I honestly think . . ."; or elicitations "Be frank about this . . ." or "Shoot straight with us . . ." (3) Reactions: The information and persons are discussed regarding their openness, truthfulness, and direct bearing on the topics. At this point, previous utterances may be identified and justified as appropriate honest sayings, prompting praise, or, as in some rare cases, the sequence is short-circuited. [This happened once when statements were evaluated as not being honest because they allegedly violated the semantics of open, truthful disclosures, thus transforming the event implicitly into lying and/or sharing.] (4) Praise: Praise, thanks, and/or respect are given for speaking honestly. Through these loosely bounded phases, being honest is conducted as a communicative event. As such, it is identified by participants as something more than an act, as an event with cultural communicative integrity.

There is a consequent to this communicative event that may be troubling to some participants, for one may be put in the position of treating as legitimate, an "illegitimate" person who has access to rare information and/or is being honest about self. In these occasions of honest speech, a moral obligation to listen respectfully is evoked as another speaks honestly, as when the audience was obliged to listen to wife abusers, male prostitutes, three persons married to each other. Resulting is a context in which improper and discreditable acts should be somewhat overlooked in favor of this valued performance of public communication. Take, for example, the nurses, the boys, the President or professor above, or child molesters, or former President Richard Nixon during his famous "Checkers Speech" (Sennett, 1978, pp. 279–281), all of whom have had their discreditable acts somewhat mitigated because they were heard to be honest. (Perhaps the most extreme example occurred when an unrepentant murderer of a Stanford professor disclosed coldly, openly, and directly the details of his heinous act.) Where being honest exudes a great normative force, an interlocutor may speak properly about his wrongdoings, make rare information available to others, and *to a degree* atone indirectly (since interacting openly) for the untoward acts. When the speaker is fully successful (unlike the murderer?), she may re-enter the scene as a legitimate actor. This way of speaking sometimes takes the tone of a cathartic confession, somewhat purging the focal actor of previous wrongdoings, with the public as the collective witness and willing recipient of those who so properly atone. As a valued form of speech in which the saying of improper things is acceptable, being honest can be easily abused if uncritically used to legitimate the illegitimate actor. This of course is less operative in extremely serious breaches (such as murder), but is operative nonetheless. How else does one account for a full hour disclosure to millions about child molestation, incest, (or murder) if not partly through an honest cultural warrant, where access to rare and/or new information and those willing to disclose it are valued? This can be a troubling consequent where some speaking and speakers are identified as honest and somewhat accepted since they have disclosed improper things in the proper social way. Further, the marginal person's face can be enhanced, if ever so indirectly and slightly, by exploiting the freedom to speak, and making valued information public in a proper honest way.

An Ambiguous Message about Relationships

In the "Donahue" scene, any person may of course be honest, give, threaten, and save one's face, as long as he or she is serious about the topic and willing to risk new disclosures about it. Yet, as a kind of speaking available equally to any member of the community, it carries in itself an unspecified relational message; speaking honestly may risk distance, as between the nurses and the audience, or engender closeness, as between the boys and their interlocutors. In other words, enactments that are *justified* as honest may communicate a range of relational messages anywhere from endearment to repulsion (Scott & Lyman, 1968). *Disclaimers* of honesty function similarly (Hewitt & Stokes, 1975), opening one to the relational unknown from submission to dominance, intimacy to distance, and so forth. But risks of distance seem to dominate as in *Tootsie* when Dustin Hoffman's character said to Teri Garr's: "I've got to shoot straight with you. I'm in love with another woman."

The relational messages in being honest are influenced by variable factors of message content, beyond the form and its meanings. So, unlike the closeness enacted in communication (Katriel & Philipsen, 1981), where the relational message is embedded in the cultural form, discourse identified as honest creates no predictable message about the quality of the relationship between interlocutors. It is this uncertain relational message that makes disclaimers such as "I've got to be honest with you . . ." sometimes unnerving, for one can not anticipate the affective valence of the message, whither anger or lust.

"Being Honest": A Personal and Informational Civility

Through such legitimations, justifications and disclaimers, being honest says something to Americans about a way of managing communication, a way of conducting the person in social conduct, especially when we explore the role of the person and the forces of society that are animated through the saying. What is constituted through enactments of this symbol, symbolic form, and its meanings? I will call the general accomplishment a kind of personal and informational civility, of which there are at least three interrelated constituent parts. First, when identified as fully honest, speaking has ignited a communal dialectic between the valued form for revealing real information and the sometimes devalued content of the disclosure. The tension animates the norm: When one has verbal resources that will inform one's interlocutors, decrease unwanted uncertainty and ambiguity, or help uncover deadly manipulations, even if they reflect discreditably on self or others, one should disclose them honestly. These are times when one should face the hard facts of the matter, stand up and honestly say the things that need to be said, but with which others may disagree, or dislike, thus risk bringing discredit to self. This is necessary sometimes regardless of the implications to self, for truth, and the reality of persons and things, is a most valued and sacred resource, and, the speaking of it, an individual's responsibility. If the individual does not bear this burden, the whole community may continue to suffer. Thus, the risks to self in "being honest" (the potential discredit the disclosure may bring) are potentially mitigated by the social value in being honest (the form in which important information is made available to one's interlocutors). The dialectic is necessary for a fully effective public enactment of honesty.[10]

Where openness is valued, uniqueness among persons assumed, and problems the topics of discussion, the dialectic places very much within the realm of public discourse. Persons feel the need to hear (or say) what others have to say (or hear) about problems because the expressive self is the preferred social value, with the sharing of unique and useful information, one's prime social right and responsibility.

The other way to frame the dialectic is—rather than from the standpoint of a potential threat to speaker's face—from the standpoint of information, where access to "hard to get" information is the main interactional concern, over the face of the speaker. The more unusual the information one holds, the more valuable one becomes as a source. For this reason, highly unusual persons—such as born-again, male go-go dancers; women who have given birth underwater; mothers who have left their families; sperm bank donors; male prostitutes—become valuable contributors. But their social value is based not solely on

---

[10] The dialectic helps explain why statements of self-praise, or self-serving truths, lack full force as "being honest" because they activate primarily one pole without the other.

concerns of face—that is to be unimpeded or approved of (Brown & Levinson, 1978)—as it is upon the status of their information as true and unusual. New information is valued and the locus of interactional concern, more than is the person speaking it. As the "unrepentant murderer" example suggests, some information may be rare and thus of value—getting the story directly or "right from the horse's mouth"— with the face of the source being of little if any value. In extreme cases, the person becomes a faceless conduit (Reddy, 1979). Getting the facts of the story becomes more important than attending to face concerns. This informational need can overshadow a low degree of positive face if the person is a holder of unusual and discreditable information. In this specific sense, the interaction attends more directly to informational needs, less directly to face concerns. By this subverting of face concerns, unusual and illegitimate persons can indirectly gain a (sometimes marginal) degree of legitimacy, since they are the sources of the valued rare information.

A second and more direct sign of civility involves "being honest" as a redress or corrective act, where the person can bring "unsayables" back *within* the constraints of the communal conversation. When one has wronged another or others, one should atone by being honest. As mentioned above, as in the nurses' disclosures that they used drugs on the job and hurt others, an honest act by an individual can—directly or indirectly—mitigate previous wrongdoings, thus purging one of (at least some of) the guilt associated with the discreditable act(s).

Third, being honest can strip the social scene of its normal etiquette and demeanor, and create a situation where the individual or self is asserted freely. There are times when social standards of politeness, routine expectations, role constraints, and so forth, are felt to be too cumbersome and restraining. One has to somehow overstep these in an effort to get down to the grit of things. One can cast these aside, at an impulse, suspending the normal social scheme of things, by being honest. Acting this way, as when an atheist disclosed that he was gay as well, lays self on the line, and provides for its assertion over the more routine constraints of social life. Thus, as honest, one is no longer obligated to uphold the more routine standards of daily conduct, but may cast them aside, and say discreditable or difficult things in a proper way.

These three sociocultural accomplishments, of sociopersonal responsibility, redress, and personal assertiveness, are acted out as honest, expressed as being honest, and create a scene of personal and informational civility. Together, they constitute in this scene, prominent strategies for *presenting and managing the person*. As the individual asserts truths, he or she can be praised, and/or may stand over and above the more routine standards for social living, present oneself openly, and if he or she was previously infelicitous, can atone. Through these activities, the individual can live in society responsibly, correct wrongdoings, and assert a personal being. The dialectic embraced with the symbol, and shown in enactments of it, mediates between this valued form for meeting informational needs and the potential discredits the disclosed content may bring to a speaker. By providing a means for accessing rare information, and by providing a degree of interactional legitimacy to some unusual or perhaps discreditable persons, the cultural communication code of being honest functions to increase the range of stateable truths and enlarge the scope of expressiveness for the person.[11] "Being honest" then comments upon the communal conversation as it provides a common and proper way in which "the individual" can assert the sometimes hard-to-get truth; it constitutes cultural speech that is heard to be open, truthful, and direct, says something about the importance of getting the story right, about stating responsibility what one believes, about doing so individually especially if one has wronged others, and about experiencing unwanted constraints of the routine society and being able to cast those aside. At a cultural level, these are some of the accomplishments that are identified, praised, and promoted as being honest, and which ground the collective enactment of a personal and informational civility.

---

[11] Compare Hart et al. (1980) discussion of the noble self, Bellah et al. (1985) discussion of expressive discourse, and Yankelovich's (1981) strong-formers.

8

"SHARING": EXPRESSING SUPPORT AND UNITY OF PURPOSE

One of the problems discussed on "Donahue" is death and how the person copes with it. One program on this general theme featured children from 12 to 16 years old whose parents had died. Donahue introduced the show by stating the problem: "It's a fact that we seem to be terrified of death in this culture. . . . One of the probably least examined features of a death in the family is the way that it affects children. What better way to find out how it affects children than to ask them." The children told the audience how a parent had died, how they found out about the death, how they reacted, how others around them reacted, whether or not they went to the funeral. The discussion began with a 12-year-old girl describing her reactions to the death of her mother (and sister) in an automobile accident. Next, a second child described how her father, a fireman, died of a heart attack while on duty. She told the audience that upon hearing the news, she "left the (living) room and went upstairs." Donahue interjected: "You ran up to your room. I see that a lot in the accounts that I've read of *very open young people who have shared with us* this very painful experience." Later, after a boy described his father's death in a plane crash, and a girl described her reactions to her father's death from cancer, Donahue said: "You're here *sharing with us* your own personal experience and that makes us smarter, not only about dealing with the pain we might sustain ourselves, but also about what we can do to help people in a situation like this."

About halfway through the show a woman author was introduced who wrote about these young people. She described the process of writing her book about children of parents who have died: "It turned out that it was sad but it wasn't depressing because the children were so anxious to talk to anybody who would listen to them. They wanted *to share* their feelings." She summarized her purpose in writing the book by saying, "other children could read the book and know they had 19 friends [the number of cases described in the book] who *shared* some of these same feelings."

The discussion about death is punctuated throughout with references to itself. Persons described the speaking as sharing. What is this kind of speaking? What are the meanings of these enactments, so labeled? What does this category of speaking accomplish for persons?

In this chapter, I will describe sharing as a cultural category about speaking, its force as an act, its meanings, uses, and form. My general purposes are to demonstrate sharing as a cultural category about, and cultural enactment of, speaking; how it is distinct from, but intimately related to being honest; and how both operate within a limited semantic system.[1]

"Sharing" As an Expressive Act of Support

"Sharing" identifies a kind of communication enactment about problems, and various responses to them. As the children disclosed their experiences surrounding the death of a parent, they expressed their feelings, and their often problematical experiences with others, making these available to others on the premise that the disclosed information could be of potential value to all of those listening. As persons listened to them, and framed their speech as sharing, they were identifying (1) a person who was making resources of self available to others, (2) speaking as an act of expressiveness, generally expressing feelings and experiences, and (3) support of one another by orienting to common purposes. These are the three general aspects of speaking that are labeled sharing.[2]

By making resources of self available to others in a tone that could support and benefit them, sharing is both enacted and identified. Consider the children above. By identifying their acts as sharing, Donahue acknowledged that their speech revealed valuable information that supported interlocutors' common purposes, "that makes us smarter." Sharing then is partly a speech act with an expressive illocutionary force (Searle, 1976, pp. 12–13), making something that is one's own, for example, one's "psychological state," available to others. More than that it entails a cultural force of support of current relations through common purposes. When used to describe a type of speech, sharing

---

[1] The following interpretations are based on 82 instances where "sharing" was used to identify a kind of speaking. Excluded from the analysis are related uses of "share" or "sharing" that are not directly about speaking, for example, Federal Revenue Sharing, "share the responsibilities," "share the benefit of excellent genes," "share expenses."

[2] All three aspects are not always relevant as we will see below.

acknowledges explicitly a potential contribution to a present relationship. Thus, sharing is not only an expression of one's inner experiences and feelings, but is also speech with a relational embrace, speaking that nurtures shared social purposes.[3]

Spoken terms that were associated with utterances of sharing were "support," "together," "loving," "caring," "affection," and "company" (in the sense of being together). Those terms opposed to sharing were "inexpressive," "divide and conquer," "divide and protect." A semantic domain is ignited with this term. It creates a sense of social cohesion which is opposed to a sense of disaffected division. As a cultural category, sharing identifies a type of "close talk" and "supportive communication" where *unity of purpose* is presumed.

The type of information shared may be personal or private, for example, one's "feelings," one's "genuine feelings," "problems," "nightmares," information about "serious relationships," "family." This type of personal information may be unflattering to the speaker—as when a guest on "Donahue" described a stage in her bout with anorexia/bulimia where she ate scraps out of her dog's bowl—but unlike "honest" disclosures the information is assumed to be of some common value to interlocutors. Sometimes the value of the information to one's interlocutors involves an assumption about the operative codes and rules in a relationship. For example, one may share one's problems with another, which assumes a valued relationship between or among interlocutors. In this sense, a speaker assumes a valued relationship between interlocutors where sharing is valued. To share in a relationship is to reinforce what is assumed to be a common value, a supportive bond. Conversely, if one does not feel close or supportive of another, then their initiation of sharing may be sensed as inappropriate or presumptuous, especially if the shared information is of questionable common value.[4]

One may also share more impersonal or public information which is important to a speaker and used to teach, inform, or meet the needs of interlocutors. Speech where impersonal information was shared on "Donahue" consisted of politicians, representatives of various self-help groups, authors of books, and members of other special groups who

---

[3] Note how "sharing" is also a possessive act in that it identifies information as a "contained thing" that one will "share" with others. See Michaels (1981) who discusses a similar event in an elementary classroom.

[4] A friend described how a colleague of his, whom he was not particularly fond of, came up to him and said, "I'd like to share something with you, I just got an article published . . ." My friend asked rhetorically about the act, "Is that sharing?" To my friend, without an assumed bond of mutual support, the act was heard less as an offer of helpful information from one to another, and more as a boast from one to another.

revealed some information that was generally unavailable to, and heard to have a common value for, the "Donahue" audience.

A Duty of "Self" to "Relationship"

By identifying speech as sharing, then, one notices an offering of some important resources to others—resources not available to others since they are contained within the speaker's self. Making verbal offerings to others displays information which is considered a distinctive part of self, is assumed to hold some common value for others, and at the same time, affirms one's support and participation in a present relationship. While others may hold information similar to one's self, no one can access it as can self. Thus, it is a duty of self to relationship to share what one has to offer. In sharing, one participates in and reaffirms the common importance of a present relationship. If one chooses not to share, one has chosen not to cooperate in a common way of creating and valuing relationship. The witholding of one's personal resources is devalued since an inexpressive self saps the common verbal good of invaluable and common commodities—the unique resources of self and its cooperative participation in a relationship. To assume that one has the same thing to say as another, or to say the same thing as another, is to violate both the communal definition of self as unique, and the valued duties of self to share in a relationship. As a popular American poster states, "Sharing just comes naturally to those who really care." Sharing, then, as a social act of speech, involves interlocutors in the offering of information that is important and unique to self (sometimes a nod or smile may suffice), in a way which supports a common purpose among those who "really care."

Two utterances which were applauded as sharing demonstrate the link between common purpose and relational bonding. A male audience member was discussing a faculty group to which he belonged. He described it by claiming

> that men have to share. I'm a faculty member in Oakland College in Des Plains and we've started a men's program that includes a fathering course, includes a men's support group where men can come and share and get support from one another. It includes some seminars by experts in the field for men and I think that's the answer. I think women have been doing that . . .

The man describes a support group where men share and get support. Given the above analyses one could infer that the speech of such a group, made coherent with the term share, would involve disclosures of information which reveal a common purpose and are of shared value to the men who gather there. The men gain support from one another through sharing; they speak in a cooperative way about their common problems; and as they share, they unite in a supportive response to them. The man, however, is not only speaking about the sharing of his group, he is also sharing as he speaks. He is disclosing information to others of "Donahue" in a content and style that in this case displays a common purpose of support. A type of bond is established with his interlocutors through his sharing. The men in his support group and the people in the "Donahue" audience rally in support of his efforts, and in praise of a common verbal style where interlocutors talk about, and display, a way to share their problems and support those present.

Second, a woman sociologist on "Donahue" described in detail how she "blamed [her] father for not working and ruining [their] family." Donahue responded to her saying: "Thanks for sharing that with us, that's very honest." On the one hand, the woman's speech was defined as sharing, as involving an offering in which a common purpose, that is, being aware and expressing feelings of resentment, could and should be supported. As sharing, the verbal offering was identified as having some value to her interlocutors, as acknowledging the problems of feelings that well up inside, especially during unemployment and its difficult consequences. Also, the woman was described as being honest. It was acknowledged that her disclosure constituted potentially discreditable behavior; it could be heard as an ungrateful criticism and anger toward her father. By defining her comment as honest, it could be praised as a direct effort to provide the audience with truthful and accurate, even if discreditable, information. By defining her speech as both sharing and honest, two aspects of her verbal performance were praised, that is, expressing feelings toward some common goal, and making accurate information available, in this case about feelings and unemployment.

Sharing may be defined as that type of speech which is open and supportive (an integrative bonding). Like honest speech, it is open, since speakers disclose some information which may be generally inaccessible to one's interlocutors. It is supportive as persons affirm those who disclose feelings and experiences toward some common purpose. It is a kind of speech where solidarity among persons and unity of purpose is assumed or displayed. It is this discursive bonding which distinguishes utterances and acts of sharing from honest speech. To be honest is to risk social alienation through candid talk which may constitute a breach. To share is to endow a conversation with a relational embrace where distance between interlocutors is minimized as their dues in support of a relationship are paid. Socially discreditable behavior is overlooked and ignored when speech is labeled sharing. In this sense, the honest category identifies bold assertions of truth, utterances which may distance one from others. In contrast, sharing identifies a disclosure of feelings and orients to a common purpose among speaker and those present; it contributes support to their present relationship.

Where the communicative exigence for honest speech invites accurate and truthful information, the one which warrants sharing is a sensed need of social support.[5] In these moments, participants create a communication climate where many disclosures related to a problem may be said in an unthreatening atmosphere. The disclosures need not be "to the point"; however, it is important that they somehow contribute to an implicit unifying ideology at hand. During moments when social division, separation, and isolation appear, sharing is warranted.

Where the purpose of honest speech is to represent reality, to be candid and truthful, the primary purpose of sharing is expressive and affiliative. Expressions of feelings and experiences are contributed in a spirit of helpfulness. Thus, the relationship itself becomes a focus of interactional concern. The climate of such speech is infused with a feeling of togetherness, commonality, and intimacy where a primary value is a contribution to the relationship among participants. A metacommunicative claim in acts identified as sharing is one of support. The tone of such acts is caring and mutual growth.

The contrast between sharing and honest speech was demonstrated in an exchange between Donahue and an expert guest. The two were discussing how a woman's response to the question: "Would you call the police [if this (long-haired Black) man was walking in your neighborhood]?" The woman responded that she would call the police because "normally in our neighborhood nobody goes walking." Her response precipitated this exchange between Donahue's guest, a Black lawyer (BL), and Donahue (D):

BL: (derogatorily) You would call the cops because nobody walks in your neighborhood. Please spare me . . .

D: At least she is being honest. She is saying I don't feel comfortable about this.

BL: No. She's not being honest.

D: She is sharing her feelings.

BL: She is not being honest about it.

D: Tell us how she is not being honest about it.

---

[5] The discursive tacking back and forth between openness and supportiveness resonates with the "dialectic" of expressiveness and protectiveness reported by Rawlins (1983).

BL: The mere fact that somebody is out of their house in her neighborhood is not a reason she would call the cops.

Since the Black lawyer did not exude support and care for the speaker (e.g., "please spare me") he suggests an event not of sharing. Thus, Donahue attempted to identify the woman's response as honest, as a direct assertion of truth. The lawyer, however, disagreed with that labeling, implying that the woman is not telling the truth directly and must be hiding her real reason. The unspoken implication that results from the lawyer's (framing of her) remarks, is an accusation of racism: the white woman would call the cops because it is a *Black* man walking in her neighborhood—it is not somebody in general, but a very particular somebody she is talking about, a Black man. This is implicated by the lawyer's accusation that the woman was not being honest. Because the lawyer refused to label the woman's speech as honest, Donahue was forced to resort to another term, sharing. This category was not directly challenged by the lawyer. Thus, there is agreement, albeit very subtle and slightly implicit, that what the woman has done is best called sharing her feelings. She has made her personal resources publicly available, she has expressed her feelings, and this act has been identified and supported, even if it was of questionable honesty.[6] Further, the premise of "unity of purpose" presumed in most acts of sharing applies equivocally here: if her statement was a dishonest sharing, as the Black lawyer's comments suggested, a subtle message of racism has been exposed, making the issue one of Black and white; if, however, she was honestly sharing, as Donahue suggested, the message is stated less as one of color than of unfamiliarity, an unknown somebody (in general) is in the neighborhood. The latter of course reaffirms the unity of most present, that is, respect others' comments as honest and speak in "noncolored" terms. But, the exchange—since not being honest and sharing were both invoked—suggests equivocal and cross-purposes, (1) the woman's act is dishonest and racist and acknowledging this exposes powerful subtleties of racism, and (2) the woman's act is honest and careful. The former is aligned with straight and honest speech that co-

---

[6] Hearing speech this way raises some questions about the way some political statements are framed. For example, in one of President Reagan's replies about the Iran–Contra Affair, he identified his discourse, in his second sentence, as "a chance . . . to share some personal thoughts with you, to speak to you the American people from the heart" (full text reported in the *New York Times*, December 7, 1986, p. 22). This occurred at a time when the President was being questioned about his honesty. Perhaps labeling his speech this way indicated subtly, perhaps unknowingly, that his following remarks were to be heard as much if not more as expressions of his personal feelings with "friends" than as direct assertions about the truth (See below).

orients to allegedly hidden racist attitudes, while the latter is aligned
with the supportive tone of sharing and functions to unify persons
behind the social purpose, that is, be nonracist by talking in color-
blind terms.

Speech where sharing was said to occur, like that of the children
whose parents had died, the author, the sociologist, the faculty member,
the audience members, may be described as unfolding in a four-step
sequence: (1) Opening: as problems are discussed and responses made
to them, interlocutors receive or express a desire for supportive disclosures of first-hand experience regarding a topic of mutual concern,
for example, persons gather to discuss death of parents. (2) Offering:
an interlocutor, or interlocutors, offer a disclosure—of personal or
impersonal information—that is important to them, and generally inaccessible, but of some potential value, to most others, for example,
the children discuss their parent's death and their personal reactions
to it. (3) Support: persons co-orient to the disclosure(s) and acknowledge
its potential value to some common purpose by identifying the act(s)
as "sharing," for example, Donahue and guest frame speech as sharing
and discuss its positive value. Often sharing occurs in a spiraling form
where various phases of offerings and support are recycled through (See
chap. 10 below). (4) Thanks: persons thank those who have disclosed
information, acknowledge the value of the comments, their mutual
support, and/or affirm the importance of speech where they share. The
general sequence of spoken acts described here suggests a verbal form
which, when properly performed, constitutes an event of sharing. The
form is not, of course, a prescription for how to share, but a description
of a processual sequencing of speech where interlocutors cooperatively
share, where they create and display a common purpose and rally in
support of one another.

The norm of interaction surrounding the above oral form can now
be stated: if one is sharing, one should disclose information that is of
common and mutual value to others in the present relationship. Conversely, if one is approached by others who desire to share, one should
listen for what is of common value in what they say. The norm attains
a force as interlocutors value the social support implicated in sharing
information and in the relationships where such disclosures occur.

The cultural term, sharing, identifies a native genre of speech that
is open (about personal or impersonal information that one uniquely
holds), and supportive (an offering of value to others that exploits a
common purpose); it is a type of speech where interlocutors are "together," "supportive," "caring," and "loving"; it involves interlocutors
in joint offerings which reaffirm their relational bond; and it unfolds
along a spiraling sequence: opening, offering, support, and thanks. These

meanings, functions, and form of sharing provide a people with a common and supportive verbal resource which they can use in confronting their everyday tasks of living, especially the articulation of their problems and various responses to them. It provides a public verbal frame in which a community of speakers identify a socially unifying feature of their spoken life. In their collective performance, a public personalness is revealed, a common way of speaking is displayed where communal actors cooperatively bond around common purposes. Sharing identifies a culture pattern in which commonly valued information is disclosed, and social support is invoked.

9

"COMMUNICATION": A RITUAL CELEBRATION

As people gathered on "Donahue" to talk, they often talked about their problems with a prominent term, "communication." For example, a male audience member was describing his recent divorce, and his quest for a new woman by saying: "I want to find out about her. I want to find out if we can communicate and I want to see the chemistry that exists." A new stepfather was asked about the difficulties of adjusting to a stepfamily arrangement. He responded: "I'm working at it. I communicate better." An expert guest described romantic relationships by saying: "[Problems occur when] you can't talk and have communication back and forth, that's the most important thing in a marriage. (Applause)" Similarly, a woman author explained: "I think marriages can stand a better chance now because communication is being encouraged by people." But, when communication fails, marriages falter, and (sometimes unusual) interventions occur. A male prostitute described his job in part by saying: "When a woman comes over to me and she is in a marriage and she is not quite communicating with her husband, and she comes to me and she is very free and very open and she does communicate with me. Then she goes back home and somewhat communicates with her husband. And sometimes the marriage does unite again." Another man described the importance of communication while he was unemployed: "Communication is the key to the whole thing. In other words, if you can communicate with your spouse, you're all set. If you can't communicate, you're in serious trouble."

What are the meanings of the term communication as it is being used by these persons? Why does its absence signal "serious trouble"? its presence, a key to success? What verbal performances are being labeled with this term? What does it accomplish for speakers?

Katriel and Philipsen (1981) have provided an insightful response to these questions. In this chapter, I will summarize their interpretations of communication, revising and extending them when necessary for present purposes, examine uses of the cultural term, relationship, that are closely aligned with communication, then interpret communication as a ritualized genre of speaking in which self, relationship, and communication itself are celebrated. My general purposes are to demonstrate how a native category of speaking is intimately linked to spoken symbols of personhood and bonding, and to interpret performances that it labels within a ritual "frame."[1]

"Communication" As a Cultural Category

Katriel and Philipsen examined American speech where clusters of terms including "real communication," "really talking," "supportive communication," and "open communication" contrasted to another cluster, including "chit-chat" and "mere talk" (1981, pp. 307–308). They showed how American persons interpreted and differentiated these two clusters, respectively, along three semantic dimensions of close–distant, supportive–neutral, and flexible–rigid (1981, pp. 307–309).

As close, communication refers to speech where interlocutors penetrate each other's "unique psychological worlds. [And] to the degree that each interlocutor makes public what was previously private information about his or her unique self image, closeness . . . is manifested" (1981, p. 308). As supportive, they described communication as speech where one approves "the other qua unique and precious individual. This is speech in which unconditional positive regard finds its natural home" (p. 308). They also describe communication as flexible, as manifesting "a willingness to listen to and acknowledge the other's presentation of self, to listen to and actively try to understand the other's evaluation of oneself, and to be willing to consider changing one's perception of self or other contingent upon the meanings which emerge in the speech event" (p. 308). In short, Katriel and Philipsen (1981) show how the cultural term communication is used to refer to speech which is close, supportive, and flexible.

Later in their description, Katriel and Philipsen show how communication can be interpreted within a ritual frame of spoken acts which pays homage to "what the culture defines as a sacred object— the definition of 'self' as experienced by any one of the participants" (1981, pp. 310–311). In what they describe as the "communication ritual," persons talk about a problem which a self is experiencing, acknowledge its legitimacy, negotiate its ingredients and implications, and reaffirm participants as individuals committed to each other's well-

---

[1] The following interpretations are based on 47 occurrences of the term, "communication," in my corpus.

being (pp. 310–313). Performances of the ritual, they argue, occur with great normative force as individuals initiate and respond to pleas for communication. Pleas for its enactment are powerfully felt since the person's self is said to be sacred and, therefore, warrants discursive attention and care.

The following discussion builds on the analyses of Katriel and Philipsen, and my own of codes of personhood. I will continue by examining a symbol of bonding, relationship, and eventually suggest that communication, as ritual, not only celebrates self but also relationships. I will show eventually that *communication functions for these persons as both the process and material of being and bonding; it is not only the how of self and relationship but also a valued social state in which these symbols of being, bonding—and speaking—are realized.*

Before beginning the analyses, two clarifications are in order. First, I am analyzing the term communication within the discourses of personhood and speaking used on "Donahue." The term has other meanings and forms in other cultural contexts and symbol systems. Second, in each instance of my corpus, communication was used by persons to conceive and evaluate their nonpresent actions. For example, a male guest described the speech of a relationship with a woman (who was not present) saying, "I communicate with her"; a stepfather described his speech at home saying, "I communicate better"; and an audience member described the speech in his marriage saying, "we communicate." Thus, unlike being honest and sharing, communication was used to refer to speaking in some nonpresent context.

"Relationship" As a Cultural Code

Several utterances demonstrate the highly praised value of communication in relationships:

1. It's extremely important in a relationship to be open, honest, and communicative . . .
2. In any relationship you have to communicate. That's the most important part of a relationship and you've got to talk about things. I've been married 3 years and I clean the house, I go to the grocery store with my wife and that's the way it should be. She works and she makes more than I do at times and it's no big deal to me but you have to communicate.
3. A woman described her relationship with her husband: The only thing that saved Craig and me is the communication. That's the

only thing that helped us. The husband replied: I think that's the key, communication. The wife: If you don't talk it will never work.
4. A mother described her relationship with her daughter and new son-in-law: It's a transition and as we've come to know each other we really are coming to understand each other and we can communicate.

The cultural term, relationship, carries a great symbolic weight in these utterances. It stands in sharp contrast to the codes of self (where meanings of separateness, uniqueness, and personality reign) and social role (where meanings of involuntary choice, obligation, and accommodation reign). The relationship symbol contrasts to these two codes by providing both valued meanings of togetherness, commonness, and sociality, and symbols of free choice and of voluntary cooperation. In combination, relationship manifests the reflexive meanings of self—as a unique construction and a common value, as an assertive and integrated whole, and as a part but not part of an impersonal whole (society or social roles), but of a personal whole (relationship). Where the personal code of self asserts an expressive independence and uniqueness, and the positional code of social role invokes a constraint which must be battled, relationship mediates an intimate terrain of "togetherness" which is discursively caressed.

An important cultural message is created with the term relationship; it carries a discursive force counter to the container metaphor of self and counter to the exemplary acts of social role. As a countermetaphor of self, relationship provides meanings of togetherness, a sense of social bonding. As a counter to social role it provides a preferred symbol of commonality that is morally preferred, because voluntarily forged. As great symbolic codes of self are highly valued and reaffirmed, and as symbols of social roles are discursively disdained, a great cultural aporia is created, an aporia which receives partial satiation with symbols of relationship.[2]

The above utterances also use a valued speech code that is aligned with relationship and is called communication. Let us now turn more specifically to this cultural category about speaking.

---

[2] One interesting speech pattern which revealed this theme involved spouses in discussions of their "relationship" with their "partner," rather than their "marriage" with their "husband/wife." The former are the preferred terms because they invoke a negotiated, voluntary sense of bonding which is distinct from "marriage," and "husband/wife," which invoke (for some) traditional expectations, constraints, in short, obligatory senses of life in society's institutions. The interpretations of "relationship" as a cultural term are more fully developed elsewhere (Carbaugh, 1984b).

To begin, it may be useful to clarify the focus of the following interpretations. Recall how Katriel and Philipsen described communication as speech which is intelligible along dimensions of closeness, supportiveness, and flexibility. They also described its form as a ritual which pays homage to what the culture describes as a sacred object, the self. One way of understanding their analysis is to view it from the symbolic system I have been attempting to describe. From this system, their interpretations are of communication from the vantage point of self. They describe the meanings and form of communication as it recognizes, validates, and celebrates self.

I complement their analyses by examining self and relationship from the vantage point of communication. I am asking: How is it that codes of the person and symbols of bonding are prominently linked to a cultural category about speaking? How is it that self, relationship, and communication are prominently aligned terms? In what follows, I will describe the meanings and form of communication as a native genre of speaking, and demonstrate its status as both an actual social state (outcome) and process (means) in which a cultural being (individual and self) and bonding (relationship) are created, as other cultural symbols and senses (social role and society) are cast aside.

Meanings of "Communication"

The speakers of "Donahue" use three semantic dimensions in conceiving and evaluating speech as communication. They are open–closed, supportive–nonsupportive, and flexible–rigid.[3] In what follows, the dimensions will be defined, refined, and applied to the personal code of self, the symbol of bonding, relationship, and the native genre itself, communication.

The first dimension, *open–closed,* suggests initially the degree to which self is made available in communication. When self is open, its personal qualities become accessible in conversation, its disclosures are unfettered by external constraints. This is speech where one is both aware and expressive about who one is; one is "open and honest," direct and truthful.[4] When one is open in communication, as was the troubled wife and the male prostitute, one's thoughts, needs, feelings, and problems become potential resources of discursive concern. Com-

---

[3] I am indebted to Katriel and Philipsen who suggested the last two dimensions (1981, pp. 307–309). The interpretations that follow are modified in light of the present corpus of materials and for purposes of this analysis.

[4] The interrelations of meanings, functions, and forms in the discourse about speaking are examined more fully in the next chapter.

munication means—in its full sense as described by the unemployed husband and his wife—not only being open about one's self, but also open to the self of others. Open communication involves a willingness to listen to other's thoughts, needs, feelings, and problems. Being open to others involves a proper respect for them, for their rights as persons. Openness in speech implies that each participant in communication has equal access to such valued discursive resources. As a result, communication is a cooperative medium for self-presentation, self-validation, and self-respect. Persons describe an openness about self, and an openness to others', when they speak of communication.

Closed speech, as attributed to some persons and especially government groups, and as invoked through the terms "normal chit-chat and mere talk," involves speech in which self or other valued information is not made available. Certain boundaries and barriers are said to operate in such speech which render this information inaccessible. Speech that is closed is speech where important informational needs such as one's and other's self go unmet.

The second dimension of communication, *supportive-nonsupportive,* suggests the degree to which persons exude care for each other and their relationship together. Speech which is supportive is speech where interlocutors bond through a relational embrace to combat with others the problematical forces which they confront—as the stepfather confronted the adjustment to the stepfamily. Supportive speech is not only an openness to other's opinions, but a commitment to bond with them, to support them, to work toward a common purpose, regardless of their particular point of view. This dimension of speech reveals an assumed common purpose, a bond between persons impervious to threat. Thus, communication involves the discursive nurturing of a close, loyal, trusting relationship between persons; it is the embodiment and expression of persons being together. Where openness highlights those features of speech where self is displayed, validated, and maintained, supportiveness invokes those features where persons bond behind common purposes. What is partly meant when persons discuss communication is a supportive bonding with others, where common purposes (rather than accuracy) is the interactional concern.

Nonsupportive speech can be heard in at least two general ways. One of these, as suggested by Katriel and Philipsen, involves speech where a neutral stance toward one's relationship with others is revealed—as in "normal chit-chat." By remaining rather aloof about one's involvement with others, one risks being interpreted as nonsupportive. Also, and rather obviously, one can be nonsupportive by criticizing the common bonds, the unspoken rules of togetherness, to which a particular social group adheres. For example, when the audience member listened to, but criticized nurses for abusing drugs, he was being open to another's position, willingly listened to it, yet did not support it. He was being open, but not supportive; he had been honest but not quite shared. One can be open about self, yet not support the common purposes at hand nor the self of others. Speech that violates the codes that bond persons together is heard to be nonsupportive.

The third dimension of communication is *flexible–rigid.* Flexibility, however, is of at least two general types. The first is a discursive willingness to be adaptable, changeable, and negotiable about self, and about the rules, codes, or agreements developed in relationship with others. When speech is flexible, the person becomes accessible in conversation, and individuals make their opinions and self-definitions malleable. Communication becomes a means toward discovering what one believes and who one is. Each personal discovery implies a flexibility to incorporate change about who one is. Communication as flexible enables the person to be displayed, negotiated, and transformed. A similar semantic is applied to the liberated symbol of bonding, relationship. Since relationships are largely arrangements of voluntary choice, they involve certain codes and rules which persons have voluntarily made. However, these consensual agreements warrant periodic negotiation and change. To the extent that speech accomplishes these necessary adaptations and changes through negotiations of persons and relations, it is identifiable as flexible and said to be communication.

There is a second general type of flexibility used in making sense of communication. The flexibility referred to here is a communicative flexibility, a flexibility in communication style. To the extent that communication occurs, interlocutors display a flexible sensitivity to the demands of the speech event. For example, some moments of conversation create an exigence where openness is warranted, where one's direct opinions and presentations, or those of others, are the pressing concern. At other moments an exigence is created where supportiveness is warranted. The degree to which interlocutors cooperatively manage the delicate balance between openness and supportiveness, between presenting the person and bonding with others, is the degree to which communication is flexibly accomplished.

Being inflexible involves speech where definitions of persons and relations are rigidly enforced. For example, "normal chit-chat" and social roles invoke meanings where restricted and rigid codes are interactively accomplished. Speech as this can be heard as rigid when it is inflexibly, inappropriately, or solely performed as either open or supportive. Any speech heard to adhere rigidly to certain definitions, codes, and styles would violate the valued sense of communication as flexible.

The three semantic dimensions suggest an interpretation of the cultural term, communication, as open, supportive, and flexible speech. As open, communication involves the presentation and validation of persons; as supportive, it implies the recognition and nurturing of a common relational bond; and as flexible, it reveals the negotiable quality of persons and relations as well as a discursive adaptability between open and supportive speech. These dimensions suggest the polysemic qualities of communication as it reflexively invokes meanings of persons and their social relations.

Relational Bonding and Personal Being

These interpretations suggest a way to understand the close alignment of relationship and communication. Specifically, the term relationship, as spoken on "Donahue," defines a type of sociation where individuals bond together uniquely (emotionally, temporally, and physically), and where they preserve the integrity of each person (respect each opinion and treat equally) (Carbaugh, 1984b). Speech of communication defines both a social outcome and process of sociation where persons bond together, support one another, negotiate and validate a sense of who each is. Both relationship and communication point to the dual functions of personal being and relational bonding. The former term defines a type of sociation in which a social means and outcome occurs (communication); the latter term defines a means and type of sociation in which a valued type of sociation occurs (relationship). In combination, the cultural terms provide cultural resources for discussing two types and one means of sociation where relational bonding and personal being are accomplished.

Both terms also provide a native response to the Hobbesian question: How is society possible? Society, in the analytical sense, is largely possible as persons communicate and forge relationships. These accomplishments involve persons in the negotiation of fundamentally important symbols, about persons, relations, and speaking. Since relationship and communication involve voluntary and flexible agreements, then interlocutors are mostly free to choose and change the nature of their relations and senses of their person. This do-it-yourself sociation simultaneously bonds individuals within the codes of choice, but at the same time reaffirms their dignity as an independent actor with a conscious communicativeness.

Society is also possible as persons communicate. Relationships do not just happen, they are said to be forged, maintained, and evaluated in and as communication (Burgoon & Hale, 1984; Millar & Rogers,

1976; Owen, 1984; Parks, 1977). This means and type of sociation is the culturally preferred act of sociality. As individuals discuss communication, they invoke a social act where separate selves are united in relationship. The communal acts of communication and relationship, moreover, do not entirely dissipate the boundaries between persons but at once recognize *and penetrate* them (unlike the positional term, role). It is this complex interaction among codes of personhood, genres of speaking, and symbols of bonding, that in this case makes society intelligible to persons, and performable by them.

"Communication" As Ritual

By treating communication as ritual (Katriel & Philipsen, 1981), a form of speech is revealed which functions in a culturally preferred way to celebrate what participants define as sacred objects—the individual self of participants, the relationship between them, and the identifiable act that distinguishes and unites them. The following description of communication is based on Philipsen's (in press) definition of ritual and several components of speech discussed by Hymes (1972). The components are used to construct an ideal type, a form of communication as ritual which captures its quintessential features. Of course, each particular performance of the ritual would deviate from the ideal, but a description of the ideal as displayed on "Donahue" should suggest features operating in particular instances of the general type. The description is organized around the following components: topic, purpose, participants, setting, act sequence, and norm of interaction.

Topic. The general topics of discussion in communication may be stated as problems of self, relationships, and/or communication, and are prompted by discussion of such things as dropping sperm count, faulty schools, absentee mothers, free-form marriage, and parent abuse. The loci of the problems are not only expressed as features of self, relationships, and communication, but also as rooted in the meanings of society and social roles. Thus, the experiencing of many problems are expressed as matters of widespread social concern, matters which warrant public communication. These general types of problems provide the common topics, the communicative exigences, which motivate individuals to communicate.[5]

---

[5] The continual verbalizing of problems can be refined by viewing the general sequencing of acts within the "show" as a social drama, especially where a phase of crisis is continually spoken thus replaying the broad extent of "the problem." Elsewhere I have interpreted the speech on "Donahue" within a social dramatic form (Carbaugh, 1984a, pp. 364–394).

The exigence which creates communication on such topics is a result of an interaction of two valued symbolic domains. On the one hand, persons are spoken as self, as choosing a life of independence, awareness, and communicativeness. But such choices render connectedness problematic which results in a problem in need of communication or aid by forging a relationship. On the other hand, bonding and supportiveness are commonly valued. However, exclusive choices for these render individuality and independence problematical, which results in more topics that warrant communication. The simultaneous demand for personal being *and* relational bonding which resides in this symbolic system, gives impulse to events of communication, events which thematize problems of self, relationship, and communication, while often rooting them in social roles or society.

Purpose. The purpose of the ritual is to manage the problematical aspects of participants' experiences by affirming the person and/or their relations in communication. The problems may not be, and on "Donahue" generally are not, solved. But they are discussed, as communication, a particular way. As Donahue frequently says, "we are trying to make some sense here." Making sense involves the recognition and clarification of a problem. In the process, interlocutors carefully examine the problem, validate those who experience it, and support a cooperative confrontation against it. The confrontation is sometimes against social roles, casting them aside since the meanings of conformity, expected dependence, and relative inexpressiveness are said to be the roots of many problems. The foremost purpose of the ritual, then, is not the solving of a substantive societal problem, of poor educational systems or unhealthy stereotypes, but the rallying of forces, a uniting together behind common purposes where persons open up, support each other, and sometimes change; the celebration of this process and social state is known as communication.[6]

Participants. Potential participants in the ritual are any individuals who are willing to communicate about a particular problem. Those who become part of the ritual are expected to be open about their experience of the problem, open to others experiences of the problem, supportive of those engaged in the ritual, willing to negotiate around and about the topic, and sensitive to the situational demands for openness and/or supportiveness. For the performance of the ritual to be effective and legitimate, participants are expected to be sincerely committed to it.

---

[6] The cultural premises of the ritual might be expressed in a rather banal way: I have problems; you have problems; we all have problems; let's talk.

Setting. The ritual may be performed in any setting where talk can be the primary focus of activity. A setting marked for, and by, communication is one where participants attend to their problems and interact properly with those who confront them.

Act sequence. The communication ritual can be heard as unfolding along a particular sequence of spoken acts. The following sequence is described using Katriel and Philipsen's (1981) adaptation of Goffman's (1967) "ritual interchange." (1) Initiation: A person or persons initiate discussion about some problem which needs to be talked about. (2) Acknowledgment: Participants in the discussion grant the problem a legitimate status by discussing it. Speech surrounding the problem becomes the primary focus of activity. The problem is heard to be an important and relevant one since participants are willing to discuss it. (3) Negotiation: The negotiation of the problem includes two general features. One involves persons who disclose about experiences with the problem and/or express opinions about it. During such discussion participants are expected to speak honestly and listen attentively in order to negotiate, clarify, and understand the nature of the problem. Since experiences and opinions about the problem are assumed to be unique and diverse, individuals are expected to speak and listen with flexibility. A second feature of negotiation involves the articulation and support of those values, opinions, or sentiments which participants share. The metamessage is something like: We are in this together. This speech provides the conversational rallying points where participants support their joint effort in confronting a difficult problem. The problem of immediate concern may focus on one participant, but what is relevant is the personal disclosures and the uniting of interlocutors, both motivated by a public and difficult problem. (4) Reaffirmation: This final phase involves the bringing together, and dismissing, of disparate views which may have occurred in the negotiation phase. Since total agreement of opinions is not expected from participants, a phase of talk is performed which minimizes differences. Participants reaffirm their commitment to each other's well-being, reaffirm the importance of communication as a way of discussing common problems, and support their shared purposes.

Norm of interaction. If a person experiences a problem, she or he should initiate the communication ritual. Further, if a person hears another who is experiencing a problem, he or she should help them enact the communication ritual (Katriel & Philipsen, 1981, p. 312). The norm is intensely felt and highly crystallized as those who express it, praise its force. In fact, communication in the above symbolic system is not only a means of presenting the person, a larger event in which to be honest and share, and "the key" to relationships, but also a valued end which symbolizes the very existence of both persons (self) and relations (relationship). To communicate is to nurture self and one's interpersonal relationships. However, those who do not communicate are heard as somewhat closed, nonsupportive, and rigid. As such, they are said to lack both the full resources of self and the key element in healthy relationships. A choice not to communicate is a choice which not only hinders the cultural presentation of self but also hinders the common performance of one's interpersonal relationships; if one does not communicate, a common and proper means of personal being and relational bonding remains absent. The normative plea for communication penetrates to a cultural core, a core where self and relationship are celebrated and praised, a core where persons and social relations find their natural symbolic home.

A folk logic in the above form deserves a comment. It can be reconstructed as follows: if one has a problem—and it is assumed that all individuals do—then one should communicate; and if one communicates, one travels a valued path toward a healthier self and better relationships. Therefore, problems are a means toward a healthier self and relationships. Of course, speakers of this discourse do not reconstruct the logic as I have done here. Yet some come close. Their pleas for communication reveal such a logic in use. After pondering it, I went back to my data and found no utterances where problems were said to lead to healthier relationships. However, I did discover several utterances where a parent or spouse expressed frustration when their potential interlocutor would not discuss problems. The expression of these frustrations implicitly defined their relationship as somewhat problematical, and implied that the child or spouse had problems they were not willing to talk about. Not talking about problems was considered problematical. Conversation constructed this way presupposes problems. Without them, a motive for communication is lacking; opportunities for growth in self and validation are decreased; moments of relational bonding are missed. But with an experience of problems, the discourse is motivated to work, communication is invoked, opportunities for self and relationship celebration are activated. The orientational system used here derives from an important and common motive, the experiencing of problems.

Communication, then, as ritual, responds to problems through a structured sequence of symbolic acts that, when correctly performed, celebrates the person (individual and self), social relations (relationships), and a native genre of speaking (communication). This is a recognized, accepted, and respected form of speech, which is identified and used by participants of "Donahue." The meanings which radiate from communication ignite a code about open, supportive, and flexible speech. Speech of participants which includes the prominent symbol, communication, can be heard as a ritualized form with symbolic meanings that pay homage to self, relationships, and communication. Interpreted this way, communication entails a regnant force which no other symbol in this symbolic universe can claim. Through communication, participants praise their most highly valued goods, their independent self and their interpersonal relationships. Perhaps any symbolic system, in principle, has such an epitomizing term (Schneider, 1976). But in this case, it is the symbolic coalescing of accepted models for persons, speaking, and relations which imbues this system with symbolic reverberations of unifying force.

If the communication ritual were meant and performed as solely the celebration of self, then its use would reaffirm cultural meanings of independence and metaphors of separateness, uniqueness, and personality. Communication would entail a collective and cooperative validation of individuals' unique and distinctive features. This is only part of what is meant. As spoken in this situation, communication artfully manages, in its meaning and form, apparently conflicting features of separateness/connectedness, uniqueness/commonness, individuality/sociality, differences/similarities, divisiveness/bonding, self/relationship. In communication, the former features are openly discussed, respected, treated equally, and therefore validated; the latter features are recognized, negotiated and supportively nurtured. Frequent testimony is given to the great power of communication as an artful means and type of sociation where the unique character of individuals, and the relations between them, are accepted, respected, and celebrated.

This view of communication is used to make heroes of some who achieve its valued meanings and forms. Great communicators or negotiators were praised on "Donahue," including former Secretary of State Henry Kissinger and former President Jimmy Carter. When they attended to situations which were said to need communication, such as the Middle East, they enhanced their public credibility. In late January of 1983, former President Carter appeared on "Donahue," and described his diplomatic style as one which relied on his forging of "personal relationships" with Begin, Sadat, and others. His diplomatic style was highly praised on the show. Also in 1983, Carter's communicative diplomacy was contrasted to the Reagan administration's. Donahue addressed Robert Dole, Republican from Kansas, saying, "It looks like the President doesn't talk to joint chiefs of staff; it looks to the world like we don't want to talk with Andropov. We've got big problems with these people running around not talking to each other. . . . Why is the President so hesitant to sit down and talk with the Soviet Union?" Dole replied, "President Carter thought it could be done that way, but it takes time to prepare." To those who share the communication code, it sounds like President Reagan is not confronting important problems which need to be "talked about." More than that, his lack of communication is a problem which they, in turn, are talking about. His diplomatic style and presidential qualities were being questioned and contrasted to former President Carter's. President Carter was shown to confront and negotiate important problems, the most difficult problems of the Middle East, demonstrating not only the positive effects of communication, but also his ability to communicate. President Reagan was being criticized for failing the test of communication. In early 1983, this criticism of the Reagan administration was acknowledged and responded to by the President's press secretary, Larry Speakes, when he was asked: "Isn't the president's job to educate the public on these [Central American] issues?" Mr. Speakes responded: "I think that communication—this goes to the heart of my job—is the key ingredient to leadership. If the president cannot communicate his policies to the American people and to the Congress—then he can't lead. That's where the president's success has been" (Interview, 1983). By aligning President Reagan's success with the cultural term, communication, an attempt was made to enhance the public image of the president as a successful communicator, as more than an actor who skillfully presents information but as a successful interactor with others, as a person who can forge cooperative relationships by enacting the communication ritual.

Communication, then, is a culturally celebrated means and state of sociation; it is an identifiable means toward accomplishing a sense of persons and relations, and it is a celebrated social state in which cultural participants, citizens and politicians alike, indicate who they are. Through communication, cultural persons and relations are realized and negotiated; in communication, self and relationship find their natural symbolic home. This cultural capacity of communication, as a regnant symbol and form, makes of it a most celebrated symbol in participants' everyday discourse, a symbol which poignantly organizes diverse experiences into an identifiable and highly respected communal performance. Thus, communication is the culturally celebrated communal event in which the valued symbols of persons (individual and self) social relations (relationship), and communication (being honest, sharing, and communication) are respected and publicly praised.

10

AMERICAN CATEGORIES ABOUT SPEAKING AND OTHER CULTURAL PATTERNS

The ethnographer of communication derives a description from a stream of discourse enacted by those observed. To begin, an attempt is made to organize the stream so that one can say, for example, of two consecutive acts or events, that one differs from the other, or of two nonconsecutive acts or events, that they are in some sense enactments of the same conduct. So, if the ethnographer claims that an activity is getting done so many times, verification of that fact involves not only a count of the times the activity occurs, but also an identification of the premises that make of the activity something distinctive from everything else, and render it intelligible as an instance of that sort. A deep sense of what activities are the "same" and what ones are "different" can follow only from a kind of cultural analysis, based on the tribal idioms of the people being studied (Frake, 1972. p. 110).

This study of an American discourse about speaking has investigated a stream of conduct following an American idiom, and proposed a way to hear three of its features, sharing, being honest, and communication. Thus, from the general stream of behavior called, "talking to each other," we now have a more refined sense of some of the talk that is labeled, enacted, and talked about.[1] In this chapter I will state more explicitly the semantic interrelations within this discourse, the functional accomplishments of each term, and the form each takes in the "Donahue" scene. The discussion responds to the general question: from the general stream of talk, what currents are talked about? I hope to demonstrate how a cultural discourse about speaking is semantically and functionally interrelated, yet occurs in distinctively identifiable forms.

---

[1] Of course, American English provides a wide array of expressions about "talk." I have not given a comprehensive analysis by any means.

The semantic structures of inclusion and contrast enacted in the use of these three American symbols is shown in Diagram 10–1.[2]

Let A, B, and C represent American talk that is labeled communication, sharing, and being honest, respectively. Then, communication can label A (including some acts of B and C), sharing the set (B or A), whereas being honest can label the set (C or A). Thus, the cultural symbols form a more or less ordered semantic system with each category related to the others.

Each term in the set has a maximum and minimal sense, such that a person may use a de-emphatic particle, "I was just being honest," as a way of specifying its minimal sense (X) but one is not obliged to

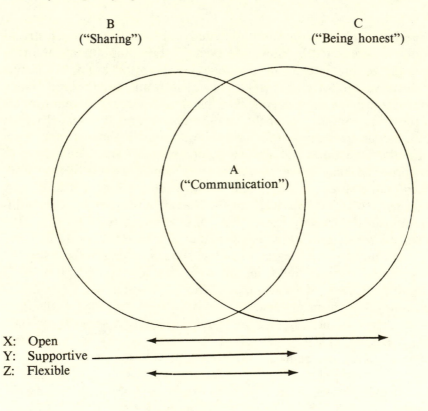

A: Speech event
B, C: Speech acts and events
X, Y, Z: Semantic Dimensions

10–1.   Semantic Dimensions in an American discourse about speaking.

---

[2] I am following closely here the analysis and wording of Frake, 1972.

use C to convey this sense. (It may also be entailed by A or B.) Likewise, one might use the term, sharing (B), to convey its minimal sense (Y), without invoking its other salient meanings. Precisely this minimal sense of sharing was invoked in the following exchange (discussed earlier) between Donahue and a guest:

Donahue: At least she is being honest. She is saying I don't feel comfortable about this.
Guest: No, she's not being honest!
Donahue: She is sharing her feelings.
Guest: She is not being honest about it.

In this exchange, there is a question about the woman's being honest, but implicit agreement about her sharing. In short, Donahue suggested the woman was being honest (being open, direct, and truthful). That category for her speech raised the ire of the guest who said, "No, she's not," leading Donahue to suggest, "She is sharing her feelings." Thus, the two negotiate the proper label for her speech, and reach an implicit agreement: she is sharing. Using this category to label her speech suggests that interlocutors were willing to co-orient to her acts as sharing (as supporting a common purpose by offering information about "strangers") but not as honest (as open, direct, and truthful statements). The content of her expressions were framed then more as an expression of feeling— that was more supportive (Y), than openly truthful (X)—with at least one person questioning her being honest (X).

In a moment, I will comment briefly on the semantic dimensions used here, but the immediate point is, users of language make subtle semantic distinctions of the kind being suggested here, with each term implying some identifiable dimension (in this case X for C), but not necessarily saying anything about the presence or absence of another (Y for C).

The general point is related to the issue of "marking" discourse at different levels of contrast, with emphatic particles, for example, "really being honest," extending the basic sense of a term, and de-emphatic particles, for example, "just being honest," specifying its more basic sense (see also Agar, 1974; Blom & Gumperz, 1972; Friedrich, 1972). In our general set, each term is marked for a dimension that is not necessarily entailed by the others:

"being honest": X = + open (+/− support)
"sharing": Y = + support (+/− open)
"communication": Z = + flexible (+ open + support)

The use of sharing prominently implies Y, but the use of being honest does not necessarily say anything about the presence or absence of Y. Likewise, the use of communication prominantly implies Z, but the use of sharing does not necessarily say anything about the presence or absence of Z (although it does of course identify one of its constituent parts).

Throughout this unit I have developed and applied the three dimensions, open, supportive, and flexible to this American discourse about speaking. Now I will summarize briefly these various meanings, XYZ; with X moving the meanings toward direct statements of truth, Y toward supportive expression of feeling, with Z orienting toward the creative interplay of these "radiants" of common meaning (Eastman, 1985).

The dimension of openness has been defined throughout as a direct disclosure of truthful and accurate information, where speech and other thoughts/actions/objects are aligned (a word to world fit). The dimension identifies enactments of forthrightness by persons, opening the interactional arena for maximal person presentation and management. This type of scene is often identified and especially prominent when a speaker brings discredit to self. Thus, when a communicative act is called being honest, and no one disputes that fact, and the person is not joking, the act is heard to be properly open, direct, and truthful. The second dimension of meaning in the set is ignited with sharing. A prominent semantic feature of sharing is an expression of feeling that supports others by orienting to common purposes. Speech that is conducted and defined this way can be heard as an act of relationship management, a kind of discursive caress of present others that rallies interlocutors behind common purposes. Thus, unlike being honest, sharing activates an explicit relational code. Sharing says of itself that there are common purposes that we are here to support. We are in, or forging, an important relationship of care and support (of others through common purposes). Communication adds a third dimension of flexibility, a dimension of enactment that renders necessary fluctuations between openness and support, self and relational management, mutually intelligible. "Really communicating" therefore necessarily implies both being truthful and direct, and being close and caring. Thus, events identified maximally as communication, are very special indeed, for they embrace in their sense a variety of powerful conduct, from self to relational management, from frank openness to caring support. That is, communication as "communication" is flexible in a deep sense.

In sum, the three cultural categories about speaking can be interpreted along three semantic dimensions, each related to important discursive accomplishments, and occurring in identifiable forms (See Diagram 10–2).

The 3 Forms and Other Culture Patterns

My purpose here is to suggest briefly a way to characterize the above discourse of speaking by reference to three forms. The notion of form extends the above discussion of meanings and functions to include the general shape or tenor of utterances, what persons generally expect and receive when speech is so enacted and labeled (Burke, 1968, pp. 29–44, 124–183, 204–212). I will sketch the three forms and discuss other culture patterns related to each.

Being honest could be called a vector of speech that is directive, a truthful proposition of some magnitude and sense. The form is used to state opinions directly, without curves, moving straight to the point without embellishing one's comments. This form enables the individual to present opinions and be respected, the self to be reflected through distinctive and sometimes discreditable features, roles to be rejected, and when several vectors are contiguously "shot," an event of honest speaking occurs (see chap. 7). It is in this sense that vectorial speech of being honest functions most prominently to bring information into the open, making it accessible to persons, but also as person management, engaging persons in various types of speaker and hearer facework including threats to the speaker's face (Brown & Levinson, 1978; Goffman, 1967). As a vectorial form of speech, then, being honest is content- and person-focused, highlighting a concern with information, with who persons are and what they owe to the topic at hand, but the concern is also oriented to cultural identity in that persons share a value in being honest as a common form of expressing the person (compare

	Semantic Dimensions	Discursive Functions	Forms
"being honest"	open	Person Management	Vector
"sharing"	supportive	Relational Management	Spiral
"communication"	flexible	Interaction Management	Linear

10–2. **Meanings, functions and forms of an American discourse about speaking.**

the direct mode and the "antistyle" of "straight talk" in Israel (Katriel, 1986).

It is noteworthy that Rosaldo (1973) has described how Ilongot "captains" (government representatives) used a vectorial form of speech to call attention to their "ruler" status, they "made a good deal of how they went right to the point, said it straight" (1973, p. 220). This "straight" speech is aligned with, and enacts, a hierarchical ordering of (an externally imposed) Philippine national life.[3]

In both being honest and the Ilongot "straight" speech, a vectorial form of directness is used. Both privilege information that may place the person within and outside the routine constraints of the present sociocultural system. In being honest, the person may enact the valued form to disclose potentially discreditable information. In straight speech, the "ruler" enacts the form as a way of displaying power (rather than traditional equality) and means of coping with a "world immensely more hierarchical and more powerful than anything [the traditional Ilongot] have been familiar with" (Rosaldo, 1973, p. 221). While there are important differences between these uses of the vectorial form, there appears to be some convergence in the use of a vectorial form to stand within yet reach beyond routine social boundaries. This suggests a potential alignment between vectorial speech and moments of social transition, perhaps even of transformation, in the sociocultural scene.

When the vectorial form becomes a stylistic preference and perhaps even a marker of cultural identity, moments of intercultural contact may be rendered problematical. As much is stated in several studies which suggest that vectorial speech forms dominate others and lead to negative evaluations of each cultural party by the other. Some degree of this phenomenon operates in meetings between Northern Athabaskans and urban Alaskans (Scollon & Scollon, 1981), Southern Athabaskans and whites (Basso, 1970), and Osage Indians and whites (Weider & Pratt, 1985).

The second form of speech considered here is a spiraling one and is demonstrated in sharing. Spiraling speech moves continuously from a point of discussion, around and about the point, sometimes even changing the central axis of discussion but with each utterance related through an assumption of "more of the same." In the "Donahue" scene, spiraling speech enables participants to speak about common purposes and unify behind them, to reveal self and affirm relationship. It is in this sense that sharing provides for a type of relationship

---

[3] It also reacts against "crooked" speech which is rich in verbal art, wit, and indirection and linked to the traditional Ilongot feeling that persons are equal and "difficult to understand" (Rosaldo, 1973, p. 221).

management, where—unlike vectors of honesty—the relations among persons are highlighted over the accuracy of information exchanged. From this vantage point, solving the problems of discussion is less important than acknowledging "we are in this together." The topics of discussion, in fact, sometimes become rather metaphorical resources for expressing "togetherness." This occurs as persons cycle through various phases of topics, sometimes returning to earlier phases, but always discussing in a supportive and cooperative tone that creates and/or reveals a unity behind common purposes.

A spiraling form of speech has been identified among Aboriginal persons in Australia (Liberman, n.d.) who, in public discourse, follow a main rule for preserving a consensus. Their discussions progress through a series of summary accounts, restatements of previous consensual statements, cycling through various expressions that persons hold in common. What the form accomplishes socially is a display of solidarity through a spiraling form, which treats consensual views and their restatement thematically. Similarly, Israelis on Friday evenings are known to engage in a national pastime, "griping parties." These occasions have been described as a "spiral pattern" of talk "proceeding from one round . . . to another" (Katriel, 1985, p. 377). Katriel discusses the "griping ritual" as like some cases of joking or anecdotal exchanges which similarly move around a common theme. What these cases suggest is a claim with at least some degree of cross-cultural generality: Encounters in spiraling forms are linked to accomplishments of shared identity or solidarity.

The third form of communication discussed here is a linear one and is called communication. The form is linear since it proceeds from one phase of talk to the next with each subsequent phase dependent upon the completion of the preceding phase. The enactment of the linear form can be noticed if an outside person enters. The participants would retrace for the outsider the progression of talk to its current phase, then continue. An elaborate summary is not needed in encounters using spiraling forms, the person can be greeted and the discussion resumed without much of an interruption. In communication, the linear form manages the identity of the person, social relations and interactions, with self, relationship, and communication itself being celebrated. The form is discussed as a way to solve problems by being open, supportive, and flexible, although its enactment on "Donahue" is limited in this regard. Thus, in addition to relating the above forms of vector and spiral to functions of social transition and solidarity, respectively, we might also relate a linear form to the social function of problem solving.

The above discourse about speaking (the system of symbols, meanings, functions, and forms) provides three instances in an American discourse of *substantial* speech, all of which are valued by persons for they accomplish important sociocultural goals. By way of contrast, we might ask: What are native sayings about relatively *insubstantial* speech? More specifically, the meanings above suggest the question: Are there kinds of speech that are relatively closed, neutral, and rigid? Several come to mind, for example, "small talk," "chit-chat," "empty words," and "lying." What are the meanings, functions, and forms of these cultural cateogries about speaking? What do they enact socially? Are there other domains of cultural categories about speaking outside the superdimension of substantial–insubstantial? If so, what do these cultural symbols tell us about situated communication practice? What do they suggest generally about principles of communication? conceptions of personhood? Hopefully, the above will serve a heuristic purpose by prompting such inquiry. There is much work to be done.

A Cultural Communication Theory of Discourses about Speaking

The above findings carry several suggestions for a renewed scope and depth in communication study, specifically about native genres of communication. With regard to scope, the study suggests consideration especially of various cultural symbols that are used as labels about communication performances; cross-cultural comparisons of the same; and investigation of instances of intercultural contact with this feature of speech in mind. With regard to depth, the report suggests exploring native meanings, functions, and forms that radiate from such communication, cultural scenes which they create and in which they are used, and links to native conceptions of the person. All such considerations can be brought to bear when one investigates native genres of communication, for they are intimately involved in the performance (Bauman, 1987; Philips, 1987). These considerations should help enrich the prospects of cultural communication theory and practice by heading us down the road with a broader scope and more powerful lens.

A few signposts should help along the way. First, levels of native genres need to be distinguished and explored further by asking, what are the general types of messages in the message? This study suggests at least three levels, three domains of intelligible meanings that occur in discourse about communication (Carbaugh, 1986), that is, communicational (e.g., what level of communication is the category labeling? An act, an event, a style? What is the structure, form, and/or meanings of communication identified by the category? Has the structure, form, or meanings changed over time?); societal (e.g., What, if any, roles and relations are aligned with the genre(s)? What institutions?); and personhood (e.g., what model for being is assumed and enacted in the performance? What are the prominent loci of motives? Bases of sociation?). These three probes can be used to refine questions about native communication genres and should prove to be valuable heuristic leads. Distinguishing levels as these can also help disambiguate some potential confusions by offering distinctive and complementary paths for inquiry (Cronen, Johnson, & Lannaman, 1982; Pearce & Cronen, 1980).

Second, the structure of native genres of communication could be explicated more fully. As of now, we could conclude: (1) native genres may occur as an act, event, or style; (2) at least three levels of messages are prominently communicable (about communication, society, personhood), (3) native genres convey messages on at least two of these levels simultaneously with one of these levels being communicated relatively indirectly; (4) the messages about communication may be communicated, relative to the other(s), directly or indirectly (Sanches, 1975).

The first point about communication events is least developed. That is, we need to explore native genres of communication at the level of particular events, acts, and styles. This path of inquiry, however, takes us beyond the city of structure. The concept of form should be helpful here as a way to organize links between discourse shapes and goals discussed above (Nofsinger, 1983; Ragan, 1983). The concept of style should provide an organization of verbal means and the selection therefrom (Ervin-Tripp, 1972), and cultural symbol should be helpful as an organization of particular frames, contexts and their common meanings (as in this report). By extending our inquiries beyond the level of acts, and including considerations of events, forms, styles, and meanings, we should be in a position better to explicate the general principles and particular practices of native genres of communication.

One approach that takes communal symbols, symbolic forms, and their meanings seriously, is demonstrated above. This cultural approach to native genres considers several features. First, by exploring communication from a cultural perspective, we can come to understand *cultural symbols* about communication, native terms about speech, and what native concepts and premises reveal about speaking. Inquiring this way helps us understand how individuals and societies weave threads into their talk, and how they discuss parts of their symbolic design. The approach keeps inquiry, early on, near the common grounds of communication, close to the people who talk on it. Second, a cultural approach as demonstrated throughout explores the *common meanings* in the sayings, the generative motives for speaking and for identifying speaking as such. Of prime interest are the publicly sensible premises that flavor the sayings, and give them a particular taste, in this case, of *truth* rather than deception (contrast Albert, 1972), of *openness* rather than artificiality (contrast Jackall, 1976), of *directness* rather than indirectness (contrast, e.g., the *parbachan* speech event reported in Brenneis, 1978). The semantics in the sayings contain rich resources that the cultural approach helps to interpret. Third, an attempt is made to identify what is accomplished through the sayings. Do the native genres *function culturally* to produce persons, manage relations and speaking? Toward what social ends? Intimacy, solidarity, structures of power? What ends are in view and which attained through native genres of speaking? Fourth, the ethnographer treats communication in part as a *symbolic form,* as symbolic action that gives shape to human energy and directs it toward its own goals. He or she sees the acts that coordinate conduct, the manners for presenting and managing persons, and the types of sociality such as that one that asserts the individual over the routine society. These considerations of cultural symbols, common meanings, sociocultural functions, and forms are needed in studies of communication, as well as in studies of discourse in general (Jacobs, 1985).

Important as well are comparative studies that explore the more general principles of native genres of communication across cultural systems of communication. A large corpus of empirical studies has been generated from around the world (Philipsen & Carbaugh, 1986), but to date there is little comparative work that explores the general principles in these cultural practices. Such study would give us perspective on what is particularly interesting about native genres in each case, as well as what is interesting more generally within and across cases.

These paths of inquiry should lead to a greater understanding of the levels, structures, and cultural functions of native genres of communication. We must continue the careful observations. We can design a better lens for the study of native genres of communication, a lens that has sharper focus as an abstract theory *and* enables our seeing into concrete human events. Such a vision would provide a way to link more closely the scope of our understanding to the particular practices of persons, making it articulate with their meanings and symbolic forms.

11

CULTURAL DISCOURSES AND COMMUNICATION INQUIRY

Common expressions are not simply the dead remains of a linguistic usage that has become figurative. They are at the same time the heritage of a common spirit, and if we only understand them rightly and penetrate their covert richness of meaning, they can make this common spirit perceivable again. (Gadamer, 1976, p. 72)

This study has explored the talk of the popular American "Donahue" show and discovered parts of it which provide models for being a person, and parts which identify ways of speaking (and also parts which display symbols of bonding). Each of these verbal resources has been investigated through systems of cultural meanings, symbolic forms, and their discursive functions.

Personhood has been symbolized through three distinct but non-exclusive cultural premises: (1) the person is an individual (individually and collectively) that is respected through a political code; (2) the individual has a self (the preferred social role from an analytical—not cultural—perspective) that reflects through a personal code; (3) self rejects "traditional social roles" through a polemical (positional) code; and (4) choice enacts individuality, personal power, and the freedom of voluntariness, thus asserting qualities of the individual and self over traditional roles. These premises, these relations among cultural symbols, symbolic forms, and their meanings, constitute a prominent discourse about personhood, a system of verbal resources that model for participants ways to conceive of and evaluate who they are.

Acts and events of speaking have been symbolized through three native genres: (1) being honest as a vectorial (straight) form of openness that prominently manages information and the person's identity; (2) sharing as a spiraling form of supportiveness that manages unique aspects of persons and their relations with others; and (3) communication as a (generally) linear ritualized form of flexibility that celebrates persons identities, their social relations, and the sacredness of open, supportive, and flexible interaction itself.

177

The relation between these discourses on personhood and speaking can be approached from several angles. From the standpoint of cultural symbols, self is preferred to be expressive, making its qualities available to others by sharing them; the contained person is expected to open up and share. Through sharing, the person is engaged in a valued form of sociation (i.e., relationship), supporting others and making self available. Likewise, the individual can be silent, inexpressive, or honest, or reject traditional roles through sharing and communication. From the standpoint of symbolic meanings, individuality and community are affirmed through various acts of openness. Expressiveness, awareness, and unique independence are understood and demonstrated openly, supportively, while dependence, conformity, and inexpressiveness are devalued and generally cast aside. From the standpoint of symbolic forms, expressions of the person are expected but not required to be open, while generally, aspects of persons may be spoken directly and truthfully, spiraled through, or more flexibly managed. The discursive functions of this system of symbols, symbolic forms, and meanings unite both discourses through enactments of person, relational, and interactional management. As personhood is modeled and ways of speaking enacted, cultural identity, a preferred type of sociation, and proper forms for communicating are constituted.[1]

The coalescing of these discourses (of personhood and speaking) into a general symbol system demonstrates the central thesis of this book: Ways of speaking a language (being open, supportive, and flexible) are intimately linked to ways of conceiving personhood (being independent, aware, and expressive). Both entail fundamental and focal properties that generate human interpretation and interaction. Both coalesce in lives of persons and societies. Both need to be integrated into our theories of language and communication. But the study is more than a study of American communication patterns. For example, the study has generated a local theory of cultural communication patterns as they

---

[1] The nature of the general claims I am making about these discourses should again be stressed. The claims are, in the weak form, about symbolizing in the "Donahue" scene, in the stronger form, about a broadly distributed patterning of American talk. I have tried to suggest the latter throughout with a sprinkling of texts from outside "Donahue," and by reference to several studies that suggest a wide distribution to the findings (e.g., Coles, 1980; Hart, Carlson, & Eadie, 1980; Hawkins, Weisberg, & Ray, 1980; Yankelovich, 1981; Veroff, Douvan, & Kulka, 1981). But the findings do not predict that persons will speak in sole terms of this general symbolic system, nor that this system will even be used. What the study predicts is the range of common meanings and identifiable forms of some prominent spoken symbols, when they are used, and suggests some of the limits of intelligibility if they are the only terms used (e.g., "the individual" makes it easy to talk all or one, but harder to talk special interests of social groups, see chap. 2).

symbolize persons and speaking; it has suggested—through some initial cross-cultural study—several hypotheses about forms of speech and their social functions (chap. 10); it has qualified several extant claims about personhood and speaking (Cushman & Cahn, 1985; Hallowell, 1955; Sennett, 1978); it has generated descriptive frameworks for interpreting cultural discourses about persons and speaking (see chaps. 6 and 10) and for comparative analyses of the same; and finally, it suggests properties of cultural discourses in general (see the introductions to units 1 and 2, chaps. 6 and 10, and below). This type of inquiry suggests how a fine-grained analysis of popular cultural scenes can be pressed into the service of local and general theories of communication.

The study has explored several focal concerns throughout, all of which are problematical from the standpoint of a cultural approach to communication study. I will conclude by briefly summarizing these focal concerns and discussing several properties of cultural discourses.

The main focal concern in the study has been the symbols that persons use when speaking. But not just any symbol was chosen, only those that held a regnant force and, as spoken, integrated "disparate parts" (Schneider, 1976, p. 204). In short, only those symbols that performed a cultural communicative function were selected for study (Carbaugh, 1983, 1985, 1988; Philipsen, in press). Exploration yielded a system of symbols in use (Bilmes, 1986) from which analyses were made of forms, common meanings, and discursive functions. Investigated were instances of action where persons were using cultural symbols, with specifiable outcomes, expressing a range of common meanings, through identifiable forms. These performances have been summarized by Bauman (1987, p. 9) as a type of "metacultural enactment, occasions in which members of society put their culture on display for themselves and others in performance" (Conquergood, 1984; Fine, 1984; MacAloon, 1984). These occasions for cultural communication, like some performances on "Donahue," make use of powerful symbolic systems, common meanings, and forms. The nexus of these concerns, cultural scenes, spoken symbols, common meanings and symbolic forms, has provided the focal problematic of this study. These concerns need further attention in our studies of human communication, especially those exploring cultural discourses.

What are cultural discourses? I will suggest that they are multilayered, polysemic, multifunctional, occur in various and particular forms, and are deeply contexted.

Cultural discourses are multilayered and systemic resources in speech.
Just as Bilmes's "discursive approach" (1986) places norms as public resources *in* talk, so the cultural communication approach adopted here places discourses as resources *in* communication. These symbolic re-

sources are multilayered and systemic.[2] Consider, for example, the cultural discourse on personhood presented in unit 1. The analysis moved among several layers, from *spoken symbols* (the individual, rights, choice, self, traditional roles), to *symbolic forms* (story, myth, metaphor), to *meanings* (of separate and common humanity, independence, awareness, and expressiveness, and dependence, conformity, and closedness), to *codes* (political, personal, polemical–positional), to their *systemic interrelatedness* in the discourse on personhood. One might isolate a symbol for close analysis, but its particular use—and thus interpretations of its "spoken life"—is always within a broader symbolic system of related symbols, forms, meanings, codes, and their interrelations. Likewise, unit 2 explored discourses of speaking as similarly multilayered and systemically related. Thus, cultural discourses are not particular words and their meanings, but systems of symbols, "their socially located meanings" (Fiske, 1983, p. 139), symbolic forms, and codes that are interrelated. One of the tasks in studies of cultural discourses is the organization of the grand symbolic complexity that persons use, coherently and intelligibly, into a useful fiction that embraces its diversity, enables its plurivocity, and places—hopefully in a productive way—such taken-for-granted resources (Hopper, 1981) into a publicly scrutable domain. The general project is the intensive and sustained rendering of cultural communication into multilayered and systematically interrelated cultural discourses.

Cultural discourses are polysemic, multivocal and coherent. Each instance of cultural symbolizing can support multiple meanings, express multiple voices, but do so—in fact if efficacious must do so—in a coherent way. For example, the *equivocal affirmation* of the individual symbol may accomplish degrees of individuality and community simultaneously (see chap. 2). Or, consider once again the dialogue between Donahue and his Black guest about the woman audience member. Was the (white) audience member being honest or not? Or was she sharing? A range of meanings were invoked as relevant to her speaking performance. Donahue initially suggested she was being open, direct, and truthful. The Black guest disagreed, suggesting she was being closed, indirect, and perhaps deceitful. Donahue then suggested that she was open and supportive, a voice that assumed an aura of considerateness for the woman's self and her willingness to speak, regardless of the truth value in her statements. The guest's voice assumed an aura of compassionateness for a cause (exposure of latent racism). Thus, the cultural terms about speaking radiated multiple meanings and gave

---

[2] While this study has explored verbal symbols, nonverbal symbols could be explored as well.

voice to multiple causes. Further, the meanings and voices were all *enabled* because of the coherence of the communal conversation, and of course equally *constrained* by it (how dare anyone sound rigid, certain, nonnegotiable, traditional, or closed?). Perhaps McKeon (1956, p. 99) summarized this quality best when he wrote: "to be of one mind is not to be of one opinion." Persons generally use only limited features of the situated meaning system when they speak, "sifting" through polysemic potentials (Bakhtin, 1981, p. 201; Ricoeur, 1981, pp. 169–170), highlighting some features while obscuring others. As a result of their selections, differences arise, tempers sometimes flare, or agreements are forged. Within the talk of "Donahue," perhaps most forcefully through the use of cultural discourses, persons may speak multiple meanings through multiple voices, and between the "Donahue" text and various audiences, several meanings and voices undoubtedly have been constructed. But at each moment of cultural discoursing, if one tunes one's ear to the communal sounds, one can be rather confident of the range of sounds in the symphony, be they playing in harmony or discord. Throughout this study (and in my daily life), I attempted to listen to how persons used the discourses inscribed here. What would one need to hear in this talk to render these features of it intelligible? Responses to this question formed the bases for the discourses analyzed here. Each discourse spanned hundreds of utterances. Each listening, multiple meanings. Thus, like Bilmes (1986, p. 116), it appears to me that there is no clear criterial attribute in the discursive life of these symbols, but there is a limited range of intelligibility that operates, a limited range of common meanings, identifiable forms, and discursive functions. The system may be used to express dissonance and disharmony, contradictions and conflict (Carbaugh, 1987), but these accomplishments cohere and are indeed coherent within the scope of the cultural conversation.

The ability of cultural discourses to embrace diverse positions and contradictions is also illustrated in several of the diagrams presented above. For example, in Diagrams 2–1 (p. 33) and 3–1 (p. 58), the upper premises are generally figured at a higher level, are foregrounded, and thus create the context for the lower premises which they contradict. In Diagram 4–1 (p. 85) however, both levels share roughly equal force with paradoxes occurring between individualized meanings and communal actions, and between communal meanings and individualized actions. Thus the kind of cultural analysis demonstrated here embraces polysemic and plurivocal qualities—and in this regard is similar to but extends Fiske (1986), lays a base for critical analyses of multiple meanings and voices, contradictions and conflicts, at several levels, as in dialogues between persons in the cultural scene, in discourses between the "Donahue" scene and its various audiences, and within the symbolic universe of America itself.

Cultural discourses thus express symbolic bases for meaning contradictions within the text, between the text and its audiences; provide for various voices to be expressed; all coherent within the systemic complexity of cultural communication (a system of discourses) itself.

Cultural discourses are multifunctional. There is much that needs to be said here (Hymes, 1962, pp. 115–124), and all I can do is demonstrate the property with the findings of this report (which at a general level point to a coalescing of what Cushman and Cahn [1985, pp. 5–18] have called the interpersonal and cultural functions of human communication).

At a general cultural level, the discourses interpreted above provide interlocutors with semantic resources for constructing personhood and speaking (and with relationship, bonding as well), with senses that display a common identity of both individuality and commonality, separateness and unity. These latter accomplishments point to a more social feature in the cultural discourses, a feature that enables persons to differentiate one from another and to unify simultaneously. Further, the discourses enable assertions of personal freedom and power, rejections of traditional forces, disclosures of discreditable information, expressions of unity behind shared purposes, negotiations of individual and relational identities through a ritualized event, and celebrations of the communication process itself. This range of accomplishments displays the currency, the cultural functioning of the discourses at cultural, social, and interactional levels, including also the various uses of the discourses to account for and disclaim, or generally to align actions (Hewitt & Stokes, 1975; Scott & Lyman, 1968; Stokes & Hewitt, 1976; Ragan, 1983).

Throughout the report I have attempted to summarize these important and various functions of the discourses with reference to *cultural accomplishments* (of cultural concepts and premises of personhood and speaking), *social uses* (in social interaction to manage persons, social relations, and interaction), and *interactional outcomes* (of symbols and symbolic forms).

While various typological schemes of the functions of communication and language have been proposed (e.g., Cushman & Cahn, 1985; Halliday, 1978; Hymes, 1962; Jakobson, 1960), my purpose here is simply to demonstrate that cultural discourses are multifunctional, with any "metacultural enactment" accomplishing several important tasks simultaneously. For a grounded understanding of cultural discourses, these "important tasks" of course need to be discovered in each case, at an emic level, rather than declared a priori. Such a procedure will enable an eventual etic kaleidoscope of functions to be arrayed, compared, and contrasted, laying a better base for further empirical investigations, perhaps even a hierarchical theory of functions (Hymes, 1962, pp. 119–123).

Cultural discourses occur in various and particular forms. That forms vary from culture to culture or from scene to scene within a culture is by now a rather uncontroversial claim. For example, within the "Donahue" scene, persons employed differing forms of personhood as well as differing forms of speaking. Metaphorical speech of self and role, as well as forms of a vector and spinal, are but two examples. These are important for they demonstrate a variety in symbolic forms, within cultural scenes, as well as across cultural discourses. Further, symbolic forms can be rendered at a more formal level as ritual, myth, social drama, or ceremony (Philipsen, in press), resulting in interpretations of the "communication ritual" (see chap. 9 and Katriel & Philipsen, 1981) or of "Donahue" as social drama (Carbaugh, 1984b, pp. 364–393). By tacking back and forth between indigenously identified forms, such as communication, and analytical categories, such as ritual, one can discover and embrace the various shapes of forms, within and across scenes, discourses, and cultures. The dual attention to indigenous symbolic shapes and formal analysis can highlight the variety and particularity of forms in cultural discourses.

Cultural discourses are deeply contexted and historically transmitted. I wish only to accentuate an implicit "axiom of particularity" that is assumed above. Cultural discourses are generally not created anew each performance, nor generally do they transform communication practices radically beyond traditional constraints. I have tried, but sense I have not developed nearly enough, some of the historical roots whence these powerful discourses derive. Certain dynamics, such as the opposition of self and roles, are easily traceable to the beginnings of our nation (which I have tried to indicate by use of Tocqueville, Robertson, and others), and perhaps are instances of a universal dynamic (see Carbaugh, N.D.). Each system of cultural discourses is not created *in vacuo,* but derives from what Gadamer might call its own history of prejudices, or better, its "heritage of a common spirit." A fuller account of the history of cultural discourses would enhance the depth of our understanding both the symbolic resources that are rather timeless across particular scenes and cultures, and those which speak a more timely voice. Historic "tracing" of cultural discourses enables a richer understanding of the context in which the discourses are used and a deeper sense of how they have developed.

In sum: Cultural discourses may be understood as multilayered, polysemic but coherent, multifunctional, various and particular in form, and historically transmitted. From my vantage point, these constitute the critical properties of cultural discourses and summarize the main problematics of this study.

Conclusion

By investigating cultural discourses that are used in a prominent American scene, I hope to have unraveled some of the layers of complexity, interpreted some of the power and heritage, explored various functions and forms, and pointed to the historical roots of some common American expressions. In the process, it seemed I was continually stepping back from those resources that expressed life for myself, my family, friends, and colleagues, but at the same time was plunging back once again into the symbolic sea. Hopefully this book has served a similar purpose for the reader, a kind of stock taking of speechways, stepping back and looking at some of the things (we as) Americans say to each other, placing them on a plane where they can be better evaluated and used more reflectively. If we do not engage in such an exercise, then we remain relatively unaware of common expressions that are our heritage, unschooled in the lessons they can teach, entrapped in these compelling forms that give shape to our lives. Holding such patterns up for scrutiny can lead to their better and more critical use, empowering people with knowledge of patterns that sometimes may oppress them, bringing them closer—in the sense of more cognizant—to something they have helped to create. Cultural discourses are powerful in their ability to define and shape human praxis. An understanding of them is necessary for the humane theory and practice of human communication.

EPILOGUE

There are, of course, limitations to a study as this. First, as in all ethnographic research, the findings are incomplete (Geertz, 1973, p. 29). I do not claim to have captured the essential feature in everyday American life, nor do I claim to have analyzed exhaustively the system of symbols described here. In fact, the resources in the cultural speech I have attempted to describe are virtually inexhaustible. Every time I have returned to the writing of this report, I find other points which could be made, should be made, and so on. I am working within the limits of such a process. However, I do claim to have discovered a prominent system of symbols, symbolic forms, and their meanings that are spoken in an American context, and to have interpreted the prominent meanings of their cultural use. There is still much work to be done. I consider the above to be an early step. As I, and others, continue similar efforts, the everyday speech of a people may gain a richer and fuller articulation, understanding, and development.

Some might criticize the above study for not treating "Donahue" as television, and for not examining its effects on the audience. They could claim: because "Donahue" is television, the dramatic action unfolds the way it does, and such action has specifiable effects on those who hear it. I agree that these are important and interesting assertions. The interactions of mediated channel, spoken code, and audience suggest important areas to research. However, this study was not designed to address these concerns. I was not asking, as some have (Lull, 1980): how does a televised medium impact spoken codes and/or the audience who hears them? I was asking: What is the nature and function of the spoken codes that are shown? The former question is important, and those interested in pursuing it may find this study helpful. For as a result of this analysis, one can hear a system of discourses that is effectively televised to a relatively large and stable audience. In fact, some of the relationships among mediated channel, spoken code, and audience may be gleaned from the above case. But this line of thinking was not the primary focus of this study. Some will say it should have been. Perhaps so. But the study has its own merits. There are diverse discourses shown on television, from call/response forms on Sunday mornings to "sex" and "violence" during prime time. A line of cultural communication research which describes the various symbolic contexts, meanings, and forms of such televised speech would complement the above concerns by extensively documenting what spoken codes are used (Fiske, 1982; Newcomb, 1984). Communicative codes as these could then be analyzed as they interact with other channels, televised or not, and specific audiences.

Some also may consider the study to be more of an ideal construction than a map of native speech. My reply would emphasize the focal concern on the patterning of "talk" in its sociocultural context, its meanings and its forms. For speech to recur with common intelligibility, it must conform to some conventional patterning like the ones herein suggested. I suppose the above interpretations could be read as prototypical cultural patterns, and if they were, I would agree that they are ideal cultural types of which each particular performance would somehow deviate. I would hope, however, that the findings presented here would be evaluated more on their descriptive adequacy, rather than be initially criticized for their systematic presentation of an ideal speech pattern.

Some might also criticize the above for its focus on a social system of speech—which de-emphasizes the role of particular speakers. Hymes (1981, p. 9), following Cassirer, has argued that the personal, the role of the performer-author, is a dimension of necessary importance in ethnographic research. To an extent, I agree. Yet, an understanding of what a particular interlocutor is saying demands an understanding of the symbolic web in which he or she speaks. So, I see the above study as a preliminary step in the understanding of what particular speakers, gathered around similar places, have said. In fact, several of the utterances described above illustrate how individual speakers have pitched and combined cultural themes in unique and revealing ways. Hearing speech this way provides a common understanding of the speech and its natural presentation, as well as an insight into the individual speaker and what they are trying to say.

During the course of the research, a few persons have asked why I have not interviewed participants and regular viewers of "Donahue." I found myself giving several replies. One was simply that I had done so—more or less informally—in the early, discovery, phase of research. This information, along with various commentaries on American life, was helpful in early formulations and in positing initial interpretations of cultural themes. My aim, however, was not to explain the *experience* of people on the show, nor to explain the reactions of viewers to the show, nor was it to interpret speech *about* "Donahue." I was trying to interpret some common speech patterns as they are naturally performed in a sociocultural context, on "Donahue." Thus, the purest data, used as stimulation and verification, were the performances of speech on "Donahue" as they were done on "Donahue." So, interviews, as were all discussions with others who commented upon the speech patterns interpreted here, were data of a second order. Important, yes, but data of a different and secondary type.

Conclusion

Perhaps Baruch Spinoza, in the *Tractatus-Theologico Politicus,* captured my sentiments best where he wrote, "I have tried sedulously not to laugh at the acts of man, nor to lament them, but to understand them." My mission has been one to hear and understand what men (and women) have commonly said as they have come to a place to speak. Hopefully, by listening to their speech this way, as a cultural resource, as a system of cultural discourses, a richer view for social science is gained. From such a view, an analyst can hear a communal conversation where others have heard individual voices. There is an analogous value for my compatriots. Interpreting our "talk" this way may provide a sense of the communal where we have not heard nor seen it before. Those of us in contemporary Western societies tend to say what we think is individual, to think what we say as individuals, but we also say what we think in a cultural voice. Further, we are taught to say what is thought individually, without thinking, nor inquiring, about what is commonly said. Rather than saying what is thought individually, my goal has been to think about, describe, and interpret what is commonly said. As such, I hope to have shown a way to hear the nexus of "talk" and American culture, to have unveiled cultural discourses that are used in an American scene and constitute part of what it is like to be a talking American, to have briefly compared aspects of these discourses across several cultures, and thus to have contributed, like Geertz and others, to the consultable record of what people, speaking in various places, have said.

REFERENCES

Abrahams, R., & Bauman, R. (1971). Sense and nonsense in St. Vincent: Speech behavior and decorum in a Caribbean community. *American Anthropologist, 73,* 762–772.

Agar, M. (1974). Talking about doing: Lexicon and event. *Language in Society, 3,* 83–89.

Albert, E. (1972). Culture patterning of speech behavior in Burundi. In J. Gumperz & D. Hymes (Eds.), *Directions in Sociolinguistics: The Ethnography of Communication.* New York: Holt, Rinehart, & Winston.

Allen, N. (1985). The category of person: A reading of Mauss's last essay. In Carrithers, M., Collins, S., & Lukes, S. (Eds.), *The category of the person.* New York: Columbia University Press.

Bakhtin, M. (1981). *The dialogic imagination.* Austin: University of Texas Press.

Baskerville, B. (1980). *The people's voice.* Lexington, KY: University of Kentucky Press.

Basso, K. (1970). To "give up on words": Silence in Western Apache culture. *Southwestern Journal of Anthropology, 26,* 213–230.

Basso, K. (1979). *Portraits of "the whiteman": Linguistic play and cultural symbols among the Western Apache.* London: Cambridge University Press.

Bauman, R. (1970). Aspects of Quaker rhetoric. *Quarterly Journal of Speech, 56,* 67–74.

Bauman, R. (1983). *Let your words be few: Symbolism of speaking and silence among seventeenth century Quakers.* Cambridge, England: Cambridge University Press.

Bauman, R. (1987). The role of performance in the ethnography of speaking. *Working Papers & Proceedings of the Center for Psychosocial Studies, 11,* 3–12.

Bell, M. (1983). *The world from Brown's lounge: An ethnography of Black middle-class play.* Champaign: University of Illinois Press.

Bellah, R., Madsen, R., Sullivan, W., Swidler, A., & Tipton, S. (1985). *Habits of the heart: Individualism and commitment in American life.* Berkeley: University of California Press.

Berger, P., Berger, B., & Kellner, H. (1974). *The homeless mind.* New York: Vintage Books.

Bharati, A. (1985). The self in Hindu thought and action. In A. Marsella, G. Devos, & F. Hsu, (Eds.), *Culture and self: Asian and western perspectives.* New York: Tavistock.

Bilmes, J. (1986). *Discourse and behavior.* New York: Plenum Press.

Blom, J., & Gumperz, J. (1972). Social meaning in linguistic structure: Code switching in Norway. In J. Gumperz & D. Hymes (Eds.), *Directions in sociolinguistics: The ethnography of communication.* New York: Holt, Rinehart, & Winston.

Bohmer, P. (1986, April 11). U. S. is at war in Central America. *Pittsburgh Post–Gazette,* p. A9.

Boggs, S. (1985). *Speaking, relating, and learning: A study of Hawaiian children at home and at school.* Norwood, NJ: Ablex.

Brenneis, D. (1978). The matter of talk: Political performances in Bhatgaon. *Language in Society, 7,* 159–170.

Brown, P., & Levinson, S. (1978). Universals in language usage: Politeness phenomena. In E. Goody (Ed.), *Questions and politeness.* London: Cambridge University Press, 56–289.

Brown, R., & Ford, M. (1961). Address in American english. *Journal of Abnormal & Social Psychology, 62,* 375–385.

Brown, R., & Gilman, A. (1960). The pronouns of power and solidarity. In T. Sebeok (Ed.), *Style in language.* Cambridge, MA: MIT Press.

Bruner, E., & Gorfain, P. (1984). Dialogic narration and the paradoxes of Masada. In E. Bruner (Ed.), *Text, play, and story: The construction and reconstruction of self and society.* Proceedings of the American Ethnological Society. Washington, DC: American Ethnological Society.

Burgoon, J., & Hale, J. (1984). The fundamental topoi of relational communication. *Communication Monographs, 51,* 194–214.

Burke, K. (1961). *Attitudes toward history.* Boston: Beacon Press.

Burke, K. (1965). *Permanence and change.* Indianapolis, IN: Bobbs–Merrill.

Burke, K. (1966). *Language as symbolic action.* Berkeley, CA: University of California Press.

Burke, K. (1968). *Counter-statement.* Berkeley: University of California Press.

Buttny, R. (1985). Accounts as a reconstruction of an event's context. *Communication Monographs, 52,* 57–77.

Campbell, D. (1975). "Degrees of freedom" and the case study. *Comparative Political Studies, 8,* 178–193.

Carbaugh, D. (1983). Oral tradition as spoken culture. In I. Crouch & G. Owen (Eds.), *Proceedings of the seminar on oral traditions.* Las Cruces: New Mexico State University Press.

Carbaugh, D. (1984a). *On persons, speech, and culture: American codes of "self," "society," and "communication" on DONAHUE.* Unpublished doctoral dissertation, University of Washington.

Carbaugh, D. (1984b). *"Relationship" as a cultural category in some American speech.* Paper presented at the annual meetings of the Speech Communication Association, Chicago.

Carbaugh, D. (1985). Cultural communication and organizing. *International & Intercultural Communication Annual, 8,* 30–47.

Carbaugh, D. (1986). *Cultural categories of speaking: A comparative analysis.* Paper presented at the annual meetings of the Speech Communication Association, Chicago.

Carbaugh, D. (1987). Communication rules in DONAHUE discourse. *Research on Language & Social Interaction, 21,* 31–62.

Carbaugh, D. (1988). Comments on "culture" in communication inquiry. *Communication Reports, 1,* 38–41.

Carbaugh, D. (n.d.). *Deep agony: "Self" vs. "society" in DONAHUE discourse.* Unpublished manuscript.

Carey, J. (1975). A cultural approach to communication. *Communication, 2,* 1–22.

Carrithers, M., Collins, S., & Lukes, S. (Eds.). (1985). *The category of the person.* New York: Columbia University Press.

Caughey, J. (1984). *Imaginary social worlds: A cultural approach.* Lincoln: University of Nebraska Press.

Chenoweth, A. (1982, June 1). Phil shares the experience—or, should transvestites be allowed to adopt Siamese twins? *Washington Post,* A17.

Chesebro, J. (1984). The media reality: Epistemological functions of media in cultural systems. *Critical Studies in Mass Communication, 1,* 111–130.

Chick, J. K. (1985). The interactional accomplishment of discrimination in South Africa. *Language in Society, 14,* 299–326.

Coles, R. (1980). Civility and psychology. *Daedalus, 109,* 133–141.

Conquergood, D. (1984). *Rhetoric and ritual: Implications of Victor Turner's dramaturgical theory for rhetorical criticism.* Paper presented at the Western Speech Communication Convention, Seattle.

Cooley, R. (1983). Codes and contexts: An argument for their description. *International & Intercultural Communication Annual, 7,* 241–251.

Corcoran, F. (1983). The bear in the back yard: Myth, ideology, and victimage ritual in Soviet funerals. *Communication Monographs, 50,* 305–320.

Corner, J. (1980). Codes and cultural analysis. *Media, Culture, & Society, 2,* 73–86.

Corrigan, P., & Willis, P. (1980). Cultural forms and class mediations. *Media, Culture, & Society, 2,* 297–312.

Craig, J. (1986, January 18). What you, the people, think about the media. *Pittsburgh Post-Gazette,* p. 7.

Cronen, V., Johnson, K., & Lannamann, J. (1982). Paradoxes, double binds, and reflexive loops: An alternative theoretical perspective. *Family Process, 20,* 91–112.

Crow, B. (1986). Conversational pragmatics in television talk: The discourse of *Good Sex. Media, Culture, & Society, 8,* 457–484.

Cushman, D., & Cahn, D. (1985). *Communication in interpersonal relationships.* Albany: State University of New York Press.

Cushman, D., & Craig, R. (1976). Communication systems: Interpersonal implications. In G. Miller (Ed.), *Explorations in interpersonal communication.* Beverly Hills, CA: Sage.

Cushman, D., & Pearce, W. (1977). Generality and necessity in three types of communication theory with special attention to rules theory. *Human Communication Research, 3,* 344–353.

Dahrendorf, R. (1968). *Essays in the theory of society.* Stanford, CA: Stanford University Press.

Darnell, D., & Brockreide, W. (1976). *Persons communicating.* Englewood Cliffs, NJ: Prentice–Hall.

Davis, P. (1982). *Hometown.* New York: Simon & Schuster.

Delia, J. (1976). Change of meaning processes in impression formation. *Communication Monographs, 43,* 142–157.

Delia, J. (1980). Some tentative thoughts concerning the study of interpersonal relationships and their development. *Western Journal of Speech Communication, 44,* 97–103.

Delia, J. Clark, R., & Switzer, D. (1974). Cognitive complexity and impression formation in informal social interaction. *Speech Monographs, 41,* 299–308.

Delia, J., O'Keefe, B., & O'Keefe, D. (1982). The constructivist approach to communication. In F. Dance (Ed.), *Human communication theory.* New York: Harper & Row.

Donahue wows Seattle: "I'm nothing without you." (1982, July 26). Seattle *Post–Intelligencer,* p. D1.

Donahue, P., & Co. (1979). *Donahue: My own story.* New York: Fawcett Crest.

Dumont, L. (1970). *Homo hierarchicus* (M. Sainsbury, trans.). Chicago: University of Chicago Press.

Dumont, L. (1985). A modified view of our origins: The Christian beginnings of modern individualism. In M. Carrithers, S. Collins, & S. Lukes (Eds.), *The category of the person.* New York: Columbia University Press.

Eastman, C. (1985). Establishing social identity through language use. *Journal of Language & Social Psychology, 4,* 1–20.

Ebenstein, W. (1969). *Great political thinkers: Plato to the present.* New York: Holt, Rinehart, & Winston.

Ervin–Tripp, S. (1972). On sociolinguistic rules: Alternation and co-occurrence. In J. Gumperz & D. Hymes (Eds.), *Directions in sociolinguistics: The ethnography of communication.* New York: Holt, Rinehart, & Winston.

Fine, E. (1984). *The folklore text.* Bloomington: Indiana University Press.

Fiske, J. (1982). *Introduction to communication studies.* London: Methuen.

Fiske, J. (1983). The discourses of TV quiz shows or school + luck = success + sex. *Central States Speech Journal, 34,* 139–150.

Fiske, J. (1986). Television: Polysemy and popularity. *Critical Studies in Mass Communication, 3,* 391–408.

Fortes, M. (1973). On the concept of the person among the Tallensi. In Germain Dieterlen (Ed.), *La notion de personne en Afrique noire.* Paris: Editions du centre national de la Recherche Scientifique.

Frake, C. (1972). "Struck by speech": The Yakan concept of litigation. In J. Gumperz & D. Hymes (Eds.), *Directions in sociolinguistics: The ethnography of communication.* New York: Holt, Rinehart, & Winston.

Friedrich, P. (1972). Social context and semantic feature: The Russian pronominal usage. In J. Gumperz & D. Hymes (Eds.), *Directions in sociolinguistics: The ethnography of communication.* New York: Holt, Rinehart, & Winston.

Gadamer, H. (1977). *Philosophical hermeneutics.* Berkeley: University of California Press.

Geertz, C. (1973). *The interpretation of cultures.* New York: Basic Books.

Geertz, C. (1976). From the native's point-of-view: On the nature of anthropological understanding. In K. Basso & H. Selby (Eds.), *Meaning in anthropology.* Albuquerque: University of New Mexico Press.

Gergen, K. (1978). Toward generative theory. *Journal of Personality & Social Psychology, 36,* 1344–1360.

Goffman, E. (1959). *The presentation of self in everyday life.* New York: Anchor Books.

Goffman, E. (1967). *Interaction ritual.* New York: Anchor Books.

Golding, P., & Murdock, G. (1978). Theories of communication and theories of society. *Communication Research, 5,* 339–356.

Gossen, G. (1974a). *Chamulas in the world of the sun: Time and speech in a Maya oral tradition.* Cambridge, MA: Harvard University Press.

Gossen, G. (1974b). To speak with a heated heart: Chamula canons of style and good performance. In R. Bauman & J. Sherzer (Eds.), *Explorations in the ethnography of speaking.* Cambridge, England: Cambridge University Press.

Grice, H. (1975). The logic of conversation. In P. Cole & J. Morgan (Eds.), *Syntax and Semantics, Vol. 3: Speech Acts.* New York: Academic Press.

Grossberg, L. (1982). Intersubjectivity and the conceptualization of communication. *Human Studies: A Journal for Philosophy & the Social Sciences, 5,* 213–235.

Gumperz, J. (1982). *Discourse strategies.* Cambridge, England: Cambridge University Press.

Habermas, J. (1976). *Communication and the evolution of society* (T. McCarthy, trans.). Boston: Beacon Press.

Hall, S. (1980). Cultural studies: Two paradigms. *Media, Culture, & Society, 2,* 57–72.

Halliday, M. A. K. (1978). *Language as social semiotic: The social interpretation of language and meaning.* Baltimore: University Park Press.

Halloran, S. M. (1982). Rhetoric in the American college curriculum: The decline of public discourse. *Pretext, 2,* 245–269.

Hallowell, A. I. (1955). *Culture and experience.* New York: Schoken Books.

Hannerz, U. (1969). *Soulside: Inquiries into ghetto culture and community.* New York: Columbia University Press.

Hannerz, U. (1980). *Exploring the city: Inquiries toward an urban anthropology.* New York: Columbia University Press.

Harrison, B. (1983, June). There's a star born every minute. *Savvy,* 46–52.

Hart, R., Carlson, R., & Eadie, W. (1980). Attitudes toward communication and the assessment of rhetorical sensitivity. *Communication Monographs, 47,* 1–22.

Hawkins, J., Weisberg, C., & Ray, D. (1980). Spouse differences in communication style: Preference, perception, behavior. *Journal of Marriage & the Family, 42,* 585–593.

Hewitt, J., & Stokes, R. (1975). Disclaimers. *American Sociological Review, 40,* 1–11.

Hitchcock, J. (1983). American culture and the problem of divorce. *Thought, 58,* 61–71.

Hopper, R. (1981). The taken-for-granted. *Human Communication Research, 7,* 195–211.

Hymes, D. (1961). Linguistic aspects of cross-cultural personality study. In B. Kaplan (Ed.), *Studying personality cross-culturally.* Evanston, IL: Row, Peterson.

Hymes, D. (1962). The ethnography of speaking. In T. Gladwin & W. Sturtevant (Eds.), *Anthropology and human behavior,* Washington, DC: Anthropological Society of Washington.

Hymes, D. (1972). Models of the interaction of language and social life. In J. Gumperz & D. Hymes (Eds.), *Directions in sociolinguistics: The ethnography of communication.* New York: Holt, Rinehart, & Winston.

Hymes, D. (1974). Ways of speaking. In R. Bauman & J. Sherzer (Eds.), *Explorations in the ethnography of speaking.* London: Cambridge University Press.

Hymes, D. (1981). *"In vain I tried to tell you": Essays in Native American Ethnopoetics.* Philadelphia: University of Pennsylvania Press.

Hymes, D. (1983). Report from an underdeveloped country: Toward linguistic competence in the United States. In B. Bain (Ed.), *The sociogenesis of language and human conduct.* NY: Plenum Press.

Hymes, D. (1986a). Discourse: Scope without depth. *International Journal of the Sociology of Language, 57,* 49–89.

Hymes, D. (1986b). The general epistle of James. *International Journal of the Sociology of Language, 62,* 75–103.

Interview with Presidential Press Secretary Larry Speakes. (1983, August 9). *USA Today,* p. 9A.

Irvine, R. (1984). *Media mischief and misdeeds.* Chicago: Regnery Gateway.

Jackall, R. (1977). The control of public faces in a commercial bureaucratic work situation. *Urban Life, 6,* 277–302.

Jacobs, S. (1985). Language. In M. Knapp & G. Miller (Eds.), *Handbook of Interpersonal Communication.* Beverly Hills, CA: Sage.

Jakobson, R. (1960). Concluding statement: Linguistics and poetics. In T. Sebeok (Ed.), *Style in language.* Cambridge, MA: MIT Press.

Jhally, S. (1987). *The codes of advertising: Fetishism and the political economy of meaning in the consumer society.* New York and London: St. Martin's Press and Frances Pinter.

Katriel, T. (1985). "Griping" as a verbal ritual in some Israeli discourse. In M. Dascal (Ed.), *Dialogue: An interdisciplinary approach.* Amsterdam: J. Benjamins.

Katriel, T. (1986). *Talking straight: Dugri speech in Israeli Sabra culture.* Cambridge, England: Cambridge University Press.

Katriel, T. & Philipsen, G. (1981). "What we need is communication": "Communication" as a cultural category in some American speech. *Communication Monographs, 48,* 301–317.

Ketner, K. (1973). The role of hypotheses in folkloristics. *Journal of American Folklore, 86,* 114–130.

Kirkpatrick, J. (1983). *The Marquesan notion of the person.* Ann Arbor, MI: UMI Research Press.

Koch, S. & Deetz, S. (1981). Metaphor analysis of social reality in organizations. *Journal of Applied Communication Research, 9,* 1–15.

La Fontaine, J. (1985). Person and individual: Some anthropological reflections. In Carrithers, S. Collins, & S. Lukes (Eds.), *The category of the person.* New York: Columbia University Press.

Lakoff, G., & Johnson, M. (1980). Conceptual metaphor in everyday language. *Journal of Philosophy, 77,* 453–486.

Lasch, C. (1979). *The culture of narcissism.* New York: Norton.

Liberman, K. (n.d.). Intercultural communication in Central Australia. In R. Bauman & J. Sherzer (Eds.), *Case studies in the ethnography of speaking.* Austin, TX: Southwest Educational Development Laboratory.

Lull, J. (1980). The social uses of television. *Human Communication Research, 6,* 197–209.

MacAloon, J. (Ed.). (1984). *Rite, drama, festival, spectacle: Rehearsals toward a theory of cultural performance.* Philadelphia: Institute for the Study of Human Issues.

Marriott, M. (1976). Hindu transactions: Diversity without dualism. In B. Kapferer (Ed.), *Transaction and meaning: Directions in the anthropology of exchange and symbolic behavior.* Philadelphia: Institute for the study of human issues.

Marsella, A., Devos, G. & Hsu, F. (Eds.). (1985). *Culture and self: Asian and western perspectives.* New York: Tavistock.

Mauss, M. (1938/1985). Une categorie de l'Espirit Humaine: La notion de personne celle de "moi." *Journal of the Royal Anthropological Institute, 68,* 263–282. [Republished in M. Carrithers, S. Collins, & S. Lukes. *The category of the person.* Cambridge, England: Cambridge University Press, 1985.]

Mead, G. (1934). *Mind, self and society.* Chicago: University of Chicago Press.

Mechling, J. (1980). The magic of the boy scout campfire. *Journal of American Folklore, 93,* 35–56.

Meyrowitz, J. (1984). The adultlike child and the childlike adult: Socialization in the electronic age. *Daedulus, 113,* 19–48.

Michaels, S. (1981). "Sharing time": Children's narrative styles and differential access to literacy. *Language in Society, 10,* 423–442.

Millar, F., & Rogers, L. E. (1976). A relational approach to interpersonal communication. In G. Miller (Ed.), *Explorations in interpersonal communication.* Beverly Hills, CA: Sage.

Mishler, E. (1979). Meaning in context: Is there any other kind? *Harvard Educational Review, 49,* 1–19.

McGee, M. (1980). The "ideograph": A link between rhetoric and ideology. *Quarterly Journal of Speech, 66,* 1–16.

McGee, M. (1984). Secular humanism: A radical reading of culture industry. *Critical Studies in Mass Communication, 1,* 1–33.

McKeon, R. (1956). Communication, truth, and society. *Ethics, 67,* 89–99.

Montgomery, M. (1984). Language and power: A critical review of *Studies in the theory of ideology,* by John B. Thompson. *Media, Culture, & Society, 8,* 41–64.

Newcomb, H. (1984). On the dialogic aspects of mass communication. *Critical Studies in Mass Communication, 1,* 34–50.

Novak, M. (1982). *The spirit of democratic capitalism.* New York: Simon & Schuster.

Owen, W. (1984). Interpretive themes in relational communication. *Quarterly Journal of Speech, 70,* 274–287.

Parks, M. (1977). Relational communication: Theory and research. *Human Communication Research, 3,* 372–381.

Parks, M. (1982). Ideology in interpersonal communication: Off the couch and into the world. In M. Burgoon (Ed.), *Communication Yearbook 5,* New Brunswick, NJ: Transaction Books.

Pearce, W. B., & Cronen, V. (1980). *Communication, action and meaning.* New York: Praeger.

Phil Donahue scores five of top 20 shows. (1986, August 20), *Daily Hampshire Gazette,* p. 31.

Philips, S. U. (1972). Participant structures and communicative competence: Warm Springs children in community and classroom. In C. B. Cazden, V. P. John, & D. Hymes (Eds.), *Functions of language in the classroom.* New York: Teachers College Press.

Philips, S. U. (1987). The concept of speech genre in the study of language and culture. *Working Papers & Proceedings of the Center for Psychosocial Studies, 11,* 25–34.

Philipsen, G. (1975). Speaking "like a man" in Teamsterville: Culture patterns of role enactment in an urban neighborhood. *Quarterly Journal of Speech, 61,* 13–22.

Philipsen, G. (1976). Places for speaking in Teamsterville. *Quarterly Journal of Speech, 62,* 15–25.

Philipsen, G. (1986a). Mayor Daley's council speech: A cultural analysis. *Quarterly Journal of Speech, 72,* 247–260.

Philipsen, G. (1986b). *The ethnography of communication: From an assumptive to an empirical foundation.* Paper delivered at the annual meetings of the American Anthropological Association, Philadelphia.

Philipsen, G. (in press). The prospect for cultural communication. In L. Kinkaid (Ed.), *Communication theory from eastern and western perspectives,* New York: Academic Press.

Philipsen, G. & Carbaugh, D. (1986). A bibliography of fieldwork in the ethnography of communication. *Language in Society, 15,* 387–398.

Philipsen, G. & Huspek, M. (1985). A bibliography of sociolinguistic studies of personal address. *Anthropological Linguistics, 27,* 94–101.

Radcliffe–Brown, A. R. (1940). *Structure and function in primitive society.* London: Cohen & West.

Rawlings, W. (1983). Openness as problematic in ongoing friendships: Two conversational dilemmas. *Communication Monographs, 50,* 1–13.

Reddy, M. (1979). The conduit metaphor. In A. Ortony (Ed.), *Metaphor and thought.* Cambridge, England: Cambridge University Press.

Richards, I. A. (1936). *The philosophy of rhetoric.* London, Oxford University Press.

Ricoeur, P. (1981). *Hermeneutics and the Human Sciences* (J. Thompson, Ed. and Trans.). Cambridge, England: Cambridge University Press.

Robertson, J. (1980). *American Myth, American Reality.* New York: Hill & Wang.

Robinson, B. (1982). Family experts on television talk shows: Facts, values, and half-truths. *Family Relations, 31,* 369–378.

Rodriguez, R. (1982). *Hunger of memory.* Toronto: Bantam Books.

Rokeach, M. (1973). *The nature of human values.* New York: Free Press.

Rosaldo, M. (1973). I have nothing to hide: The language of Ilongot oratory. *Language in Society, 2,* 193–223.

Rosaldo, M. (1982). The things we do with words: Ilongot speech acts and speech act theory in philosophy. *Language in Society, 11,* 203–237.

Rosaldo, M. (1984). Toward an anthropology of self and feeling. In R. Shweder & R. LeVine (Eds.), *Culture theory: Essays on mind, self, and emotion.* Cambridge, England: Cambridge University Press.

Rosenthal, P. (1984). *Words and values: Some leading words and where they lead us.* New York: Oxford University Press.

Rousseau, J.-J. (1762/1978). The social contract. In F. Baumer (Ed.), *Main currents of western thought.* New Haven and London: Yale University press. (Originally published, 1762.)

Rushing, J. (1983). The rhetoric of the American western myth. *Communication Monographs, 50,* 14–32.

Sacks, H. Schegloff, E. A., & Jefferson, G. (1974). A simplest systematics for the organization of turn-taking for conversation. *Language, 50,* 696–735.

St. George, R. (1985). "Heated" speech and literacy in seventeenth-century New England. *Seventeenth Century New England,* 275–322.

Sanches, M. (1975). Introduction to metacommunicative acts and events. In M. Sanches & B. Blount (Eds.), *Sociocultural dimensions of language use.* New York: Academic Press.

Sanders, R. (1987). *Cognitive foundations of calculated speech: Controlling understandings in conversation and persuasion.* Albany: State University of New York Press.

Schneider, D. (1976). Notes toward a theory of culture. In K. Basso & H. Selby (Eds.), *Meaning in anthropology.* Albuquerque: University of New Mexico Press.

Schneider, D. (1980). *American kinship* (2nd ed.). Chicago: University of Chicago Press.

Scollon, R., & Scollon, S. (1981). *Narrative, literacy, and face in interethic communication.* Norwood, NJ: Ablex.

Scott, M., & Lyman, S. (1968). Accounts. *American Sociological Review, 33,* 46–62.

Scruton, R. (1979). The significance of common culture. *Philosophy, 54,* 51–70.

Searle, J. (1969). *Speech Acts.* Cambridge, England: Cambridge University Press.

Searle, J. (1976). A classification of illocutionary acts. *Language in Society, 5,* 1–23.

Season of the locust. (1982, August 23). *Newsweek,* 60.

Seitel, P. (1974). Haya metaphors for speech. *Language in Society, 3,* 51–67.

Sennett, R. (1978). *The fall of public man.* New York: Vintage Books.

Shanahan, E. (1986, September 15). Being honest. *Daily Hampshire Gazette,* 6.

Sherzer, J. (1977). The ethnography of speaking: A critical appraisal. In M. Saville–Troike (Ed.), *Linguistics and anthropology.* Georgetown University Round Table Series on Language and Linguistics.

Sherzer, J. (1983). *Kuna ways of speaking: An ethnographic perspective.* Austin: University of Texas Press.

Shore, B. (1982). *Saláilua: A Samoan mystery.* New York: Columbia University Press.

Shweder, R., & Bourne, E. (1984). Does the concept of the person vary cross-culturally? In R. Shweder & R. LeVine (Eds.), *Culture theory: Essays on mind, self, and emtoion.* Cambridge, England: Cambridge University Press.

Shweder, R., & LeVine, R. (Eds.). (1984). *Culture theory: Essays on mind, self, and emotion.* Cambridge, England: Cambridge University Press.

Sigman, S. (1980). On communication rules from a social perspective. *Human Communication Research, 7,* 37–51.

Singer, M. (1980). Signs of the self: An exploration in semiotic anthropology. *American Anthropologist, 82,* 485–507.

Smith, L. (1978). An evolving logic of participant observation, educational ethnography and other case studies. In L. Schulman (Ed.), *Review of Research in Education.* Chicago: Peacock Press.

Stewart, J. (1983). Interpretive listening: An alternative to empathy. *Communication Education, 32,* 379–391.

Stokes, R., & Hewitt, J. (1976). Aligning actions. *American Sociological Review, 41,* 838–849.

Stross, B. (1974). Speaking of speaking: Tenejapa Tzeltal metalinguistics. In R. Bauman & J. Sherzer (Eds.), *Explorations in the ethnography of speaking.* Cambridge, England: Cambridge University Press.

Takao, S. (1976). Language and behavior in Japan: The conceptualization of personal relations. *Japan Quarterly, 23,* 255–266.

Taylor, C. (1977). Interpretation and the sciences of man. In F. Dallmayr & T. McCarthy (Eds.), *Understanding and social inquiry.* Notre Dame, IN: University of Notre Dame Press.

Taylor, C. (1985). The person. In M. Carrithers, S. Collins, & S. Lukes, (Eds.), *The category of the person.* New York: Columbia University Press.

Thompson, J. B. (1984). *Studies in the theory of ideology.* Cambridge: Polity Press.

Tocqueville, A., de (1835/1945). *Democracy in America.* New York: Vintage Books. (Originally published, 1835.)

Turner, V. (1969). *The ritual process: Structure and anti-structure.* Ithaca, NY: Cornell University Press.

Turner, V. (1974). *Dramas, fields, and metaphors: Symbolic action in human society,* Ithaca, NY: Cornell University press.

Urban, G. (1984). Speech about speech in speech about action. *Journal of American Folklore, 97,* 310–328.

Urban, G. (1986). Ceremonial dialogues in South America. *American Anthropologist, 88,* 371–386.

Varenne, H. (1977). *Americans together.* New York: Columbia University Press.

Varenne, H. (1984). Collective representation in American anthropological conversation about culture: Culture and the individual. *Current Anthropology, 25,* 281–300.

Varenne, H. (1986). *Symbolizing America.* Lincoln: University of Nebraska Press.

Veroff, J., Douvan, E., & Kulka, R. (1981). *The Inner American: A self-portrait from 1957 to 1976.* New York: Basic Books.

Verschueren, J. (1985). *What people say they do with words.* Norwood, NJ: Albex.

Verve, style, courage bring raves for stars. (1983, May 16). *USA Today,* p. 2D.

Weaver, R. (1964). *Visions of order: The cultural crisis of our time.* Baton Rouge: Louisiana State University Press.

Weaver, R. (1970). *Language is sermonic* (R. Johanneson, R. Strickland, & R. Eubanks, Eds.), Baton Rouge: Louisiana State University Press.

Weider, D. L., & Pratt, S. (1985). *On being a recognizable Indian among Indians.* Paper presented at the annual meetings of the International Communication Association, Honolulu.

Weiler, M. (1984). The rhetoric of neo-liberalism. *Quarterly Journal of Speech, 70,* 362–378.

Western, D. (in press). *Self and society: Narcissism, collectivism, and the development of morals.* Cambridge, England: Cambridge University Press.

White, G., & Kirkpatrick, J. (Eds.). (1985). *Person, self, and experience: Exploring Pacific ethnopsychologies.* Berkeley: University of California Press.

Wierzbicka, A. (1985). A semantic metalanguage for a crosscultural comparison of speech acts and speech genres. *Language in Society, 14,* 491–514.

Witherspoon, G. (1977). *Language and art in the Navajo universe.* Ann Arbor: University of Michigan Press.

Wittgenstein, L. (1958). *Philosophical investigations* (G. Anscombe, Trans.). New York: Macmillan.

Yankelovich, D. (1981). *New rules: Searching for self-fulfillment in a world turned upside down.* New York: Bantam Books.

AUTHOR INDEX

A

Abrahams, R., 122, 123, *189*
Agar, M., *189*
Albert, E., 124, 175, *189*
Allen, N., 115, 116, *189*

B

Bakhtin, M., 107, 181, *189*
Baskerville, B., 106, *189*
Basso, K., 12, 172, *189*
Bauman, R., 12, 123, 125, 174, 179, *189*
Bell, M., 124, *189*
Bellah, R., 93, 97, 100, 142, *189*
Berger, B., 13, 42, 53, 61, 107, 113, *189*
Berger, P., 13, 42, 53, 61, 107, 113, *189*
Bharati, A., 40, 115, 119, *189*
Bilmes, J., 179, 181, *189*
Blom, J., *189*
Boggs, S., 11, *190*
Bohmer, P., 134, 135, *190*
Bourne, E., 17, 18, 19, 115, 116, 119, 120, *198*
Brenneis, D., 11, 123, *190*
Brockreide, W., 72, *191*
Brown, P., 30, 124, 141, 171, *190*
Brown, R., 93, 102, *190*
Bruner, E., 39, *190*
Burgoon, J., 160, *190*
Burke, K., 6, 21, 85, 127, 171, *190*
Buttny, R., 74, *190*

C

Cahn, D., 113, 117, 179, 182, *191*
Campbell, D., 14, *190*
Carbaugh, D., 6, 8, 62, 105, 129, 156, 160, 161, 174, 179, 181, 183, *190, 191, 196*
Carey, J., 6, *191*
Carlson, R., 72, 142, 178, *193*
Carrithers, M., 17, *191*

Caughey, J., 19, 40, 118, *191*
Chenoweth, A., 3, 191
Chesebro, J., 8, *191*
Chick, J.K., 11, *191*
Clark, R., 72, *192*
Coles, R., 14, 178, *191*
Collins, S., 17, *191*
Conquergood, D., 179, *191*
Cooley, R., *191*
Corcoran, F., 8, 107, *191*
Corner, J., 8, *191*
Corrigan, P., 8, *191*
Craig, J., 4, 90, *191*
Cronen, V., 8, 175, *191, 196*
Crow, B., 2, *191*
Cushman, D., 69, 90, 117, 179, 182, *191*

D

Dahrendorf, R., 100, *191*
Darnell, D., 72, *191*
Davis, P., 13, 134, *191*
Deetz, S., *195*
Delia, J., 72, *192*
Devos, G., 17, *195*
Donahue, P., 3, 13, 127, 130, *192*
Douvan, E., 13, 99, 178, *199*
Dumont, L., 16, 17, 19, 87, 114, 119, 120, *192*

E

Eadie, W., 72, 142, 178, *193*
Eastman, C., 7, 170, *192*
Ebenstein, W., 100, *192*
Ervin-Tripp, S., 175, *192*

F

Fine, E., 179, *192*
Fiske, J., 8, 180, 181, 186, *192*
Ford, M., 93, *190*
Fortes, M., 15, *192*

SUBJECT INDEX